THE
SUBVERSIVE
FAMILY

by the same author

THE THEATRE OF POLITICS

VERY LIKE A WHALE
THE MAN WHO RODE AMPERSAND
THE CLIQUE

FERDINAND MOUNT

THE SUBVERSIVE FAMILY

An Alternative History of Love and Marriage

THE FREE PRESS
A Division of Macmillan, Inc.
New York

Maxwell Macmillan Canada
Toronto

Maxwell Macmillan International
New York   Oxford   Singapore   Sydney

To William, Harry and Mary

Copyright © 1982, 1992 by Ferdinand Mount

The Free Press
A Division of Macmillan, Inc.
866 Third Avenue, New York, N.Y. 10022

Maxwell Macmillan Canada, Inc.
1200 Eglinton Avenue East
Suite 200
Don Mills, Ontario M3C 3N1

Macmillan, Inc. is part of the Maxwell Communication Group of Companies.

First American Edition 1992

Printed in the United States of America

printing number

1 2 3 4 5 6 7 8 9 10

Library of Congress Cataloging-in-Publication Data

Mount, Ferdinand
    The subversive family: an alternative history of love and
marriage / Ferdinand Mount.
        p.   cm.
    ISBN 0-02-921992-2
    1. Family—History.   2. Love—History.   3. Marriage—History.
    I. Title.
HQ503.M68   1992
306.8—dc20   92-30779
                                                            CIP

The author and publisher are grateful to the editors of *Encounter* for permission to reprint extracts from 'The Dilution of Fraternity', first published in October 1976.

CONTENTS

PREFACE TO THE AMERICAN EDITION

When this book was first published in Britain, it was variously described as "anarchist", "romantic", "reactionary", "ludicrous", "magnificent", "apocalyptic" and "a joy because it vindicates the natural affections". On closer inspection, these wildly discordant responses sorted themselves out into three clearly marked—and highly revealing—groups.

The first (and I like to think the largest) group of readers seemed to experience a pleasant shock, or at any rate a tremor, of recognition. The version of the history of the family which I described corresponded to suspicions, intimations, stray pieces of evidence that had come their way in the course of their researches or their daily lives. Material which the conventional wisdom had instructed them to disregard as trivial, marginal or "merely anecdotal" could, it seemed, be collated and arranged to constitute an alternative history of family life, one in which personal affection and private aspiration played a rather larger part and impersonal social forces were not always dominant; a history in which the notorious, supposedly inexorable progress from feudalism to capitalism, and from the extended family to the nuclear family, began to dissolve.

All this was anathema to the second group of readers, who, if not themselves actually marxists, had come to rely rather heavily on the scheme of social history which Marx and Engels had left behind. Some of these critics frothed with rage; others affected a weary superiority. Any attempt to suggest that personal affection (or even, to use the word which must not be spoken, Love) might be an important and continuing factor in human history was to be dismissed as bourgeois sentimentality.

From some Catholics and traditional moralists came a different, indeed, almost opposite criticism. This third group of readers agreed that, yes, the family was a bulwark of independence against the State and a refuge from the storms of history, but it was the Church that had built this refuge, and I was mistaken in lumping the Church in with the other oppressive forces menacing family life. Far from being too cosy, sentimental and conservative in its approach, my book showed a dangerous streak in its refusal to understand the positive social role played by Christianity.

As for its implications for the present and the future state of marriage and the family, the quasi-Marxists accused me of an absurd complacency about the survival of an institution which was bound to crumble away. The traditionalists accused me of complacency too, although of a different type. They shared the belief that the family was crumbling, but they also believed that it could be revived if only the old social cement was remixed and generously applied: divorce made more difficult, abortion forbidden, and so on.

To carry the story up to the present date is simple enough. As the study of social history becomes ever more popular, an increasing body of evidence tends to support the conclusions first given coherent expression by Dr. Peter Laslett and the Cambridge Group for the History of Population and Social Structure.

Many of my themes have since been given securer underpinning in such scholarly works as Keith Wrightson's *English Society* 1580–1630, R. B. Outhwaite's *Marriage and Society,* Martine Ségalen's *Love & Power in the Peasant Family,* and the diverse and distinguished writings of Linda Pollock, Richard Smith and, especially, Alan Macfarlane. I certainly would not dare to claim that a new consensus reigns, but it is clear that the old conventional wisdom, once so widely shared by social historians, anthropologists, and literary scholars, has had to be rearranged a little.

As for the here and now, the evidence of the intervening decade only reinforces my tentative conclusions about the enduring appeal of "popular marriage", that is, *fallible* marriage in which equality, privacy and independence are sought, with an indifference to risk and a concentration of desire which pays little or no attention to social expectations.

I wish here only to repeat—with a little more emphasis for those who missed it the first time—that freedom is not the same as happiness. The quest for liberty always has a bleak and lonely aspect. This insistence on making and unmaking our own relationships without let or hindrance from society is anything but a soft option. Nor is the project undertaken because it offers a greater assurance of contentment, either for ourselves or for our children, than our forefathers enjoyed.

To claim that, in our part of the world, marriage was never a purely commercial arrangement but always aroused the most intense human emotions is not to claim that those emotions were always pleasant. There never was a golden age in which brutality, neglect and desertion were unheard of. And we have small reason to expect that there ever will be.

The modern insistence on liberty in personal relationships derives from that most modern, most protestant of reasons, the dignity of the individual. It is likely to be reversed only by a wholesale return to the ideals of a collective, tribal society. And anyone who sees such a development shimmering on our present horizon must have a bizarre set of binoculars.

In setting out its alternative version, this book does not claim that this is the way we ought to be. It contents itself with claiming that, in North-West Europe especially but elsewhere too, this is the way we were, are and, most probably, will go on being.

This is a strictly European history. It has hardly a word to say about America. Yet what applies to the British Isles, to Scandinavia and to Germany must apply with still greater force to the United States; for when we come to chart the social world of modernity, we in Europe have to recognise that we may be its sources and its tributaries, but America is the main channel. The traditions of family life which were carried across to the New World were stripped down to their essentials and stand there to this day as plain and unadorned as the furniture in a New England parlour. This book might even serve as a prologue to that great history of the American Family which has yet to be written.

INTRODUCTION

The family is a subversive organisation. In fact, it is the ultimate and only consistently subversive organisation. Only the family has continued throughout history and still continues to undermine the State. The family is the enduring permanent enemy of all hierarchies, churches and ideologies. Not only dictators, bishops and commissars but also humble parish priests and café intellectuals find themselves repeatedly coming up against the stony hostility of the family and its determination to resist interference to the last.

As with any other underground movement, the authorities try to suppress any mention of its popularity or even of its existence. History has to be rewritten, photographs retouched to blot out embarrassing figures. Looking in from the outside, we have to read between the lines of official condemnations and prosecutions. For the history of the family we have to rely much of the time on the records and propaganda of Church and State. That is not unlike trying to find out about Christianity in the Soviet Union and having access only to *Pravda* and *Izvestia*.

Now this is an unfamiliar way of looking at things. From childhood on, we are taught a very different picture of the family. Schools and newspapers and broadcasters lead us to think of the family as *propping up* the established order. In speeches and sermons, you will hear the family praised as a 'bulwark' – of Society, or the State, or True Religion, or Socialism. Politicians all emphasise that they are 'on the side of the family'. The Synod of Bishops in Rome in 1980 discussed 'the role of the Christian family in the modern world'. The presumption was that the family was, in its essence or at its best, a specifically Christian institution.

Now and then, it is true, one or two writers have noticed that the family can be used as a last ditch from which to resist the State. De Tocqueville remarked that 'as long as family feeling is kept alive, the opponent of oppression is never alone'. D. H. Lawrence, although falling victim to the partial illusion that Christianity had elevated the condition of marriage, also saw that marriage created private space for the individual:

> It is marriage, perhaps, which had given man the best of his freedom, given him his little kingdom of his own within the big kingdom of the State . . . It is a true freedom because it is a true fulfilment, for man, woman and children. Do we then want to break marriage? If we do break it, it means we all fall to a far greater extent under the direct sway of the State.[1]

But most people do not usually think like that. Most people take it for granted that 'subversion' means rebellion against the 'Establishment' and that this Establishment is nothing more than the family writ large, with all the hypocrisy and stuffiness of family life. Most of us accept at face value the claims of those who present themselves as the real subversives, feminists, anarchists, hippies, utopians and radicals – people who are rebelling against the 'conventional' customs and obligations of the family.

Yet there is a snag here. For was not Jesus himself something of a radical, perhaps even a sort of hippie? And did not Plato, for centuries the mentor of our governing classes, draw up the first blueprint of a commune? And was not Karl Marx a bit of a bohemian? And did not all of them say some rather unpleasant things about marriage and the family?

Yet these – and others like them – are the prophets who have filled the minds and moulded the conventions of the Establishment. Every time you go to Church or, in the Soviet Union, to a meeting of the Young Communist League or perhaps even to a branch meeting of your political party, you will find that you are required to assent to some remarkable propositions. And the first is usually that thou shalt have no other God but me – no other cause or faith or loyalty. You are to renounce all other worldly goods and attachments and follow the flag or the Cross or the Crescent or the Hammer and Sickle. And what is the one centre of worldly goods and attachments that stands mutinously opposed to all this renouncing and following? The family and only the family.

How then does it come about that we stand grouped in family pews at these occasions? Why does the priest or politician speak so warmly of the family?

The society we live in has been shaped by a series of powerful revolutionary movements, some religious, some purely political, some a mixture of both. After seizing power over men's minds and then over their bodies, these revolutionary movements have hardened into orthodoxies. The ideas of Plato, Jesus, Marx, Lenin, Mao, Hitler and the numerous other nationalist demagogues of the last hundred years have all gone through much the same sequence of attitudes towards the family.

This book is about that sequence and its consequences for the family and for the lives of its members. And the sequence runs as follows:

First, *hostility and propaganda to devalue the family*. The family is a source of trouble. It could distract apostles or potential apostles from following the new idea. The family is second-best, pedestrian, material, selfish. Alternative families are promoted – communes, party cadres, kibbutzes, monasteries.

Second, *reluctant recognition of the strength of the family*. Despite all official efforts to downgrade the family, to reduce its role and even to stamp it out, men and women obstinately continue not merely to mate and produce children but to insist on living in pairs together with their children, to develop strong affections for them and to place family concerns above other social obligations.

Third, *collapse of efforts to promote the alternative pseudo-families*. Communes, crèches, kibbutzes, monasteries and nunneries lose the enthusiasm of their founders and decay. Either their numbers dwindle, or their members become cynical and corrupt, or both.

Fourth, *a one-sided peace treaty is signed*. The Church or State accepts the enduring importance of the family and grants it a high place in the orthodox dogma or ideology. That does not mean that the family is allowed to live its natural life. On the contrary, the Church or

3

State still insists on defining what is good for the family and what makes a Good Family.

Fifth, *history is rewritten* to show that the Church or State *always* held this high conception of the family. The family is redefined as essentially Christian, or Communist, or Fascist or whatever – despite the fact that the earliest apostles are on record as having loathed and despised the family.

Sixth, the family gradually manages to *impose its own terms*. The constricting, unnatural or impractical terms which were forced upon it gradually buckle under continuous social pressure – until the guardians of Church or State have no choice but to yield, while busily continuing to rewrite history and to maintain that the new concessions were always somehow implicit in the True Faith.

At each stage, we must take note of the element of conscious manipulation which has gone into the formation of official dogma. And in trying to estimate, say, what lay people thought of the Church, we must not be deluded by the apparent security and self-confidence implied by soaring cathedrals and broad monastic acres. Even the comfortable, traditional faith of country people should not mislead us into imagining that the authority of the Church, even in the Middle Ages, ever went wholly unresented or unchallenged. We can no more write a true history of marriage on the assumption that the Church's rules were universally respected than we can write a history of Soviet Russia on the assumption that Stalin's constitution of 1936 has been consistently revered. Whole realms of official humbug, grudging popular conformity and unashamed bureaucratic cynicism never appear in the official records.

What we must never forget is that there is always a power struggle in progress. The ceaseless efforts of bishops and abbots to maintain and enlarge their authority cannot be separated from the rest of the life of the Church, nor from the Church's efforts to impose Christian morality and ecclesiastical law upon secular society. For the Church had in the first place attained real secular authority – and hence the opportunity to impose its own codes of behaviour – only by capturing the centres of worldly power in a series of spectacular coups: the conversion of the Emperor Constantine, the conversion of Clovis, King of the Franks, the conversion of Ethelbert, King of Kent, and so on throughout what was to become Christendom. Without such royal connection and support, both military and financial, Christianity rarely progressed beyond scattered communities of holy men with groups of pious lay followers.

Although it is impolite to say so, nearer our own day this technique of achieving influence by converting top people has been copied not only by the Jesuits but also by Moral Rearmament. The secular power of the Church was almost always imposed from the top.

That is why, however different its ideals and motives, the Church's techniques of acquiring and maintaining power may fairly be compared with those of the Bolsheviks or any other revolutionary party which aims to take power by seizing control of the central apparatus of government. The revolutionaries capture the royal palace and the radio station. The Church captures the conscience of the king and, through him, quickly gains a monopoly of the means of communication. Naturally, many devout communities of holy and honest men and women continue to exist, just as there still exist today academic communities of honest Marxists; but it is not through such communities that the Church or the Communist Party comes to power; still less is it through any kind of democratic process. How many cases are there of a heathen nation adopting Christianity by majority vote?

For most nations, the experience of conversion has been collective and more or less compulsory; it has resembled the experience of the English people being marched to and fro under successive Tudor sovereigns – Catholic under Henry VIII, Protestant under Henry and Edward VI, Catholic again under Mary, and Protestant again under Elizabeth. Each time, the official – supposedly divinely sanctioned – attitude towards marriage and divorce changed too, keeping roughly in step. The divorce laws proposed by Cranmer, which were never enacted because of the death of Edward VI, were much the same as the divorce laws we have today. Had Edward lived only a few months longer, English social history in the next four centuries might have been rather different.

Similar to-ings and fro-ings have taken place in Soviet Russia, although compressed into less than seventy years, and also in Communist China over an even shorter period. We are more conscious of these shifts of orthodoxy in Russia and China, because they are so violent and recent, than we are of the remarkable changes in Church dogma on marriage and divorce, which have often been spread out over centuries and have been more cunningly disguised.

Meanwhile, ordinary families have struggled on, trying to lead their lives in what seems to them the natural way, under the shadow of uncomprehending, indifferent or actively hostile authority. The hostility of Christianity to the family dates back 2,000 years. The hostility of historical Marxism has been continuous and unwavering. If we place Marxism in the tradition of previous collective utopias, its anti-family thrust is as old as Plato.

There is nothing mysterious or hidden about this hostility. The only surprise is that we do not remark on it more. The doctrine, the leaders and the most zealous followers of new revolutionary movements all agree on this indifference or aversion to the family. The doctrine calls for new loyalty 'higher' than and in opposition to the natural loyalties of family. This new loyalty – to God or the Church, to the Nation, to the Party or the Ideology – awards maximum points to those who forsake all other ties; not merely are those whose faith most sharply cuts them off from home and parents and children most warmly commended, it is part and parcel of the practice of the new movement that you cannot do your work properly if you are still encumbered with old loyalties.

All this derives naturally from the personality and position of the leader or leaders. To put it mildly, revolutionary leaders have tended not to enjoy ordinary home lives. They may be ascetic celibates, such as Jesus, or libertines, such as Mussolini and Napoleon, or a little of both such as Mao and Stalin, or something altogether more complicated such as Hitler.

The early apostles too tend to share something of the unusual personal character of the leader. The early Christians were linked with and drew some of their doctrine and many of their members from the ascetic sects of the desert, most notably the Essenes; these sects tended to be celibate and to regard marriage and indeed all family ties as gross, fleshly and sinful.

The old Bolsheviks, for their part, contained a large bohemian element – young men and women who believed in free love and free living and expected Communism to provide a permanent means of enjoying both; Lenin himself had an ascetic side which was, as we shall see, at war with the bohemian Bolsheviks but he shared their general impatience with bourgeois ties and with the allegedly repressive and warping nature of bourgeois marriage.

The early Nazi movement contained a number of homosexual semi-gangsters who hoped to find personal liberation and salvation in collective political action. Hitler later found these people an embarrassment when he had to present the Nazi Party as officially pro-family; but he retained a certain loyalty to them, and the Nazi ideology never shook off that footloose, sexually deviant character which they had helped to imprint upon it.

There is therefore nothing accidental or haphazard about the anti-family bias of the ideologies which have proved most influential in our history. Both in their early leaders and their original theories, they have been strongly and characteristically marked by an urge to *get away from* the family.

In this flight from the family, every available means of transport has been pressed into service. Religion, history, economics – all have been commandeered to prove that family life is unnatural, unnecessary or bad for us. Just as Christianity in its heyday instructed us to look beyond the gross ties of flesh and blood, so now the modern secular theologies, such as sociology and psychology, can be used to teach that the family is a prison which is liable to warp our true humanity. The language may change. The message of revolt is the same.

The history of human thought and fancy is full of sustained efforts to prove that we are not part of the animal kingdom. These efforts range from the censorship of sexual matters and euphemisms for excretion to the claim that, in some sense, we do not die as animals do. Modern people, proud of being unlike their grandparents, are unafraid to talk about sex. Death is now in danger of losing its position as the last taboo.

But even the most outspoken people, in fact particularly the most outspoken people, hesitate to talk with complete candour about the part their families play in their lives. More lies are spoken and written about family life than any other subject. And these lies have soaked through into our ideas of history, so that family life has come to be one of the most embarrassing aspects of being human, misread and misunderstood by reason of that privacy which is its protection and its core.

Introduction

The Myths

The history of the family in past times is hard to unearth. Often it is hidden away from our prying eyes. What did married people feel about love and marriage in general – and about each other in particular – two hundred or five hundred or a thousand years ago? What did they feel about their children and about their parents? We do not and cannot know for sure. After all, we are not even sure what married people today think about these subjects.

When the facts are so difficult to establish, it is not surprising that curious beliefs should abound and should gain a firm hold in the textbooks. Some of these beliefs about the history of the family are very curious indeed. When you come across them for the first time, you may feel like rubbing your eyes and saying, not without a hint of incredulity: is this what scholars really believe the past was like? Did our ancestors really think and act like this?

The sort of beliefs I am referring to include the following:

- That the family as we know it today – the so-called 'nuclear' family of husband, wife and children – is an historical freak unknown to other centuries and other parts of the world.
- That in past centuries most people lived instead in large 'extended' families amongst a crowd of grandparents, brothers-in-law, aunts and cousins; that it was the Industrial Revolution which broke up these gregarious clans and created the isolated, inward-looking nuclear family.
- That among 'primitive' tribes marriage as we know it is uncommon or unknown; and that people live in clans or groups which are often cheerfully promiscuous and devoid of jealousy.
- That most marriages used to be entirely arranged by the parents of the bride and groom; and that the bride and groom had no choice in the matter.
- That young people used to marry or be married in their early teens.
- That romantic love was invented by the troubadours of mediaeval Provence; and that it applied only to the adulterous love of a knight or minstrel for a married lady who was not his wife.
- That child care and the interest in childhood are inventions of relatively modern times; that in the old days, so many children died as babies that mothers became indifferent to their loss and grieved little; that children used to be regarded as adults in miniature.

- That divorce is a modern development and indicates a decline in the strength of the family; that divorce used to be regarded with horror.
- That Church and State have always been steadfast upholders of the family; that the Roman Catholic Church in particular always esteemed the family very highly.
- That the appearance of communes, squats and kibbutzim is a new development which may bring about the collapse or transformation of the family.

These beliefs hang together. Taken as a whole – and they often are taken as a whole – they form a large part of what the established textbooks tell us about ourselves and our history.

Yet every one of these beliefs is now under fierce attack among specialists in the relevant fields – among social, economic and ecclesiastical historians, historical demographers, anthropologists, mediaevalists, literary critics and so on.

Some of these beliefs are regarded by scholars as so utterly exploded as to be scarcely worth discussing. Others are still hotly contested. In others again, the question is whether we have been looking at the right sort of evidence or whether that evidence is a fair sample. Unfortunately, these doubts and demolitions have, for the most part, been confined to academic circles; they have not found their way into the general assumptions which underlie public discussion in newspapers, parliaments and paperbacks.

In fact, many of the texts which are still recommended to students continue to rehash the old theories. Feminist pamphlets continue to quote Engels on the family. Literary critics continue to quote C. S. Lewis on the troubadours. Social historians continue to refer to Philippe Ariès on childhood in olden times. You still hear sociologists refer to 'the nuclear family' as something peculiar to our generation.

This last belief, for example, will be encountered all over the place. Shulamith Firestone writes in *The Dialectic of Sex*:

> The modern nuclear family is only a recent development. Ariès shows that the family as we know it did not exist in the Middle Ages, only gradually evolving from the fourteenth century on. Until then one's 'family' meant primarily one's legal heredity line, the emphasis on blood ancestry rather than the conjugal unit.[2]

Introduction

Germaine Greer writes in *The Female Eunuch*:

> In fact the single marriage family, which is called by anthropologists and sociologists the *nuclear* family, is possibly the shortest lived familial system ever developed. In feudal times the family was of the type called a *stem* family: the head was the oldest male parent, who ruled a number of sons and their wives and children.[3]

Popular sociologists and anthropologists still blindly repeat the famous assertion of Sir Edmund Leach that the nuclear family system 'is a most unusual kind of organisation and I would predict that it is only a transient phase in our society'.[4]

Progressive churchmen, such as the members of the British Council of Churches Working Party, describe the 'isolated nuclear family' as a 'socially conditioned pattern' and complain that 'this small unit, shaped to a great extent by the economic pressures of a consumer society, is presented to us in advertising and writing as an ideal, self-contained entity.'[5]

These things are said – and said over and over again – with blithe certainty. I quote from well-known recent texts, but these are only the latest repetitions of what Marxists and Darwinists were saying a hundred years ago. Yet to the best of our available knowledge, these beliefs, and many others like them, are simply not true.

My excuse for writing this book is first to present to a general audience, however briefly, some of the reasons why the theories are no longer accepted by specialists. I shall try, as fairly as I can, to describe the state of current research. Most of what I am saying is not new to specialists in the relevant fields. Considering these fields as part of a single estate – the estate of marriage – may be new.

I shall also argue that, in the light of these fresh historical conclusions, we ought to look at marriage and the family from a different angle. We must start afresh. And we must be a little more sceptical.

We must not take at face value the pronouncements of politicians and popes and poets. For the history of the family is a furtive affair, marked by manipulation, dishonesty and sophistry – as well as by cruelty and indifference to individuals.

My approach is intended to be marked by two features which distinguish it from a great deal of writing on the subject. First, we shall mostly be working *from the inside looking outwards*. Wherever appropriate, we shall present evidence of how married people talked and wrote about the family – rather than relying on pronouncements of those in authority who regarded it as their duty to control and supervise the family and who, during the Christian era at least, were mostly outsiders, in the personal as well as the public sense, since they were celibate.

Secondly, we shall try to *resist abstraction*. I hope to present the evidence fairly straightforwardly, draw only conclusions which follow directly from that evidence and refrain from the temptation to build up comparative psychological and ideological structures to represent what the French call the 'mentalités' of married people then and now. If this approach seems simple and a little pedestrian, that may have its advantages.

It may also seem that I spend an excessive time on the more distant past (where the evidence is often scanty) and relatively little on the nineteenth and twentieth centuries where the evidence is plentiful and the subject of more pressing concern. The reason is that our myths often go deeper than we know and if they are to be grubbed up, they must be grubbed up from the roots. Besides, it is possible that when we have cleared the ground of certain persistent misconceptions, some vexed questions about the present will look a little simpler, and that what may legitimately be said can be said quite simply and briefly. At least I hope so.

For my own part, I started out on this enquiry holding very different views from those I now hold – particularly about the attitudes of the Church and the position of women in times past. I hope others may be, if not converted in the same way, at least provoked to question.

In writing this book, I am grateful to all those scholars whose primary research has provided me with my material, even where my conclusions differ sharply from theirs. To none do I owe a greater debt than to Dr Peter Laslett and the Cambridge Group for the History of Population and Social Structure – whose researches provide the statistical underpinning for the whole book.

My final borrowing from Dr Laslett must be to echo his view that 'we do not understand ourselves because we do not know what we have been, and hence what we may be becoming.'

PART ONE

THE MYTHS

1
MARRIAGE AND THE CHURCH

Jesus says: 'If any man come to me, and hate not his father, and mother, and wife, and children, and brethren, and sisters, yea, and his own life also, he cannot be my disciple.'[1] And again:

Think not that I am come to send peace on earth: I came not to send peace, but a sword. For I am come to set a man at variance against his father, and the daughter against her mother, and the daughter in law against her mother in law. And a man's foes shall be they of his own household. He that loveth father or mother more than me is not worthy of me: and he that loveth son or daughter more than me is not worthy of me.[2]

To this day I remember as a child the shock of first coming across these texts. The tone is so fierce, so unyielding. It was explained to me that Jesus was merely laying down the practical conditions of discipleship in forceful terms. He meant only that nobody could hope to be an effective or wholehearted disciple without giving up family concerns. I found and find this interpretation unconvincing. And in any case, it does not escape the problem. For the New Testament uncompromisingly states that to be a disciple of Christ is a *higher* calling than to be a kind and loving member of a family. If the two were alternatives of equal value, we would expect to find corresponding eulogies of marriage and family life in the Gospels.

There are none. 'Suffer the little children to come unto *me*' – not unto their parents – is the message. It is hard to deny that all those sectarians whose demands have caused family rifts and human tragedies – the Plymouth Brethren, the Moonies and the Rev. Jim Jones – *can* claim scriptural authority, however foully they may have abused it.

The Anglican marriage service contains only two specific references to the Gospels: the Marriage at Cana[3] and Jesus's remarks on divorce.[4] The party at Cana starts unpromisingly: 'And the third day there was a marriage in Cana of Galilee; and the mother of Jesus was there: and both Jesus was called, and his disciples, to the marriage. And when they wanted wine, the mother of Jesus saith unto him, They have no wine. Jesus saith unto her, Woman, what have I to do with thee? mine hour is not yet come.' The impression is given – indeed the story would lack point without it – that Jesus is in somewhat irritable mood at being distracted from His work and is annoyed by His mother's request and that He turns the water into wine partly to pacify her and partly to demonstrate that He is who He is (it is His first miracle). The miracle in no sense could be taken to uphold, endorse or glorify the institution of marriage itself, rather than the marriage feast.

The only direct quotations from Jesus in the Anglican marriage service come from Mark 10: 6–9: 'But from the beginning of the creation God made them male and female. For this cause shall a man leave his father and mother, and cleave to his wife; And they twain shall be one flesh: so then they are no more twain, but one flesh. What therefore God hath joined together, let not man put asunder.'

This is certainly an endorsement of marriage as a biological imperative and a social institution. However, it comes in answer to a trick question from the Pharisees about the legality of divorce. It is hard to read it as a positive assertion of the *spiritual* importance of marriage – something which is wholly absent from the Gospels.

Do the Epistles have a higher opinion of the married state? St Paul does tell husbands to love their wives 'as their own bodies' and 'as Christ loved the Church'; men must love their wives 'and be not bitter against them'.[5] Wives are to 'submit yourselves unto your own husbands, as unto the Lord. For the husband is the head of the wife, even as Christ is the head of the church';[6] young women are to be taught by the aged women 'to be sober, to love their husbands, to love their children, To be discreet, chaste, keepers at home, good, obedient to their own husbands, that the word of God be not blasphemed.'[7]

What is in question here is decent social behaviour so as not to disgrace the young Church at a precarious stage in its growth. When St Paul turns to spiritual priorities, his message is quite different:

> It is good for a man not to touch a woman . . . I would that all men were even as I myself. But every man hath his proper gift of God, one after this manner, and another after that. I say therefore to the unmarried and widows, It is good for them if they abide even as I. But if they cannot contain, let them marry: for it is better to marry than to burn . . . the fashion of this world passeth away. But I would have you without carefulness. He that is unmarried careth for the things that belong to the Lord, how he may please the Lord: But he that is married careth for the things that are of the world, how he may please his wife. There is difference also between a wife and a virgin. The unmarried woman careth for the things of the Lord, that she may be holy both in body and in spirit: but she that is married careth for the things of the world, how she may please her husband.[8]

Marriage for St Paul is unmistakably an *inferior* state. Existing marriages are to be maintained, but only as a concession to human weakness and as a social expedient. Some Christians in Corinth regarded all sexual intercourse as improper, even within marriage – an un-Jewish view, but one frequently found among ascetic sects such as the Essenes. Hans Lietzmann writes in his *History of the Early Church* of Paul's view: 'It was a question of opposition to "this world" to which marriage really belonged: any idea of uplifting marriage into the spiritual sphere, as among stoic thinkers, was foreign to the Pauline horizon.'[9] Cardinal Jean Daniélou is equally candid: 'The superiority of virginity to marriage had never been questioned. But during the first two centuries certain thinkers had gone much further than that; being a Christian seemed to them to imply virginity. Married persons who did not separate could be only imperfect members of the Church. In the heterodox sects this doctrine was the expression of a total condemnation of creation, but it seems clear that tendencies of this kind existed at the very heart of the Church.'[10]

This 'Encratist' tendency – which also included abstention from flesh and wine – was not confined to heterodox sects, but expressed a much more general movement. Pseudo-gospels in Egypt, Palestine and Rome furthered Paul's obsessive esteem for virginity and burst out into polemics against marriage, which was spoken of as 'bitter grass'. The Marcionites admitted to baptism only virgins or married people who had taken a vow of chastity. The Montanists taught that sexual abstinence was an obligation for all Christians. The spirit of evil was linked, as it had been among the Essenes, with sexuality.

Gradually, however, the Church yielded to reality in the interests of increasing its flock. Dionysius of Alexandria wrote to the Bishop of Knossos 'to exhort him not to impose on the faithful the heavy burden of continence as an obligation, but to take account of the weakness of the majority'. Encratism began to die out, except among the extreme and heretical sects. Clement of Alexandria at the beginning of the third century wrote a whole book to show that marriage was fully compatible with the Christian life.

Yet this accommodation to reality, this taming of the ascetic element in Christianity, this 'civilising' of its origins never quite wiped out the stern code of the desert. Throughout the third century, apocryphal Acts of the Apostles continued to glorify virginity and the separation of married couples in the service of God. When the Emperor Septimus Severus issued an edict forbidding Christians to make converts – the first legislation directed specifically against the Christians – it was, according to Daniélou, largely because of these anti-family views: 'At the moment when Severus was reforming the laws on marriage and trying to strengthen the family, these Christians condemned marriage and urged all their brethren to practise continence.'[11]

Even Tertullian, later to be one of the first inventors of a specifically Christian endorsement of marriage, upheld virginity as the expression of total Christianity.

And when Tertullian did speak highly of marriage, it was only of marriage entirely controlled by the Church: 'How can we describe the happiness of this marriage which the Church approves, which the oblation confirms, which the blessing seals, which the angels recognise, which the Father ratifies?'[12] A whole Christian liturgy had been substituted for the idolatrous parts of the Roman matrimonial rites.

Moreover, the new discipline was considerably stricter than the old. Not only did Tertullian condemn divorce, polygamy and abortion; he warned against mixed marriages with pagans who might interfere with Christian duties.

Gradually, marriage began to be sanctified and absorbed into official Christian ritual. In the fourth century, the custom began of solemnly blessing the bride and groom as soon as they had been married, accompanied by rites taken over from pagan customs; at Rome, a veil was placed on the heads of the married couple, the *velatio conjugalis*. And in the fourth century too, in the reign of Constantine, the Church began to exert influence on the legal code: married men were forbidden to keep concubines, adultery and rape were treated severely and obstacles were put in the way of divorce, which had become relatively easy.

What must be kept in mind is how long this process took. For centuries, marriage was regarded as a second-best, a potential distraction from the love of God. As late as the sixteenth century, the Council of Trent, the starting-point of the Counter-Reformation, denounced those who claimed that 'the marriage state is to be placed above the state of virginity, or of celibacy, and that it is not better and more blessed to remain in virginity, or celibacy, than to be united.'

For centuries, the Church was absorbed in a double task: to elaborate a conception of Christian marriage which could survive in the lay world without sacrificing too much of the Christian regard for chastity, and to gain control of the legal and social institutions governing marriage. In England, the Church did not succeed in its claim to exercise exclusive jurisdiction in matrimonial cases until the eleventh century. For hundreds of years after that, poor people continued to marry without benefit of clergy. At the same time, the Church's rules about who was and was not permitted to marry became more and more niggling and constrictive. The Table of Affinity which survives in the Book of Common Prayer is only a fragment of the huge corpus of mediaeval law governing what constituted a legitimate marriage. For a few centuries – not many out of two thousand years of Christianity – the Church exercised more or less total control over marriage.

But not for long. The Reformation was at least in part a revolution against celibacy. Calvin's view would have been incomprehensible to the mediaeval Church and even more so to the early Christians:

As for me, I do not want anyone to think me very virtuous because I am not married. It would rather be a fault in me if I could serve God better in marriage than remaining as I am . . . But I know my infirmity, that perhaps a woman might not be happy with me. However that may be, I abstain from marriage in order that I may be more free to serve God. But this is not because I think that I am more virtuous than my brethren. Fie to me if I had that false opinion![13]

From this moment on, the Church began gradually to accommodate itself to sexuality. Among the Puritans, marriage began to be glorified not just as another, equally good way of serving but as a better, fuller way. And this idea of the sexual life as fulfilling and completing God's purpose naturally permitted the growth of the idea of sex as something good in itself.

All this, however, entailed a considerable amount of rewriting of history. For example, Ernst Troeltsch in his monumental *Social Teaching of the Christian Churches* describes the views of the early Church thus:

Alongside of this influence of Christian thought upon the idea of the Family there were, however, the quite different ideas of Christian asceticism and the ideal of celibacy. This dual character of the Christian sex ethic was already apparent in the thought of Paul, and under the influence of asceticism and monasticism it led to a grotesque exaltation of sexual restraint, which again led to the well-known ideas about the danger inherent in the female sex and to a low estimate of women – these ideas certainly arose out of the overstrained imagination of monasticism, and not out of the thought of Christianity.[14]

Grotesque they might be by our present standards, but Cardinal Daniélou has described these tendencies as 'existing at the very heart of the Church'. And so they obviously did. The only conclusion to be drawn from the New Testament is that all the enthusiasm went into celibacy and that the acceptance of marriage was always grudging and conditional. Troeltsch, the most influential of modern social historians of the Church, was engaging in pious wishful thinking. He was smoothing out the tortured disputes of the desert ascetics in order to present an unchanging picture of 'Christian marriage' which has no basis in reality.

You can feel the strain caused by this endeavour when you read

Troeltsch's triumphalist account of how St Thomas Aquinas 'integrated' the family within the Church:

> The incorporation of the Family into the central religious purpose of the Church consists in this: so far as possible the purely sexual side is ignored, since the aim of marriage is limited solely to the rational reproduction of human beings, and thus of members of the Church; the wedded state itself becomes a symbol of the union of Christ and the Church. In both respects the ascetic limitation of the sex instinct is effective, since marriage becomes solely an institution for reproduction, and a symbol of the spiritual unity of love. In all other respects its sacramental character brings it under the ecclesiastical marriage law, which the Church tries to extend as far as possible in opposition to the civil marriage law; it is also greatly influenced by the widespread power of the confessional. Since, moreover, the Church penetrates the personal relationships within the family with the Christian virtues of love, raising these above their natural union to the religious union of love, the family becomes the original form of, and the preparation for, all social relationships.[15]

But did the family *want* to be incorporated? How could husband and wife ignore the purely sexual side? In what sense can the wedded state become a symbol of the union of Christ and the Church? The wedded state exists in itself, for human purposes, and did so long before Christ came on earth. And have not those civil marriage laws, which the Church struggles so hard to supplant by its own, evolved out of human experience of marriage? And, put like that, does not 'the widespread power of the confessional' suggest a kind of intrusion and interposition between husband and wife which contradicts the whole purpose of marital union? Is there not, in short, something both domineering and sneaky about this whole 'incorporation'? Above all, can this take-over be regarded as divinely ordered when the Church's attitude is itself so recently evolved and remains in permanent flux? Is there not a crippling dishonesty – intellectual and moral – running through the whole business?

It is perhaps the bitterest of ironies that Cardinal Daniélou, the most honest of Church historians, should have died in a brothel. The Church tried to cover that up too.

Fear and distrust of sexual relations have always pervaded and distorted the Church's view of everything to do with marriage. And to understand ecclesiastical logic, it has always been essential to start from the fear and distrust. Take St Paul's attitude to divorce. Under the Roman Empire, divorce was common and legally quite simple to obtain. Paul by contrast discouraged divorce as far as possible, because a second liaison compounded the uncleanness, *not* because marriage was a sacred thing. Just as St Matthew inserted adultery as the sole ground for divorce,[16] so St Paul says, if you must divorce, at least do not marry again: 'Art thou loosed from a wife? seek not a wife.'[17] There is no question of marriage being so sacred as to need the protection of the gravest ordinances. Rather, marriage presents such a perilous distraction and such an occasion for sin that it must be carefully controlled; in modern terms, St Paul's teaching is comparable more to the regulations governing betting shops and pubs than to any doctrine of the spirituality of the married state.

Even within the married state, the early Church saw great temptations. St Jerome wrote:

> In the case of the wife of another, truly all love is shameful; in the case of one's own, excessive love. The wise man should love his wife with judgement, not with passion. Let him control the excesses of voluptuousness, and not allow himself to be carried away precipitately during intercourse. Nothing is more infamous than to love one's wife like a mistress.[18]

Nor did the Church entirely succeed in hiding its low view of marriage. People were well able to put two and two together, and the Church's grudging, distrustful attitude was still evident long after bishops and priests had been forced to make the tactical switch and to elevate the avoidance of uncleanness to 'Holy Matrimony'. Milton, for example, was aware of the intellectual dishonesty involved and exposed the contradiction in *The Doctrine and Discipline of Divorce*:

> It was for many ages that marriage lay in disgrace with most of the ancient doctors, as a work of the flesh, almost a defilement, wholly denied to priests, and the second time dissuaded to all, as he that reads Tertullian or Jerome may see at large. Afterwards it was thought so sacramental, that no adultery or desertion could dissolve it.[19]

The sole conclusion to be drawn from the law on divorce, Milton thought, was that the Church cared only about the control of sexual behaviour and little or nothing about 'the acts of peace and love, a far more precious mixture than the quintessence of an excrement'. This dishonesty contradicted and undermined the spirit of Christian doctrine.

Nor was this teaching an eccentric invention of the Church fathers, restricted in time and place. St Paul himself warns us not only against fornication and uncleanness but also against 'inordinate affection'. This tradition of distrust of passion even within marriage survives unmistakably to this day in the words of Pope John Paul II: 'Adultery in the heart is committed not only because the man looks in this way at a woman. But also if he looks in this way at a woman who is his own wife, he would commit adultery in his heart'[20] – a sentiment which goes one step further than the words of Jesus in St Matthew's Gospel.

Pope John Paul's words created a considerable stir at the time, but they do not seem to depart at all from the traditional teaching of the Church. Pius XII stated that even in marriage

> Couples must know how to restrict themselves within the limits of moderation. As in eating and drinking, so in the sexual act, they must not abandon themselves without restraint to the impulse of the senses . . . Unfortunately, never-ending waves of hedonism sweep over the world and threaten to drown all married life in the rising flood of thoughts, desires, and acts, not without grave dangers and serious damage to the primary duty of man and wife. Too often this anti-Christian hedonism does not blush to raise this theory to a doctrine by inculcating the desire to intensify continually enjoyment in the preparation and carrying out of the conjugal union, as though in matrimonial relations the whole moral law were reduced to a regular completion of the act itself and as though all the rest, no matter how accomplished, remained justified in the pouring out of mutual affection, sanctified by the sacrament of matrimony . . .[21]

Nor have these restrictions on the expression of feeling within the family circle been applied solely to sexual love between husband and wife. J. L. Flandrin, in his brilliant studies of the Catholic manuals for confessors between the fourteenth and nineteenth centuries, quotes several examples of confessors forbidding other forms of immoderate feeling:

An anonymous work entitled *Exercices spirituels qui se font en l'église Saint-Etienne-du-Mont* (1667) enjoined friendship between parents and children, not love. Moreover, when the word 'love' is used by the writer, it appears in the inventory of sins that children can commit, to warn them against any excess of this sentiment: 'If, owing to an immoderate love towards one's father or mother, one has not worried about offending God.' Conversely, it was a commonplace of the age to compare fathers who were insufficiently strict with their children 'to monkeys that kill their little ones through hugging and cherishing them too much.'[22]

Montaigne noted with a half-raised eyebrow:

The affection which we have for our wives is quite legitimate: nevertheless, theology does not neglect to curb and restrain it. I think I have read in the past in the works of Saint Thomas, in a passage in which he condemns marriages between kinsfolk within the prohibited degrees, this reason among others: that there is a danger that the affection that one has for such a woman may be immoderate; for if marital affection exists there entire and perfect, as it should do, and one overburdens this further with the affection that one owes to one's kinsfolk, there is no doubt that this addition will transport such a husband beyond the bounds of reason.[23]

Husbands and wives were and are to be loved *in moderation*. Only God is to be loved immoderately, boundlessly.

Once the Church had decided to exert total control over marriage, confessors found themselves led into curious byways. It might be simple enough to ban all variations on standard coitus, but it does seem curious that masturbation and *coitus interruptus* should have come to be classed along with sodomy and bestiality as the most grave of sexual sins – worse than fornication or adultery.

And the Church's prime concerns – chastity and the avoidance of sin – sometimes had unpleasant consequences for the children. Fromageau posed this problem in his *Dictionnaire des cas de conscience*. 'Jeanne, having had a first child by her husband, wishes to feed it herself; but, since her husband wishes to demand of her his conjugal rights, she asks whether she is obliged to satisfy him during all the time that she is nursing her child, or whether she can refuse him without sinning?' After setting out the arguments, he concludes: '*The wife should, if she can, put her child out to nurse,* in order to provide for the frailty of her husband by paying the conjugal due, for fear that he may lapse into some sin against conjugal purity.'[24]

Even if putting the child out to wet-nurse might mean neglect and death, as it frequently did, the need to keep the husband pure was regarded as more important. The 'conjugal due' was not the maintenance of your family and the nurture, cherishing and educating of your children; it was regular sexual intercourse, to keep both partners free from sin or the temptation to sin. If the consequence of regularly paying this conjugal debt was too many mouths to feed, that was preferable to sexual impurity.

The family was to be controlled for the avoidance of individual sin. It was always a secondary and subordinate instrument of the Church's purpose. Family relationships and responsibilities did not exist in their own right. And if the Church's teaching led to suffering, poverty and even death within the family, then those misfortunes were sent from God.

Modern churchmen have attempted to bury such embarrassing passages in the history of the Church. Yes, they will say, it is true that some of the hermits and desert fathers in the early Church had some rather curious ideas, but the mainstream of the Church always espoused the tradition of 'Be fruitful and multiply' and of the twain becoming one flesh. To quote the title of the Report of the British Council of Churches Working Party, 'God's Yes to Sexuality' can be found throughout the Church's history. All one can say is that at times it seems to have been a very faint and grudging Yes.

And one cannot help noticing that even today the same devious tactics are still at work:

> The Bible, both Old and New Testaments, is part of what is given to us, our tradition, and as such we must be guided by it. But just as the biblical writers did not regard their tradition as static, fixed or dead, neither can we regard our tradition as any less dynamic . . .[25]

This licenses the modern churchman to choose only the bits that suit his case. Now that we are to appreciate the joyous communion of human sexuality at its full worth, all the prohibitions on sexual conduct are to be discarded:

> The tendency hitherto has been to regard the heterosexual orientation as normal and all others as deviations from that. It is now more

usual to think of all forms of sexual identity and orientation as on a spectrum of individual manifestations of sexuality, in all its variety . . . While heterosexual orientation may be taken as a statistical norm, and the expected outcome of development, it cannot however be concluded that other patterns of sexual behaviour or expression are necessarily inferior or harmful, or morally bad.[26]

Marriage is simply one form of intimate relationship. Nowhere do the biblical writers 'affirm that this particular relationship is the only way for all women and men for all time. If this were so we should surely expect the record to point to a marriage of Jesus himself.'[27]

Even the symbolic use of marriage in the Bible 'is not a family image which can be used to support and uphold the nuclear family'.[28] In fact, the churches are to be rebuked for lagging behind the changes taking place in society and for trying to enforce Victorian morality or seeming to extol 'the self-enclosed nuclear family, living by middle-class values and conventions'.[29]

These 'dynamic' reinterpretations of the Bible all radiate a strong distaste for marriage and the nuclear family and its code. 'The quality of faithfulness of one to another which is required needs examining in the light of modern lifestyles and experience. Ideas of fidelity in marriage built around sexual faithfulness alone seem too narrow a concept, particularly for our time.'[30]

The fifteen members of the British Council of Churches Working Party were drawn from various denominations – Church of England, Roman Catholic, Methodist, Baptist. Some were married, some with children, we are told; some were celibate, some were homosexual, some were clergy, some laity. But what they all share is a manifest impatience with the demands and loyalties of the family:

Certainly living as a family is important, but is chiefly so when it points beyond itself and acts as one intersection among many others in the human network. Sometimes apparently strong families contribute little to society at large, falling all too easily into the trap of living for themselves alone . . .

Priorities in the use of time and talents need to be examined in the light of Christian commitment to society, of which commitment to the family is but one part. The assumption that family must always come first in terms of money, time and care, is not always fruitful. It is interesting that in the struggles of some great Christians the

family apparently came off badly, as for example in the lives of John
Wesley, Elizabeth Fry or David Livingstone . . .

The New Testament itself points away from exclusive concentration on family concerns towards other outward-looking possibili-
ties. Jesus is presented as warning us that ties of kinship are not
necessarily the most important in God's Kingdom, and proclaiming
that his brothers and sisters are 'all those who do God's will'. There
are times when it is right and necessary to break the bonds of family,
or to be free, however painfully, to relinquish claims upon another
member of it.[31]

This at least appears to be theologically correct. If we compare
the tolerance and compassion extended here to homosexuals and
adulterers and the *intolerance* towards those who put their families
first, it becomes clear that the underlying attitude of the Church is the
same as ever.

The family is still the enemy of *all* Christian churches. The family is
still the main distraction from the love of God. Scholars who have
recently investigated the Church's attitude to homosexuality in the
Middle Ages have found, if not tolerance, at least relative indifference. Although homosexuality was supposed to be no less a sin than
the heterosexual transgressions of fornication and adultery, in practice it was not denounced or punished with anything like the same
vigour. This may, I suppose, be partly because many clergy then and
now have inevitably themselves been homosexual, but it is surely also
because homosexual relationships do not present the same distraction
from the life of the Church. Above all, they do not present the danger
of having children. Nothing is more remarkable in *God's Yes to
Sexuality* than the fleeting and perfunctory references to children. The
truth is that sex is much less of a danger than parenthood is to religious
observance; modern churchmen have learnt to capitalise on the sexual
element in ecstatic religious experience instead of being ashamed of it.
But the cares and duties of parenthood are as remote as ever from the
religious sphere.

Above all, having children involves *planning*. Parents have to take
thought for the morrow and lay up treasure on earth, not only in the
material sense but in the sense of devoting time and emotion to the
upbringing of their children. Love, attention and forethought have to
be invested in huge quantities. The Christian message that faith will

free us of worry about the future does not fit in with the parental message that it is *right* to worry, that our children cannot be left to look after themselves.

It is not, and never has been, the Church's restrictions on sexuality which have constituted the basic threat which Christianity poses to the family. It is the carefree attitudes of the Sermon on the Mount:

> Lay not up for yourselves treasures upon earth . . . Behold the fowls of the air: for they sow not, neither do they reap, nor gather into barns; yet your heavenly Father feedeth them . . . Consider the lilies of the field, how they grow; they toil not, neither do they spin: And yet I say unto you, That even Solomon in all his glory was not arrayed like one of these . . . Take therefore no thought for the morrow: for the morrow shall take thought for the things of itself. Sufficient unto the day is the evil thereof.[32]

The irreducible, ultimate element in religious faith is the insistence that we are created things; male and female created He them; without God we are nothing. And yet, when men and women have children and become parents, they unmistakably become *creators*, incompetent, accidental and partial creators, no doubt, but creators none the less. It is their inescapable duty, and, with luck, their occasional delight to care and watch over their creations; even if this creative power is partly illusory because chromosomes and chance decide the whole business, parents cannot act *as if* it is illusory; they cannot sincerely believe in their ultimate helplessness. They must behave like shepherds, however clumsy, and not like sheep, however well trained.

The Sermon on the Mount is a wonderful, intoxicating sermon. But it is a sermon for bachelors.

2

THE STATE
AND THE
FAMILY

The contempt for marriage and the family is no less fierce in the teachings of Marx and Engels. The *Communist Manifesto* says:

On what foundation is the present family, the bourgeois family, based? On capital, on private gain. In its completely developed form this family exists only among the bourgeoisie. But this state of things finds its complement in the practical absence of the family among the proletarians, and in public prostitution. The bourgeois family will vanish as a matter of course when its complement vanishes, and both will vanish with the vanishing of capital . . .

The bourgeois clap-trap about the family and education, about the hallowed co-relation of parent and child, becomes all the more disgusting, the more, by the action of Modern Industry, all family ties among the proletarians are torn asunder; and their children transformed into simple articles of commerce and instruments of labour . . .

Our bourgeois, not content with having the wives and daughters of their proletarians at their disposal, not to speak of common prostitutes, take the greatest pleasure in seducing each other's wives. Bourgeois marriage is in reality a system of wives in common and thus, at the most, what the Communists might possibly be reproached with is that they desire to introduce, in substitution for a hypocritically concealed, an open legalized community of women.[1]

According to the *Manifesto*, published in 1848, the family under capitalism could be written off in two sentences: among the upper classes, it was an inhuman, corrupt, commercial arrangement; among the lower classes, it did not exist.

All this is elaborated in Engels's *The Origin of the Family, Private Property and the State* – a late work sometimes treated with embarrassment by academic Marxists, but still stubbornly influential and much quoted in Soviet Russia and in the Women's Movement. Engels claimed that he had been working on Marx's notes after the latter's death; some Marxists say he had oversimplified Marx's conclusions, but the phrasing of the *Communist Manifesto* of nearly forty years earlier shows that the differences can have been only relatively minor. Apart from these two cases, the references to marriage and the family in the voluminous writings of Marx and the early Marxists are scant and cursory. Indeed, Engels was consciously trying to fill a gap – much as St Paul was.

This is no coincidence. For Marxism as for Christianity, the family is a corruption or at best a distraction. It is only our tiresome biological legacy and its attendant practical social problems which force our attention to turn to these secondary matters; the family is both a symptom and a cause of human weakness.

Nor can we avoid distasteful comparisons. However horrible we may find Adolf Hitler and Nazism, we cannot deny a certain similarity between the Nazis' attitude towards the family and the attitude of the Christian Church. For both, the family is essentially secondary and subordinate. Hitler wrote in *Mein Kampf*:

> Even marriage cannot be an end in itself, but must serve a greater goal, the increase and conservation of the species and race. That is its only purpose and task. For that reason, early marriage is correct because the marriage of young people still has that strength from which alone may come a healthy posterity capable of resistance.[2]

Later on, Hitler specifies the purpose of marriage and the way in which it should be controlled and guided by the State:

> The generation of our notorious present-day weaklings will of course cry out in protest and moan and wail about attacks on the most sacred human rights. I say no, there is only one most sacred human right, and this right is at the same time the most sacred duty,

namely, to see to it that the blood is kept pure in order that by the preservation of the best in humanity the possibility of a nobler development of its essence may be provided.

A people's State will therefore as a first priority raise marriage from the level of an enduring shame to the race, so as to consecrate it as an institution which is designed to forge images of the master and not monstrous abortions half-way between man and ape.[3]

Protest against this sacred programme on 'so-called humane grounds', according to *Mein Kampf*, is really only special pleading from 'degenerates and weaklings' and 'from those healthy beings who can buy in any chemist's shop the means to stop producing healthy progeny, while cripples and syphilitics freely reproduce themselves'.[4]

Now this ghastly stuff did not stop at propaganda. Within a year of his coming to power in 1933 as *Reichskanzler*, Hitler had a sterilisation law passed. The entire Reich was swiftly organised to stamp out 'hereditary defects'. A doctor who failed to supply the required information lost his right to practise. A whole corpus of marriage law was instituted. Individuals could apply for sterilisation, or it could be asked for by legal guardians, doctors or prison governors; persons judged to be dangerous sexual criminals were castrated. Those who were considered healthy were not permitted to ask to be sterilised.

A licence was necessary for marriage; applicants needed a health certificate; a German could not marry a Jew, and such a mixed marriage contracted before the law had been introduced could be dissolved on that ground alone.

These horrific prohibitions are burnt into our memory. But less often remembered are the positive means by which the Nazi state sought to encourage 'healthy' families. Young men were discouraged from marrying until after they had completed their six months' duty in a labour camp and their two years in the army. Professional men on long courses of study were not permitted to marry until the age of twenty-five, unless they had private means. Industrialists and government departments, however, warned their employees that 'at 26 a bachelor has reached the place where he can expect no further advancement in position or wages until he has shown himself capable of assuming responsibility by taking his place in German society as a husband and a father.'[5]

The State, in other words, sought to exercise total control over

31

marriage and the family in the interests of racial improvement. The ends and results were uniquely appalling. But the claim of the State to know best and to possess supreme authority over the institutions of marriage and the family is by no means unique or even unusual.

In Prussia itself, there had long existed similar 'guidelines' prescribing when and whom to marry. The parson's blessing was not enough. Authority had to give its approval too. An edict of 1739 forbade noblemen to marry the daughters of peasants. In Württemberg, in the eighteenth century, cripples and blind persons were not permitted to marry at all. Artisans had to have completed their apprenticeships. Students in many institutions were forbidden to marry before graduation and even afterwards until they had obtained a job. Nowhere in Protestant Germany was it possible to marry without parental permission, just as Luther had prescribed.

In twentieth-century Britain we too are familiar with comparable prohibitions, if on a much smaller scale. In British regiments it has usually been forbidden to marry without the commanding officer's permission. In England, young people over the age of consent but under twenty-one could not marry without their parents' approval – hence the elopements to Gretna Green where the more permissive Scottish law reigned.

These restrictions dwindle by comparison with the constraints placed upon the marriage of unfree peasants by the feudal system. Throughout Western Europe, it was forbidden to marry outside your lordship or *familia* without your lord's permission; indeed, in many places it was forbidden to marry at all without permission. The lord could and did withhold his consent, particularly in the case of serfs who wanted to 'marry out', thus depriving him of labour to work his land. Parents were held responsible for children who disobeyed this law. Heavy fines known as the 'formariage' were payable. In any case, in many countries, the lord exacted a marriage tax on all weddings of serfs' daughters, in or out of the lordship. In England, this tax was called 'merchet' and was regarded as 'of all manorial exactions the most odious', according to the great mediaeval historian Sir Paul Vinogradoff. The abolition of such obligations and taxes – a key test of servile status – was one of the prime demands in peasant uprisings.

Paradoxically, it is from these obligations and taxes that we can deduce our first evidence that peasants married for love. For the customary legal and financial obstacles to 'marrying out' were so severe that they might have been expected to deter the half-starved serfs from ever attempting such a thing. But marrying out was a frequent occurrence and highly tiresome for lords. In fact, it happened so often that complex and hotly disputed rules were drawn up to deal with the consequences. The children of a 'mixed marriage', for example, were to be brought up on the manor to which the mother belonged; or, according to another view, they were to be shared between the two manors when they were old enough to work, the eldest to the father's manor, the next to the mother's and so on. When the marriage produced only one child or an odd number of children, the rules became more complex still, and still more of a deterrent.

The most striking proof that love could hurdle such obstacles is the feudal rule governing marriages between a free person and an unfree person. The children of such marriages were usually held to be unfree, and often the free parent thereby became at least partially unfree too – the least advantageous sort of match imaginable, and yet it happened, so often in fact that both the French and the Germans had a phrase for it: '*le mauvais emporte le bon*' and '*Das Kind folgt der ärgeren Hand*' (the child follows the worse side of the family). The point of this rule, which derives from Roman law, is clear: the interests of the ruling class demanded that the serf pool should not be drained by upwardly mobile serfs marrying out.

We must never forget how rare it has been in the past thousand years for marriage to be unaffected by official pressure. Apart from a ban on bigamy and a minimum age of consent, today we regard it as grossly oppressive for the authorities to try to put any restrictions on whom and when we choose to marry. Such freedom is hard to find elsewhere in the history of the last thousand years. More often, marriage has been regulated by the authorities to serve some external purpose: the increase or decrease of the national population, the breeding of an invincible race, the maintenance of a well-defined class structure, the improvement of national prosperity or national moral fibre, the fulfilment of God's purpose, the avoidance of impurity or degeneracy.

'Marriage cannot be an end in itself' – the words are Hitler's, but they might just as well be those of any Communist dictator or any pope or bishop.

In the Encyclical Letter of Pius XI on 'Christian Marriage', the subordinate nature of marriage is made very clear:

. . . let us recall this immutable, inviolable, and fundamental truth: Matrimony was not instituted or re-established by men but by God; not men, but God, the Author of nature, and Christ our Lord, the Restorer of nature, provided marriage with its laws, confirmed it, and elevated it; and consequently those laws can in no way be subject to human wills or to any contrary pact made even by the contracting parties themselves. This is the teaching of Sacred Scripture; it is the constant and universal Tradition of the Church; it is the solemnly defined doctrine of the Council of Trent, which uses the words of Holy Scripture to proclaim and establish that the perpetual indissolubility of the marriage bond, its unity and its stability, derive from God Himself.[6]

The makers of Soviet Russia were in a somewhat different situation. Like the early Christians, many of the old Bolsheviks were hostile or indifferent to marriage, though of course for opposite reasons. They often believed in free love, which was regarded as a 'Gift of the Revolution'. Many nineteenth-century socialists had subscribed to the view that sex was or ought to be as simple and trivial a satisfaction of physical needs as drinking a glass of water. As for the family, at one time or another, Trotsky, Alexandra Kollontai, Lunacharski and Krylenko all subscribed to the view that it would wither away in due course. The radical view was summarised by A. Slepkov, an influential Leningrad party member:

Bourgeois ideologists think that the family is an eternal, not a transitory organization, that sexual relations are at the basis of the family, that these sexual relations will exist as long as the two sexes, and since man and woman will both live under socialism just as under capitalism, that therefore the existence of the family is inevitable. That is completely incorrect. Sexual relations, of course, have existed, exist, and will exist. However, this is in no way connected with the indispensability of the existence of the family. The best historians of culture definitely have established that in primitive times the family did not exist . . . Similar to the way in which, together with the disappearance of classes, together with the annihilation of class contradictions, the state will disappear, similarly to that, together with the strengthening of the socialist economy, together with the growth of socialist relationships, together with the overcoming of earlier pre-socialist forms, the family will also die out. The family is already setting out on the road to a merging with Socialist Society, to a dissolution into it. An openly negative attitude toward the family under present conditions does not have sufficient grounding, because pre-socialist relationships still exist, the state is still weak, the new social forms (public dining rooms, state rearing of children, and so forth) are as yet little developed, and until then the family cannot be abolished completely. However, the coordination of this family with the general organization of Soviet life is the task of every communist, of every Komsomolite [member of Communist Youth League]. One must not shut oneself off in the family, but rather, grow out of the family shell into the new Socialist Society. The contemporary Soviet family is the springboard from which we must leap into the future. Always seeking to carry the entire family over into the public organizations, always a more decisive overcoming of the elements of bourgeois family living – that is the difficult, but important task which stands before us.[7]

Lunacharski, the Commissar of Education, wrote as late as the early 1930s:

Our problem now is to do away with the household and to free women from the care of children. It would be idiotic to separate children from their parents by force. But when, in our communal houses, we have well-organized quarters for children, connected by a heated gallery with the adults' quarters, to suit the requirements of the climate, there is no doubt the parents will, of their own free will, send their children to these quarters, where they will be supervised by trained pedagogical and medical personnel. There is no doubt that the terms 'my parents,' 'our children,' will gradually fall out of usage, being replaced by such conceptions as 'old people,' 'children,' and 'infants.'[8]

This, according to Lunacharski, was to be an essential part of the transition to the new society – 'that broad public society which will replace the small philistine nook, that little philistine apartment, that domestic hearth, yes, that stagnant family unit which separates itself off from society.'[9] A genuine Communist would avoid such a permanent pairing marriage and would seek to satisfy his needs by ' . . . a freedom of the mutual relations of the husbands, the wives, fathers, children, so that you can't tell who is related to whom and how closely. That is social construction.'[10]

Although these ideas were popular and indeed acted on by enthusiastic young Communists, they did not, strictly speaking, form part of the party line. Lenin recoiled from the glass-of-water theory as completely un-Marxist and, moreover, anti-social:

> To be sure, thirst has to be quenched. But would a normal person normally lie down in the gutter and drink from a puddle? Or even from a glass whose edge has been greased by many lips? But the social aspect is more important than anything else. The drinking of water is really an individual matter. But it takes two people to make love, and a third person, a new life, is likely to come into being. This deed has a social complexion and constitutes a duty to the community.[11]

Free love, according to Lenin, was a degenerate bourgeois fantasy: 'The revolution calls for concentration and rallying of every nerve by the masses and by the individual. It does not tolerate orgiastic conditions so common among d'Annunzio's decadent heroes and heroines. Promiscuity in sexual matters is bourgeois.'[12] He had little time for discussion on the subject:

> I was told that sex problems are a favourite subject in your youth organisations too, and that there are hardly enough lecturers on this subject. This nonsense is especially dangerous and damaging to the youth movement. It can easily lead to sexual excesses, to over-stimulation of sex life and to wasted health and strength of young people.[13]

Mens sana in corpore sano was Lenin's motto. But the Soviet leaders were busy and, as Trotsky wrote in 1923, 'the party did not and could not accord specific attention to questions of the everyday life of the working masses.'[14]

The after-effects of civil war and the new sexual freedoms combined to produce social chaos, a great number of unwanted and abandoned children, venereal diseases and also – a factor not to be underestimated – millions of shocked and puzzled peasants, particularly women, who regarded the new freedoms as dangerous and unhealthy.

The Communist Party began rapidly to change its tune. By the time

Beatrice and Sidney Webb published *Soviet Communism: A New Civilisation?* in 1935,

> In the Communist Party and among the Comsomols, sexual prom-
> iscuity, like all forms of self-indulgence, has come to be definitely
> thought contrary to communist ethics, on the grounds enumerated
> by Lenin; it is a frequent cause of disease; it impairs the productiv-
> ity of labour; it is disturbing to accurate judgment and inimical to
> intellectual acquisition and scientific discovery, besides frequently
> involving cruelty to individual sufferers. Stability and mutual
> loyalty have become steadily more generally enforced not only by
> public opinion but also, so far as Party members and Comsomols
> were concerned, by the ordinary Party sanctions. Disloyalty in
> marital relations, and even exceptional instability have become
> definite offences against communist ethics, leading not only to
> reprimands but also, in bad cases, to expulsion.[15]

Trade union leaders were urged to take more interest in the private
lives of their members, including attitudes towards wives and children. In 1935, 1936 and 1944, new laws were introduced to compel
divorced parents to contribute towards the maintenance of their
children, to make abortion illegal and divorce itself more difficult and
expensive. Homosexuality became a criminal offence in 1934. In
1936, *Pravda* commented that, 'Marriage is the most serious affair in
life.'[16]

Stalin had changed direction and everyone else had to change too.
Entirely spurious interpretations were dredged up to prove that Marx
and Engels had never been against the family. The new scapegoats
came in handy here:

> The enemies of the people, the vile fascist hirelings – Trotsky,
> Bukharin, Krylenko and their followers – covered the family in the
> USSR with filth, spreading the counter-revolutionary 'theory' of
> the dying out of the family, of disorderly sexual cohabitation in the
> USSR, in order to discredit the Soviet land.[17]

Why did Stalin turn? No doubt it was partly because the family had
stubbornly refused to die out, and its official revival would be
generally popular and help to deal with genuine social problems; but
the main reason was surely that the regime had simply allowed too
large an area of Soviet life to escape its control. It was not only that the

Soviet concept of 'free marriage' – involving divorce and abortion at will – had proved a social failure. It was rather that no fully articulated Soviet attitude towards marriage and the family existed at all. The only answer was, so to speak, to 'patriate' the family – to glorify it as a popular, essentially *Russian* institution.

In other words, on this question as on so many others, Stalin resorted to compromise between Marxism-Leninism and the Russian tradition. The family was good because it was created by the Russian people; hence it was good because it was socialist too.

By this compromise between dogma and tradition, the Soviet regime effectively assumed control of marriage and the family. In just the same way, the Christian Church, after its initial indifference and hostility, had assumed control by redefining the natural biological origins of marriage as ordained of God in the Garden of Eden – and not, as the very early Christians had thought, as simply the impulses of our lower natures and a perpetual occasion of sin. Of course, the official rules were and are quite different under the two regimes; divorce and abortion remain easy in the Soviet Union; the Church still disapproves of both. But the overarching control is the same. So is the rewriting of history.

And so, alas, is the lingering aura of bad faith, the unavoidable suspicion that the regime attaches a lower importance to marriage and the family than it pretends to. Yet ideologues continue to deny that any problem exists. Soviet spokesmen continue to pretend that Marx and Engels look down benignly on the Soviet family. It is not merely parish priests quieting their simple flocks and popes and Synods who have asserted that the Church must be accepted as the protector and director of family life.

How do they manage this evasion? What are the strategies for sidestepping the apparent conflict between family and ideology?

The strategies are of two types: the historical and the moral.

The historical strategy argues that the family as we know it – the 'nuclear family' – is a temporary and fleeting historical development. There is nothing eternal or natural or god-given about it. All these institutions which we take for granted – marriage, 'parenting' within the family, separate households based on the 'marital unit' – are of relatively recent origin and will in time pass away.

Sir Edmund Leach, anthropologist, Reith Lecturer and former Provost of King's College, Cambridge, is not alone in believing that the nuclear family 'is a most unusual kind of organisation and I would predict that it is only a transient phase in our society'.[18] Lawrence Stone concludes his massive work, *The Family, Sex and Marriage in England 1500–1800*, with this judgment on the evolution of the family as we know it:

> However one assesses it in moral terms, for better or for worse, it is certainly one of the most significant transformations that has ever taken place, not only in the most intimate aspects of human life, but also in the nature of social organization. It is geographically, chronologically and socially a most restricted and unusual phenomenon, and there is as little reason to have any more confidence in its survival and spread in the future as there is in that of democracy itself.[19]

Less cautiously, Edward Shorter concludes *The Making of the Modern Family*:

> Towards the end of the eighteenth century, a transformation in domestic life occurred, the shift from traditional to nuclear family. I argued that 'capitalism' was the driving force behind that change. What master variable is at work today though, I must say, is unclear . . . In the 1960s and 1970s the entire structure of the family has begun to shift. The nuclear family is crumbling – to be replaced, I think, by the free-floating couple, a marital dyad subject to dramatic fissions and fusions, and without the orbiting satellites of pubertal children, close friends, or neighbours . . . just the relatives, hovering in the background, friendly smiles on their faces.[20]

Because the nuclear family is such a recent and accidental development, we are told, it is not only mortal and transient but also of secondary importance. It cannot claim to be superior or immune to other imperatives, such as the worship of God or the interests of State or the progress of society. Even if the family as we know it may have certain good points along with its flaws, it is for the State or Church to define what those good points are. The fact that families themselves may desire to perpetuate or enlarge certain family customs and practices is not in itself a good reason for allowing them to do so. We do not need to argue that the family exists *for* the State; all we need say is that the State *knows best* and has the moral and historical authority to guide and direct the development of the family and its attendant institutions.

It is the State which knows whether families should have more babies or fewer babies. Sometimes the State changes its mind very rapidly on this question; at one moment, official wisdom may be that it is imperative for the future development of the nation to replace dead heroes – as it has been in France since the First World War; a few years later or a few miles away over the border, officials may be worrying whether there will be too many mouths for the nation to feed.

The examples I have given so far have mostly come from states which were or are totalitarian, or at any rate authoritarian. These are the most relevant for this part of our enquiry, for in times past most states were authoritarian and took it as a matter of course that they should control the institutions of marriage and the family. The history of liberal regimes in the West since the mid-nineteenth century has been a story of gradual but accelerating relaxation of control.

All the same, it is remarkable how long even Western governments have clung on to their power over marriage. The most striking example is the state control of divorce – which in England was only transferred *to* the State from the Church courts in the mid-nineteenth century against severe opposition from Gladstone and other high churchmen. The real relaxation in the laws of divorce did not reach England – and many other Western European countries – until well after the Second World War.

The retention of these strict controls was defended not primarily on utilitarian grounds, such as the welfare of the children and the protection of deserted wives. These were regarded as important, just as they are today. But the authorities were perfectly well aware that many childless couples or couples with grown-up children might well wish to get divorced *by mutual consent*; in practice, these categories have formed a high proportion – almost one-third – of couples divorcing under modern liberalised divorce laws.

The real primary objection was that easier divorce would damage the *nation*. As late as 1956, the Royal Commission on Marriage and Divorce argued that 'to give people a right to divorce themselves would be to foster a change in the attitude to marriage which would be disastrous for the nation.' Even today, something of this attitude lingers in a report from the Society of Conservative Lawyers which argues that not only does the present rate of marriage breakdown 'represent a deep well of human misery' but 'the financial cost to the State of the present rate of marriage breakdown is capable of absolute proof and is already an intolerable burden. *On that ground alone*, it is clearly important that more marriages should be preserved and preserved in stability . . . The fundamental factor in the changes of the past decade is that the State has withdrawn from preserving marriages and protecting children and it is now time to consider whether the State should resume that responsibility.'[21] (My italics.) The interests of the State – economy, orderliness – are to Conservative lawyers apparently of such importance that they should outweigh public opinion which has 'continued to demand easier divorce laws'. We are told, in elegiac tones, that 'in the space of a decade the Law and the Church, the two pillars which supported marriage, have both collapsed.'

As we have seen, the Church's support for marriage was always somewhat backhanded. The Law's support – derived in the case of England directly from mediaeval canon law and therefore scarcely distinguishable from the Church's – simply took the form of banning divorce for all except the few people rich enough to hire a good lawyer. Neither the Law nor the Church ever grappled with the idea – common in almost all pre-Christian and non-Christian societies – that any serious conception of marriage must include provision for dissolving disastrous marriages.[22] The belief that it is the State's business to control marriage and divorce dies very hard. This is because the idea that marriage is an *independent* institution with a life of its own is extremely distasteful to the State as it is to the Church – neither of which lightly tolerates any rival for power over human hearts.

In fact, when the family shows a will of its own, that will is to be regarded as froward, contrary, wilful in the popular sense. For the moral objection to the family is that it is a *selfish* institution; it puts its own interests first. That is why, we are told, among Christ's first followers, in the beginning at least, 'all that believed were together, and had all things common' and 'the multitude of them that believed were of one heart and of one soul: neither said any of them that ought of the things which he possessed was his own; but they had all things common.'[23]

Socrates in Plato's *Republic* argues more thoroughly why the family and private property should be seen as threats:

Then the community of wives and children among our citizens is clearly the source of the greatest good to the State? Certainly. And this agrees with the other principle which we are affirming – that the guardians were not to have houses or lands or any other property; their pay was to be their food, which they were to receive from the other citizens, and they were to have no private expenses; for we intended them to preserve their true characters of guardians.

Right, he replied. Both the community of property and the community of families, as I am saying, tend to make them more truly guardians; they will not tear the city in pieces by differing about 'mine' and 'not mine'; each man dragging any acquisition which he has made into a separate house of his own, where he has a separate wife and children and private pleasures and pains; but all will be affected as far as may be by the same pleasures and pains because they are all of one opinion about what is near and dear to them, and therefore they all tend towards a common end.[24]

Thus an excessive devotion to family is just as selfish as excessive devotion to yourself; both are at the expense of the wider community.

Before we examine more carefully these two anti-family strategies, the historical and the moral, there is one further point to be noted. The two strategies contradict each other.

If the family as we know it – the nuclear or conjugal family – is a fleeting phenomenon of modern history, destined to pass away as suddenly as it has come, why is it that the *moral* objection to the family has taken much the same form over the past 2,500 years? According to the historical critique, in 400 B.C. no such thing as the selfish, private nuclear family of modern industrial society ought to have existed. Society in the Holy Land ought to have been dominated by tribal systems. The procreation of children would accordingly have been a mechanical matter, carried out according to social rules without emotional commitment.

Yet it is precisely the emotional commitment which seems to have alarmed the philosophers and ascetics of these times. It might be possible to extract from these expressions of alarm some indication that these ancient families were a little more extended, that their members felt rather more strongly about their remoter kinsmen than we do. But the evidence suggests that this is a quibble. Ancient critics of the family may have been disturbed by the trouble caused by warring clans, but their primary and unmistakable worry concerned the emotional intensity of the *nuclear* family – the strength of sexual passion and intimacy between husband and wife and the passionate determination of parents to protect and prefer their own children. It was in fact this intensity, this concentration of the tight-knit, small unit which provoked the criticism; any larger, more extended family might have been easier to integrate into a communal society.

Both anti-family strategies cannot be entirely right at the same time. Either the moral objections to the family have always been true and relevant because, so far as we can trace back, something comparable to our type of family has always existed, in which case the historical critique is not only irrelevant but false; or the moral objections have been irrelevant throughout most of human history, because the family as we know it has existed only for the past two or three centuries.

But is either of the strategies correct? We shall have to examine each separately.

3

IS
THE FAMILY
AN HISTORICAL
FREAK?

Engels bases his history of the family on the findings of the latest nineteenth-century anthropologists, in particular those of the American, Lewis Morgan. Indeed, the subtitle of *The Origin of the Family, Private Property and the State* is 'in the light of the researches of Lewis H. Morgan'. Like most of his contemporaries, Morgan was heavily Darwinian and took it for granted that the same type of evolutionary scheme must apply to the development of man's social arrangements as to his physical development. The family, according to Morgan, 'represents an active principle. It is never stationary, but advances from a lower to a higher form as society advances from a lower to a higher condition.'

The first stage in Morgan's scheme – enthusiastically adopted by Engels – is an era of communal promiscuity: 'unrestricted sexual freedom prevailed within the tribe, every woman belonging equally to every man and every man to every woman'.[1] This is both the oldest and most idyllic form of family life, an emotional Garden of Eden:

And what, in fact, do we find to be the oldest and most primitive form of family whose historical existence we can indisputably prove and which in one or two parts of the world we can still study today? – group marriage, the form of family in which whole groups of men and women mutually possess one another, and which leaves little room for jealousy.[2]

In the mid-nineteenth century, polygamy was widely regarded among radicals and anarchists as the natural and habitual state of the great majority of primitive mankind. Charles Fourier, in his savage attacks on the hypocrisy and brutality of marriage in France, takes this for granted:

> If polygamy merits the attacks levelled against it by the philo-
> sophers, how is it that they have found no means of eliminating the
> barbarian societies which keep five hundred million men in a state
> of polygamy? How is it that among the three hundred million
> people who live in savagery and civilization, the former frequently
> practise polygamy and regard it as a virtue, while the people of
> civilization are clandestine polygamists despite the fact that they
> claim to regard adultery as a vice?[3]

The findings of the fledgling science of anthropology seemed to confirm the travellers' tales of the eighteenth century. The practice of free love in real places such as Tahiti was held to prove that monogamy was not natural.

That is why this first stage is valuable to Engels, not because it evokes a lost golden age of natural freedom, such as might appeal to Utopians and other romantic spirits, but because it purports to establish, right from the start of human history, that monogamy is not *natural* and that there is no continuous line of development to the human from the animal kingdom. Thus any evidence that most animals prefer monogamy may be ruled out as beside the point. This primitive promiscuity represented a *break* with the animal kingdom.

To establish this break is tactically crucial. It is one of the main reasons why Marx remains so enduringly popular and why even today his admirers persist in repeating his most utterly exploded assertions about human history. For the charm of Marxism is that it liberates you from nature – and from the duties and restrictions of the family.

It is essential for the view of human development proposed by Marx and Engels that man should be freed from the legacy of any biological imperative. We are the makers of our own history; there is nothing in our physical or genetic make-up which could limit or direct the course of that history. Nothing 'comes naturally' to us. Indeed, the whole idea of 'human nature' as something fixed and enduring is to be dismissed as sentimental twaddle, like telling your future by the stars.

Marxists manage this argument by making a cunning shift in the way they define 'natural'. What we normally mean by 'doing what comes naturally' is nothing so instinctive and automatic as a knee-jerk or the physical functions of breathing, sweating and excreting, but an action which can be placed rather nearer the instinctive end than the voluntary end of the range of human actions. We do not suppose that such actions and feelings are the same as purely physical reflexes. 'Doing what comes naturally' can be avoided; a person can be *denatured* by physical or psychological pressures. Rats in cages do funny things which they do not do in the wild. Not all males in any species are sexually attracted to females. Not all mothers love their babies.

The knowledge of such deviations from natural behaviour does not prevent us from saying that 'it is natural for rats to do such-and-such' or that 'it is natural for males to be sexually attracted to females'. Whatever the language we use to explain natural behaviour – we may talk of instinctual drives, or of biological programming – the purpose of invoking the idea of nature is to contrast it with *unnatural* behaviour resulting from untoward or abnormal outside forces. If we *always* behaved naturally, and could behave in no other way, the idea would be much less useful; we would simply say 'Human beings/rats *do* x or y'; it would be like talking about a blink or a knee-jerk.

The Marxist trick is to shift the definition of nature along the range until it means virtually the same as instinct. At that point, the Marxist can say 'nature is an illusion' – because people can and do behave unnaturally, often violently so and in great numbers. Because some mothers are cruel or indifferent to their children, the idea of a maternal instinct as being natural to women must be rejected. Because in most societies a percentage of men and women are homosexual, we must reject the idea that heterosexual behaviour is natural. Therefore, we are triumphantly informed, nothing we do is natural; everything is the product of environment.

But the commonsense idea of nature is in no way damaged by the argument that so-called natural human behaviour needs, at least in part, to be learnt by example or precept. So does much natural animal behaviour. It is easier to be an affectionate mother if you knew affection as a child; happy marriages breed happy marriages. To say this is to do no more than observe that water prefers to run downhill. The fact that a natural tendency may be either blocked or helped along by outside interference does not prevent it from being natural.

Curiously enough, the Roman Catholic Church also relies upon the notion of an *historical break* with nature and biology, although the Church's intention is somewhat different. The Catholic tradition is based upon the assumption that primitive societies became promiscuous, and that marriage had to be *rescued* by Christianity. This rescue was both a spiritual advance and a restoration of the natural institution laid down by God in the Garden of Eden. Pope Leo XIII in *Arcanum* (1880) described the pre-Christian history of marriage thus:

> The corruption and change which overtook marriage among the Gentiles seem almost incredible, inasmuch as it was exposed in every land to floods of error and of the most shameful lusts. All nations seem, more or less, to have forgotten the true notion and origin of marriage . . . plurality of wives and husbands, the abounding sources of divorces, brought about an exceeding relaxation in the nuptial bond.[4]

While the Church's version of history is designed to prove the specifically Christian character of marriage as we know it, Engels has to demonstrate that marriage was continuously developing under the influence of social and economic change. Each stage of human society must be reflected by some dramatic change in the institution of marriage.

The group marriage of primitive society was accordingly succeeded in Engels's scheme by 'pairing marriage'. This was the feature of 'the age of barbarism':

> In this stage, one man lives with one woman, but the relationship is such that polygamy and occasional infidelity remain the right of the men, even though for economic reasons polygamy is rare, while from the woman the strictest fidelity is generally demanded throughout the time she lives with the man and adultery on her part is cruelly punished.
>
> The marriage tie can, however, be easily dissolved by either partner; after separation, the children still belong as before to the mother alone.[5]

This pairing marriage is sharply distinguished from modern monogamy.

> The pairing family, itself too weak and unstable to make an independent household necessary or even desirable, in no wise

destroys the communistic household inherited from earlier times. Communistic housekeeping, however, means the supremacy of women in the house; just as the exclusive recognition of the female parent, owing to the impossibility of recognizing the male parent with certainty, means that the women – the mothers – are held in high respect.[6]

The transition from the pairing marriage to modern monogamy is produced by the most dramatic event of all – the one which has guaranteed the continued popularity of Engels and Morgan:

The overthrow of mother right was the *world historical defeat of the female sex*. The man took command in the home also; the woman was degraded and reduced to servitude; she became the slave of his lust and a mere instrument for the production of children . . .

The establishment of the exclusive supremacy of the man shows its effects first in the patriarchal family, which now emerges as an intermediate form. Its essential characteristic is not polygyny . . . but 'the organization of a number of persons, bond and free, into a family under paternal power for the purpose of holding lands and for the care of flocks and herds . . . Those held to servitude and those employed as servants lived in the marriage relation.'[7]

With the patriarchal family, we reach the second great stage in the historical critique. The patriarchal family is what is also commonly called 'the extended family', which is widely imagined to have filled the world until the coming of the industrial world and modern times. In the patriarchal family, several generations of the descendants of a single father, together with their wives, live in one homestead and work in the same fields.

So far love does not come into it. Engels refers repeatedly to the 'small part individual sex love, in the modern sense of the word, played in the rise of monogamy'.[8] And even when monogamy in our modern sense did emerge, 'It was not in any way the fruit of individual sex love, with which it had nothing whatever to do; marriages remained as before marriages of convenience. It was the first form of the family to be based not on natural but on economic conditions.'[9] And its purpose was brutally economic, to secure the supremacy of the man.

Love, according to Engels and to many other popular historians, was invented by the troubadours of Provence and celebrated not married love but adulterous passion. It was the rise of the bourgeoisie, with all its hypocrisies and contradictions, which brought sex love into marriage.

This, then, is the Engels pattern: first of all, promiscuous group marriage, then matriarchal pairing marriage, then the patriarchal extended family, then bourgeois monogamy and then and only then the integration of sex love and marriage.

Now the historical truth of this pattern is disputed not once but from start to finish, and by a variety of observers. To start with, anthropologists have firmly denied that group marriage was the rule in primitive society. On the contrary, they argue again and again that this deduction by Morgan and his Victorian contemporaries, Bachofen and Sir John Lubbock, was based on a total misunderstanding of tribal customs and institutions. Westermarck in his *History of Marriage* (1891) asserts that, on the contrary, monogamy is the rule almost everywhere; even where polygamy or any other variant of sexual, parental and social relations is found, monogamy continues to be the normal rule of life. Westermarck's counter-attack began in Engels's lifetime; the *Origin of the Family*, indeed, contains replies to some of Westermarck's early assertions about monogamy in animals. Nor does Westermarck accept that these lifelong marriages were without affection; he lists a string of cases of devotion in tribal society – lovelorn fiancées, griefstricken widows and widowers and so on.

Among the instances cited, I cannot resist quoting:

Among the Indians of Western Washington and North-Western Oregon, says Dr. Gibbs, 'a strong sensual attachment undoubtedly often exists, which leads to marriage, as instances are not rare of young women destroying themselves on the death of a lover.' The like is said of other Indian tribes, in which suicide from unsuccessful love has sometimes occurred even among men. Colonel Dalton represents the Pahária lads and lasses as forming very romantic attachments; 'if separated only for an hour,' he says, 'they are miserable.' Davis tells us of a negro who, after vain attempts to redeem his sweetheart from slavery, became a slave himself rather than be separated from her. In Tahiti, unsuccessful suitors have been known to commit suicide; and even the rude Australian girl sings in a strain of romantic affliction –

'I never shall see my darling again.'[10]

The intensity with which Westermarck argued against the hypothesis (in Volume I, chapters IV–VII in particular) may perhaps be partly attributed to the moral shock of Morgan's claim upon Victorian susceptibilities, but his argument has been sustained with increasing firmness by the great masters of modern anthropology – Malinowski, Radcliffe-Brown and many others. In fact, Malinowski admired Westermarck for having so promptly demolished the myth of group marriage.[11] Robert H. Lowie, too, received Malinowski's respect for refuting Morgan. Indeed, Lowie's summary of the case against Morgan, deployed in *Primitive Society* (1929), remains the accepted view of anthropologists:

When evolutionary principles, having gained general acceptance in biology, had begun to affect all philosophical thinking, it was natural to extend them to the sphere of social phenomena . . . For the mid-Victorian thinker it was a foregone conclusion requiring only statement, not proof, that monogamy is the highest form of marriage in the best conceivable universes; and it was equally axiomatic that early man must have lived under conditions infinitely removed from that ideal goal. So Morgan made no pretense at producing empirical proof of pristine promiscuity, which in fact he assigned to the period when man was still hovering near the border line between humanity and a lower organic stage. He advanced promiscuity as a *logical postulate* precisely as some evolutionary philosophers advance the axiom of spontaneous generation; and thereby placed it beyond the range of scientific discussion.[12]

Lowie's conclusions are uncompromising. He asserts that, contrary to Morgan, the family came first, before tribe or clan:

The reversal of the traditional sequence is one of the safest conclusions of modern ethnology . . . Sexual communism as a condition taking the place of the individual family exists nowhere at the present time; and the arguments for its former existence must be rejected as unsatisfactory . . . we are justified in concluding that regardless of all other social arrangements the individual family is an omnipresent social unit. It does not matter whether marital relations are permanent or temporary; whether there is polygyny or polyandry or sexual license; whether conditions are complicated by the addition of members not included in *our* family circle: the one fact stands out beyond all others that everywhere the husband, wife and immature children constitute a unit apart from the remainder of the community.[13]

Modern students of Engels almost all accept that Morgan and his contemporaries are not the securest foundation upon which to build a history of marriage. David McLellan says that, as Morgan's ideas on primitive sexual promiscuity, group marriage and the priority of the matrimonial family are 'extremely dubious', it is not surprising that the section on the family is the weakest part of Engels's book.[14]

All the same, Marxists and particularly Marxist feminists are inclined to let Engels off the hook by saying: 'Even if he didn't get it quite right – because the historical material available to him was so inadequate – he and Marx were right about the way history works.'

For example, Sheila Rowbotham writes of Engels and his theories about the origin of the family:

The fact that his anthropological data is inadequate does not mean that the ideas he expresses and the attempt to integrate his Marxism with an anthropological study of the family should be ignored. To dismiss his anthropology as simply outdated is comparable to the complacency which says of Marx's *Capital* that the economics are old-fashioned. Having understood the limits of *The Origin of the Family*, the most important question, that of method, remains. The arguments against Engels very quickly become arguments against any attempt to discover historical pattern and factors for change.[15]

But surely it *does* matter whether Engels's anthropology and Marx's economics are correct ('old-fashioned' is a rather evasive word). And if they are not correct and if the generality of evidence suggests either that there is no straight-line pattern of development to be found or that there is a pattern but that it is an entirely different one, or that there is no useful steady connection between economic development and family structure, then we surely ought to think again.

With all unsatisfactory theories of history, there must eventually come a stage at which the general line can no longer be sustained because it cannot be sustained at enough of its individual supporting points. If the hypothesis of primitive promiscuity cannot be supported, therefore, it is all the more important for Marxism as a whole that Engels should be shown to be right about his great transition from the extended to the nuclear family.

4

THE MYTH OF THE EXTENDED FAMILY

The damage to Engels's doctrine could be limited if it were possible to show that its weaknesses were confined to the earlier stages. Unfortunately, there are equally boggy patches in the middle of his historical scheme, in the area surrounding 'the patriarchal family'. Engels quotes examples of the patriarchal family among the Southern Slavs and here and there in other parts of the world. But in North-Western Europe, the evidence for this kind of extended family, where several generations of brothers and sisters and their spouses live under the same roof, is coming more and more to be questioned. In one way or another, G. P. Murdock, Peter Laslett, Alan Macfarlane, Emmanuel Le Roy Ladurie and many other scholars have cast considerable doubt on whether these extended families were ever the norm in those parts of the world where the Industrial Revolution started – which are precisely the parts which must have gone through the extended-family stage if the Marx–Engels scheme is valid.

The sceptics make two points: first, the nuclear family is *universal*. Wherever more complicated forms exist, the nuclear family is always present as well. Second, in England and North-Western Europe, the nuclear family was the *standard* situation – a simple family living in its own house.

In *Household and Family in Past Time* (1972), one of the most crushing and total refutations of any orthodox wisdom in recent history, Laslett writes:

In England and elsewhere in Northern and Western Europe the standard situation was one where each domestic group consisted of a simple family living in its own house, so that the conjugal family unit was identical with the household . . . in spite of the important differences which comparison reveals . . . this standard situation seems to have obtained to a remarkable extent everywhere else.[1]

Earlier scholars on both sides of the Atlantic had come to the same conclusion. G. P. Murdock: 'The nuclear family is a universal human grouping.' Marion Levy: 'Most of humanity must always have lived in small families.' But it is the statistical studies of household size pioneered by Dr Laslett and his colleagues at the Cambridge Group for the History of Population and Social Structure which have finally demonstrated conclusively that the nuclear family was always the normal family. According to Marion Levy, 'The general outlines and nature of the *actual* family structure have been virtually identical in certain strategic respects (size, age, sex and generational composition) in all known societies in world history for well over 50 per cent of the members of these societies.'[2]

Sentiment or tradition or official morality might prescribe other types of household. For example, there might exist a tradition that married couples with children ought also to look after their parents by taking them into their homes as honoured guests; but in most societies, this was a tradition more honoured in the breach than the observance, for the simple reason that most married couples in traditional society could not afford to feed their parents. Most old people died alone, in the workhouse or in wretched poverty.

Contrary to the conventional wisdom, it is only *since* the Industrial Revolution and pre-eminently in industrial towns that married couples have started living with their parents in any great numbers. The extended family, in Western Europe at least, is a *modern* development in as much as it exists at all. Michael Anderson in his studies of industrial Lancashire, the heartland of the Industrial Revolution, suggests that this startling increase in parents and grandparents living together occurred for strictly economic reasons. For the first time, parents who both worked at the mill were earning enough to feed the grandparents; in return, the grandparents could act as babyminders for them or their neighbours and perhaps perform a few odd jobs as well. Moreover, the children could remain at home longer than they had in rural pre-industrial England because their earnings would contribute towards the household expenses – whereas in the country, there would be enough work on the farm for only a small minority to stay at home until they married. Despite its barbarities and deprivations, one thing that the Industrial Revolution did *not* do was break up families.[3]

The rate of illegitimacy is one of the indicators most frequently taken by historians to show the quality of family life. In particular, the proportion of children born illegitimate is supposed to demonstrate how living in cities and working in factories tend to corrupt the morals of the young, destroy parental control and lead to a general sense of aimlessness and lawlessness, or 'anomie', which can only result in sexual licence.

Unfortunately, as Peter Laslett points out, 'It is simply not true, in fact, that living in towns or cities, or migrating to such population centres, has always been directly and positively correlated with illegitimacy, during the so-called sexual revolution, or at any other time.'[4]

In Scotland, Germany and England at least, the rate of illegitimacy was always higher *in the country* – most remarkably so in some parts of rural Scotland, where the strict morality of the kirk seems to have gone almost unheeded. And in many other European countries – Austria, Belgium, Denmark, Germany, Italy, the Netherlands, Sweden and Switzerland – the rate of illegitimacy actually fell, often quite sharply, throughout the period of maximum industrialisation, the late nineteenth and early twentieth centuries.

In 1845, when bastardy in England and Wales was at its highest point before the twentieth century, most London districts were among the least bastard-prone in the land; the highest rates of illegitimacy were often to be found in the remotest parts of Cumberland and Wales. Even the new industrial cities, so notorious in Victorian fiction for the looseness of moral behaviour, cities such as Manchester, Liverpool and Newcastle, were well down the Registrar-General's list. Whitechapel and Bethnal Green, the direst of the East End's slums, were below the national average for illegitimacy throughout the nineteenth century. Up to 1930, rural districts had far higher bastardy rates than the cities. Thereafter the loss of rural population and the growth of suburbia make the comparisons less valuable.[5]

Here at least there is no evidence for assuming that moving to industrial cities weakened family life or sexual morality, contrary to the automatic assumptions of novelists such as Dickens and Disraeli and sociologists such as Marx and Engels. Marx may have had a child by his maid, Engels may have seduced the girls in his father's mill, but the great majority of urban courtships and pregnancies ended in marriage between young people of equal social station.

By contrast, in pre-industrial society, the classic case of the unmarried mother was of the girl in domestic service, living away from home, made pregnant by the young farmhand, also living away from home in service, the couple being prevented from marrying by poverty and perhaps also by their conditions of service. Wage labour in the factory, whatever its other horrors, did not suffer from those constraints.

The freedom to marry was a genuine freedom and one which came to many young people only after moving to the city. It was this new freedom which contemporary moralists, though not the most acute observers such as Mrs Gaskell, were all too ready to confuse with immorality, suffering as they did from the naive illusion of the well-to-do that physical squalor is bound to breed moral squalor.

In reality, it would be truer to say that such records as we have of life in Lancashire mill-towns and the like bear witness to a moral tenacity in face of continuous hardship which is as poignant as any record of heroism in war or captivity.[6] And the principal object of that tenacity was to keep the family together through thick and thin.

One of the deepest myths about the past is that there was a time when we were all part of one harmonious community and, because we were all one, we were entirely open to and with each other. There was no privacy in this golden age. The wish to be private was then regarded as bad, anti-social.

Sometimes this golden age is located in the South Seas, sometimes in Western Europe in the Middle Ages. We are invited to look back to the way our ancestors lived together in one great smoky room, and slept in the same bed and saw each other perform all the bodily functions without shame or embarrassment. This myth survives partly by the pretence that everyone lived in the great halls of the nobility. In fact, in most Western countries, the average family dwelling has been the cottage or hovel. Moreover, even where dwellings were closely huddled together or were actually part of the same structure – the Mexican ziggurat, the modern apartment block – we must not assume that the sense of privacy was any less sharp. Law in past time – the common law of England, the German 'Mirrors' of Justice, the Roman private law – is permeated by a strongly marked sense of private territory.

What are all these disputes about hedges and walls, about wayleaves and easements, about drains and overhanging trees, even about ancient lights, if they do not show a ferocious sense that the full possession of property included the right to be private, secluded – so much so that even the air and the light above your garden were your own inalienable possession?

Modern law, far from entrenching and intensifying this privacy, is often weaker and vaguer on these subjects. The mediaeval English law against eavesdropping was in fact recently repealed without any serious effort to replace it by some provision which would deter the modern methods of bugging and photocopying.

I do not wish to swing to the opposite extreme and try to argue that modern life is in most respects far *less* private than life 500 or 1,000 years ago. But it is true that many of the supposed instances of the public, social world we have lost are somewhat shaky.

The family wedding, for example. It is almost a cliché to compare a modern wedding in a registry office attended 'only' by the immediate family with the huge cluster of neighbours and relations which was supposed to attend almost every happening in the mediaeval village. Yet such hard evidence as there is continually prompts the opposite comparison. Marriage in the Middle Ages, as we shall see, was still popularly regarded as a *private* ceremony, to the despair of the Church authorities. Poverty and poor communications meant that mediaeval families saw far less of their cousins and kinsfolk. Economic factors dictated that a great proportion of the population, in some countries the majority, lived not in large bustling villages but scattered settlements or in isolated farms and cottages. Of course, in all rural societies up to and including the present, we can find examples of village festivals, of village solidarity and of village moral and social pressure upon young people; picturesque ceremonies such as the charivari and dancing round the maypole delight folklorists and anthropologists. But to represent these ceremonies, important though they might be in the life of the village, as either essential to or the most important thing in the life of the *individual* is mere fancy.

And even in those societies in which the family appears to be more extended and the community more all-embracing, we should be wary of assuming that the basic family unit was a large one lacking any sense of privacy. Often the African village may be more like a friendly apartment block than the warm tribal community in which people live, eat and sleep together with no separation between families. Professor Goody warns:

> We have to be very careful about contrasting a so-called *zadruga* type of unit, which consists of, say, a fortress of 100 persons, with an 'extended family' that comprises a small farm, a conjugal family and a few attached relatives . . . the former is likely to be a multi-celled version of the latter, the cells coming together for protection, for administrative convenience, or simply because that was the way the house had been built in the first place; permanent stone dwellings structure family composition in much more radical ways than mud huts and bamboo shelters, for the latter constantly change their shape according to the number and nature of those who live there.[7]

These *zadrugas* were Balkan villages which seemed intensely tribal to the outsider and captured the imagination of Victorian anthropologists – and indeed of Engels – as representing the kind of intimate community which the modern 'isolated nuclear family' had lost, at great expense of happiness and psychic health. Modern research into these *zadrugas*[8] suggests that life inside them was more carefully and subtly compartmentalised than nostalgic outsiders had grasped and moreover that the *zadruga* was not and is not in decline, as nostalgia had suggested, but on the contrary cheerfully persists even in modern Yugoslavia. Professor Goody concludes that:

> It is not only for England that we need to abandon the myth of the 'extended family' – as the term is often understood. In one form or another this myth has haunted historical and comparative studies since the time of Maine and Fustel de Coulanges, whether the work has been undertaken by historians, sociologists or anthropologists. Whatever the shape of the kin groups of earlier societies, none were undifferentiated communes of the kind beloved by nineteenth century theorists, Marxist and non-Marxist alike. Units of production were everywhere relatively small, kin-based units.[9]

Rodney Hilton, in *Bondmen Made Free*, says that it is the inescapable conclusion from the examination of the abundant manorial documents of the thirteenth century that:

> By the thirteenth century, or even earlier, the normal family in most parts of western Europe was not the extended family consisting of all the descendants of common great-grandparents – or beyond – with their wives and children living together. Instead, we often find grandparents, the married eldest son and heir with his wife and children, together with the unmarried members of the second generation. If the grandfather were active he might run the holding; or he might have made way for the heir, but still live on the holding. On the death of the grandparents, the family would become a two-generation nuclear family until the pattern repeated itself with the maturity and marriage of the heir.[10]

Hilton does say that extended families may have existed in earlier times, as the older school of mediaeval historians, most notably Marc Bloch, used to believe: 'In the badly documented era from the sixth to the tenth or eleventh century some peasant households might have been much bigger and more cohesive than they were in the central middle ages.'[11] 'Some' and 'might' are the crucial words, alas, in view of the documentation; Hilton quotes a ninth-century French family consisting of two brothers and their wives, two sisters and fourteen children, but he also says that the document from which this example comes suggests a predominance of nuclear families on the estate among the tenants.

It always seems to be the case that the more that historians know about a period in the history of Western Europe, the more they discover that the nuclear family is the normal way of living. Then and now, of course, there are all sorts of exceptions and variations, involving adult brothers and sisters and grandparents; some of these variants may have arisen because the farmhouse happened to be large, or because there was no other dwelling available, or because the family was unusually close-knit and affectionate, or for agricultural or financial reasons, or for protection or because someone was old or bedridden. But 'the family' then seems to have been little different from the family now as far as numbers and residence go.

Laslett argues that:

The wish to believe in the large and extended household as the ordinary institution of an earlier England and an earlier Europe, or as a standard feature of an earlier non-industrial world, is indeed a matter of ideology. The ideology in question, it is suggested, is not to any extent a system of norms and ideals present in the minds of the men and women of the past who actually made the decisions giving their domestic group structures their characteristic forms.[12]

Why have so many historians, sociologists and ideologues succumbed to this myth over the past hundred years? During most of that time, there was after all very little evidence either way. Let us try to offer a few reasons for the myth. Some will be technical, concerned with the type of evidence that *was* available and the treatment historians gave it. Others, however, will be emotional, concerned not only with attitudes to the past but with perceptions of the present, feelings of nostalgia, malaise or resentment; these are less easy to establish. Let us start with the more concrete technical reasons.

Historians who still talk in terms of 'the evolution of the family from the (to us) impersonal, economically bonded and precarious extended family group of the sixteenth century to the smaller, affectively bonded nuclear unit that had appeared by the end of the eighteenth century'[13] usually turn out to be talking about the *upper classes* only. Indeed, Lawrence Stone says as much in the introduction to the abridged Pelican version of *The Family, Sex and Marriage, 1500–1800*:

> The nature of the surviving evidence inexorably biases the book towards a study of a small minority group, namely the literate and articulate classes, and has relatively little to say about the great majority of Englishmen, the rural and urban smallholders, artisans, labourers and poor. But the consequences are mitigated by the fact that everything suggests that the former were the pacemakers of cultural change.[14]

But how can we know that the upper classes were the pacemakers when we know so little about the rest? Again, Professor Stone himself says: 'When dealing with the sexual behaviour of the lower orders, the historian is forced to abandon any attempt to probe attitudes and feelings, since direct evidence does not exist.'[15] Besides, coming nearer our own time, the layman is tempted to infer that it was the other way about; has not upper-class marriage become more openly affectionate and less dynastic and property-oriented, in other words, more like working-class marriage?

At all events, this scarcity of evidence does not seem even to slow up Professor Stone. In no time at all, he is deducing that:

> Social relations from the fifteenth to seventeenth centuries tended to be cool, even unfriendly . . . at all levels men and women were extremely short-tempered . . . familial emotive ties were so weak that they did not generate the passions which lead to intra-familial murder and mayhem . . . What is being postulated for the sixteenth and early seventeenth centuries is a society in which a majority of the individuals who composed it found it very difficult to establish close emotional ties to any person.[16]

In which case, the audience at the Globe must have been alternately bored stiff and bewildered by *Romeo and Juliet* or *Antony and Cleopatra*. 'At all levels'? 'A majority of the individuals'? How could he know?

Social relations cool? Familial emotive ties so weak that they did not generate the passions which lead to mayhem? Let us pluck from 1527–8, near the very beginning of Professor Stone's period, just one of the famous series of letters from Henry VIII to Anne Boleyn:

> Mine own sweetheart, this shall be to advertise you of the great elengeness [loneliness] that I find here since your departing; for I ensure you methinketh the time longer since your departing now last than I was wont to do a whole fortnight. I think your kindness and my fervency of love causeth it; for otherwise I would not have thought it possible that for so little a while it should have grieved me. But now that I am coming towards you, methinketh my pains be half released, and also I am right well comforted in so much that my book maketh substantially for my matter; in looking whereof I have spent about four hours this day, which caused me now to write the shorter letter to you at this time, because of some pain in my head; wishing myself (specially an evening) in my sweetheart's arms, whose pretty dukkys [breasts] I trust shortly to cusse [kiss].
> Written with the hand of him that was, is, and shall be yours by his will,
>   H.R.[17]

Even amongst the upper classes, social relations were not always tepid. We may step three hundred years further back, to the account by Berthold the Chaplain of the life of St Elizabeth of Hungary who married Ludwig IV of Thuringia in the 1220s. 'They loved one another with an astonishing passion,' we are told; 'she kissed him a thousand times upon the mouth.' When he was away visiting his far-flung estates, she founded a soup kitchen and a hospital. When he died in 1227, just after he had joined the crusaders assembling in Southern Italy, she ran through the castle utterly crazed with grief, crying, 'Dead, now is the whole world dead to me.' The point of the story is not merely that we are expected to admire her for all her good works and for having remained faithful and loving, but that we are expected to admire him too for getting angry with his courtiers who urged him to take mistresses during his long absences from home and telling them: 'I have a wife and I keep troth with her.'[18]

It does not matter how much historical accuracy there is in Berthold's lives of St Elizabeth and Ludwig. For our purposes, what matters are the emotional attitudes which are depicted for our edification and admiration. And we are clearly instructed that at the beginning of the thirteenth century love within marriage, fully articulated, passionate sexual love, was a familiar and admired phenomenon in the nobility. Similarly, Henry's passionate letters to Anne Boleyn show that at the beginning of the sixteenth century an educated prince was far from reluctant to express his love on paper in terms both intensely erotic and sentimental. There is nothing frozen, tepid or mechanical about the tone.

Professor Stone seems to be in no way unusual among historians of the family. Edward Shorter, a breezy American historian, prefaces his book *The Making of the Modern Family* (1977) by saying:

> I want to convey to the reader a massive modesty about its contents. We are talking here about the private lives of anonymous, ordinary people. Many were scarcely able to read. None wrote books about what they did or felt. Reconstructing the record of their family experience is bound to be a chancy business. Very little is certain, and the evidence, far from anchoring indisputably my proposition about sentiment and affection, trembles feebly in the wind.[19]

Quite so. Time and again, Professor Shorter confesses endearingly that he only has evidence from one or two countries (usually France), and from a period rather too late for his purposes (usually the nineteenth century). Quite often he cheerfully skates over the evidence presented in books which he has actually read. For instance, in defiance of almost all recent research, he continues to insist that 'Households in traditional Europe were somewhat larger and certainly more complex – in the sense of sheltering more than the simple, conjugal unit – than are modern households.' Well, to the best of our knowledge, they were not.

Yet Professor Shorter is even less impeded by the dearth of evidence than Professor Stone. He discovers not one, but two 'sexual revolutions'. And off he goes: 'Popular marriage in former centuries was usually affectionless, held together by considerations of property and lineage.'[20] 'The great surge of sentiment begins earlier in the cities than in the countryside, and sooner among the middle classes than the lower, but before this secular unfolding commences, relations between men and women in the household seem to have been affectionless everywhere in France.'[21] 'In traditional society, mothers viewed the development and happiness of children younger than two with indifference . . . Nor did these mothers often (some say "never") see their infants as human beings with the same capacities for joy and pain as they themselves.'[22] The 'massive modesty' seems to have evaporated.

I refer to these well-known works by highly esteemed scholars not so much to pick holes in their conclusions as to draw attention to their remarkable *impatience*. They cannot wait to draw out from the scanty material the most emphatic demonstration of a great transition from the 'extended family' of 'traditional society', with its loveless and grasping attitudes, to the 'nuclear family' of today based on affection – and, crucially, on to a further transition to a freer, floating type of relationship, in fact, to the end of marriage as we know it.

It is not as if there were anything novel or original about this theory. Professor Stone and his publishers refer to the evolution of *the* family in the terms quoted earlier, and his publishers claim that 'this is a work that challenges all conventional views hitherto held about English society at that period'. On the contrary, it *restates* the conventional views of those who wish to keep the family in its place as an historical accident.

The truly unconventional and subversive view would be to argue that the nuclear family is older than Jesus and Plato and Marx and

63

Engels, let alone older than the Industrial Revolution, and that the nuclear family – with all its drawbacks, difficulties and dangers – is a biologically derived way of living which comes naturally to us and which generates an emotional force of enduring and unquenchable power.

5

MATCHMAKING AND LOVEMAKING

'A single man of large fortune; four or five thousand a year. What a fine thing for our girls!' Almost everyone remembers Jane Austen's Mrs Bennet, desperate to marry off her daughters to the richest men who can be found, and her delight when a new prospect, Mr Bingley, takes the neighbouring estate of Netherfield. Most of us have at the back of our minds a general picture of the typical marriage in times past as an alliance arranged by the parents. The notions of marrying for love and of betrothal as an act of free choice between the betrothed seem essentially modern. The further back we go in history, the more we expect to find young people married off without their wishes being consulted, often against their will and sometimes as children too young to know their own minds.

In tracing the development of the modern attitude, we have to ask: *when* did the idea that it was right to marry for love begin to creep in? Obviously the old attitude must have sunk deep into the way people spoke and thought about marriage, so that it should not be too difficult to establish when the new idea – so central to modern notions of freedom, individuality and happiness – began to gain ground.

Clearly, in Jane Austen's day the new idea was already full-blown. Mrs Bennet is a silly woman, worldly, feather-headed, unable to understand the real best interests of her daughters; the attitude which Jane Austen expects readers of *Pride and Prejudice* to share with her heroine Elizabeth is that, while you must behave prudently and thoughtfully in matters to do with marriage – and not run off with Captain Wickham like her sister Lydia – marriage ought to be based on mutual affection and esteem and to be the result of free choice on both sides.

We are sometimes told that this attitude to marriage was something rather new – something perhaps to do with the individualism of the Enlightenment and the eighteenth century generally. But a moment's thought will show that this cannot be true. Exactly similar attitudes are to be found in almost all Shakespeare's comedies.

In *The Merry Wives of Windsor*, Page objects to his daughter Anne marrying Fenton, a riotous young gentleman, on the grounds that he must be after her solely for her money:

Fenton.	He doth object, I am too great of birth,
	And that my state being gall'd with my expense,
	I seek to heal it only by his wealth.
	Besides these, other bars he lays before me,
	My riots past, my wild societies;
	And tells me 'tis a thing impossible
	I should love thee but as a property.
Anne.	May be he tells you true.
Fenton.	No, heaven so speed me in my time to come!
	Albeit I will confess thy father's wealth
	Was the first motive that I woo'd thee, Anne:
	Yet, wooing thee, I found thee of more value
	Than stamps in gold or sums in sealed bags;
	And 'tis the very riches of thyself
	That now I aim at.[1]

Meanwhile, Page is in fact trying to marry Anne off to Slender, and Mrs Page is trying to marry her to Dr Caius – in both cases for money. But these stratagems come to nothing. And the triumphant Fenton rebukes his in-laws in the final scene:

Fenton.	You would have married her most shamefully,
	Where there was no proportion held in love.
	The truth is, she and I, long since contracted,
	Are now so sure that nothing can dissolve us.
	The offence is holy that she hath committed,
	And this deceit loses the name of craft,

Of disobedience, or unduteous title,
Since therein she doth evitate and shun
A thousand irreligious cursed hours,
Which forced marriage would have brought upon her.[2]

True love triumphs. If this really does reflect a new popular attitude, then it is an attitude which seems to have become entrenched long before the supposed 'Sentimental Revolution' of the eighteenth century. But there can surely be no denying that this was a *popular* attitude, that forced marriage, marriage for money and the treatment of women as mere pieces of property was already regarded as *wrong* in the Elizabethan age.

Now it is true that this might also suggest that at one time arranged marriages *had* been more normal and that their discrediting might have been relatively recent. Indeed, historians such as John Hajnal in *European Marriage* have argued that the scanty statistical evidence does indicate 'a fundamental change in marriage habits over much of Europe between 1400 and 1650'.[3] If so, there is not much sign of such a change in England where the earliest parish registers, dating from 1538 onwards, show that men and women married in their middle or late twenties. The age at which people marry is an almost infallible guide to whether the match is arranged or not. Arranged matches are always associated with a very early age of marriage, often in the middle teens. Lawrence Stone says emphatically that, although the upper classes married quite early in Elizabethan times,

> Among the plebs, the age of marriage followed a remarkably different pattern. It has now been established beyond any doubt that all over north-west Europe, with some unexplained regional exceptions, the middle and lower classes of both sexes married remarkably late, certainly from the fifteenth century onward. This created a pattern which was 'unique for all large populations for which data exist or reasonable surmises can be made.' A very large quantity of evidence for France, some for Italy, and a certain amount for England and America, proves that among small property-owners and labourers the median age of first marriage was very high in the sixteenth century and went even higher in the seventeenth and part of the eighteenth centuries, rising from twenty-seven to twenty-eight for men and from twenty-five to twenty-seven for women.[4]

This point was first published widely in Peter Laslett's *The World We Have Lost* (1965). Dr Laslett traces the source of the delusion to *Romeo and Juliet*:

> My child is yet a stranger in the world,
> She hath not seen the change of fourteen years;
> Let two more summers wither in their pride
> Ere we may think her ripe to be a bride.

Capulet says this in the second scene of the play. But whatever he said and whatever he felt, his child Juliet did take Romeo to husband at about her fourteenth birthday. Juliet's mother left her in no doubt of her opinion:

> Well, think of marriage now; younger than you,
> Here in Verona, ladies of esteem,
> Are made already mothers: by my count,
> I was your mother much upon these years
> That you are now a maid.

So she had been married at twelve, or early thirteen, and all those other ladies of Verona also. Miranda was married in her fifteenth year in the *Tempest*. It all seems clear and consistent enough. The women in Shakespeare's plays, and so presumably the English-women of Shakespeare's day, might marry in their early teens, or even before; and very often did.[5]

Yet, Laslett asserts, this is not true. 'We have examined every record we can find to test it and they all declare that, in Elizabethan and Jacobean England, marriage was rare at these early ages and not as common in the late teens as it is now. At twelve marriage as we understand it was virtually unknown.'[6]

This fits in with Professor Stone's entirely logical argument that 'because the key to the system of controlled marriage was the exchange of property, it theoretically follows that children lower down the economic scale would enjoy greater freedom of choice.'[7] No doubt there were middle-class parents with a little property to bestow who did try to ape upper-class custom and control their children's choice of spouse. But whether this was a new argument is hard to say. What we do know is that in the sixteenth century, the earliest period for which we have reliable evidence, arranged marriages were the exception rather than the rule among the middle and even more so among the lower classes. And the loveless marriage dictated solely by considerations of property was already considered shocking – at least outside the upper classes.

Thomas Becon wrote in about 1562 of the cause of the low esteem in which marriage was held: 'First as touching men of nobilitie, wee see dayly by experyence that they fore the moste parte marrye theyr chyldren at theyre pleasure whan they are verye yonge even to suche as wyll geve them moste mony for them, as men use to sel theyr horses, oxen, sheepe or any other cattel. Who that wyl geve most mony, shalbe soonest sped.'[8]

A century earlier, there is no sign of any change in popular attitudes. *The Boke of Good Manners*, translated by Caxton from the French and reprinted four times from 1487 onwards, says emphatically that marriage is ordained 'for to love each other', quotes stories of loving spouses in antiquity and decries 'the great abomination to see in many marriages so little faith and loyalty as now is. But I believe that one of the causes among the other is that the marriage be not duly made but for money or other evil cause.'[9]

In *The Ship of Fools*, a European best-seller of 1494, Sebastian Brant wrote:

> Who has one ground to take a wife;
> Her money, which he weds for life,
> Is ever plagued by woes and strife.

The normal pattern of such foolish marriages is:

> Thus often marriages begin
> With wooer setting out to win
> Whatever's hidden in her coffer,
> Not what her heart and soul can offer;
> And if a man so badly wive it,
> His happiness will not survive it.
> Far better in the desert dwell
> Than start on earth one's life in hell,
> And brook an angry harridan
> Whose captiousness will sap a man.[10]

Brant – who does not strike us as a particularly original satirist – treats as a familiar type 'the swain who barters off his youth for gain'.

So the contrast of spiritual poverty and material wealth can only depend on an assumption that wisdom consists in *not* marrying for money. Go back a century again, to the 1370s, and the obscure Shropshire lay clerk, William Langland, the author of *Piers Plowman*; for Langland too, a married man with a daughter, true marriage was 'for love, and not for property'.

We have to bear in mind this popular prejudice against marrying for money when we read the most celebrated documents of the time, such as the fifteenth-century Paston Letters. The meticulous historian Stanley Bennett in *The Pastons and Their England* remarks that 'Many readers will be heartily tired of, and repelled by, the insistence on financial and worldly matters shown by both men and women in discussing marriage proposals.'[11] Yet Bennett himself makes several important caveats, first that it was only among the nobility and landed classes that these marriages of convenience were the rule; and the Pastons were a highly ambitious, not to say greedy family of Norfolk squires who clawed their way up to the peerage over a period of 250 years. The letters date from the period of the Wars of the Roses when both life and the title to property were extremely insecure. A misalliance could prove fatal.

Yet even amongst the Pastons, there is another theme being played, often highly discordantly, alongside the talk of jointures, dowries, settlements and 'livelodes'. It is most clearly and urgently expressed in a letter of 1473 from Sir John Paston to his brother, also called John: 'I pray you take good heed to my sister Anne, lest the old love atween her and Pampyng renew.'[12] Only three days earlier, he had written the same warning in nearly the same terms to his brother – an indication of his state of panic. There was a decent commercial match in prospect for Anne – William Yelverton. All would be ruined if her 'infatuation' for Pampyng was allowed to take its course.

But parents *were* pleased if a suitable match also turned out to be a love match. Sir John Paston writes to his mother, expressing the hope that the complicated negotiations for the marriage between his brother John and Margery Brews should speedily come to a successful conclusion, 'whereof I would be as glad as any man; and am better content now that he should have her than any other that ever he was heretofore about to have had, considered her person, her youth, and the stock that she is come of, the love on both sides, the tender favour she is in with her father and mother . . . '[13]

There was indeed love on Margery's side. She wrote to John as 'Right worshipful and well-beloved Valentine' and vowed that if he would be content with the modest dowry which was all her father would part with and with 'my poor person, I would be the merriest maiden on ground'.[14] After they had been married, in 1477, she wrote: 'I pray you that ye will wear the ring with the image of St. Margaret, that I sent you a remembrance till ye come home; ye have left me such a remembrance that maketh me to think upon you both day and night when I would sleep.'[15] And in another letter she wrote: 'Sir, I pray you, if you tarry long at London, that it will please (you) to send for me, for I think (it) long since I lay in your arms.'[16]

Such sweet outbursts may not be statistically frequent in the Paston Letters or in the few other precious bundles of mediaeval letters that have come down to us. But that is hardly surprising. The great bulk of these letters are between noblemen and their men of business, not between newly wed husband and wife, and they are concerned primarily with the huge volume of disputes about inheritances, boundaries, rents, titles to property, religious quarrels, military dispositions, debts and supplies of food and clothing. Such letters are naturally somewhat dry. When you remember too that letters were often dictated to clerks, because the nobility and gentry lacked either the time or the capacity to write (although they could read), and had to be carried by messengers who could ill be spared from other duties, it is no wonder that the majority of letters should be matter-of-fact.

What is more relevant is that in letters where we should expect to find expressions of intimacy and affection, we do find them. The famous *Lisle Letters* include a series of letters between Arthur Lisle, Henry VIII's Lord Deputy at Calais, and his wife Honor from the two brief periods when they were separated in the 1530s. He was an elderly soldier and diplomat, probably in his early sixties; she was in her forties; both had been married before. Yet their letters suggest an intense love. His begin 'Sweete hart' or 'Mine own swete hart' or 'My very heart root and entirely beloved bedfellow'. He says, 'I do as much long for you as doth the child for his nurse,' and 'I think so much on you I cannot sleep in the night.'[17]

Nor can she. Lady Lisle ends one letter from Calais (her husband is back in England pleading his cause with Thomas Cromwell and the King): 'Once again sweet heart, I bid you farewell, as she that doth endure with as little sleep as any woman living, and so shall continue till your coming.'[18]

She feels the constraint of communicating through scribes and wishes that her husband would write to her in his own hand

> not to require of you to take so much pain as to write to me of your own hand in or for all your business or necessary affairs, but only at your own pleasure of such secret things as it shall please you to advertise me of, and at your convenient leisure to signify unto me part of your gentle heart, which unto me shall be most rejoice and comfort.[19]

That the Lisles were not freakish in their closeness and readiness to express their love appears from a letter written from Calais by one of those embarrassing scribes, Thomas Rogers, to his own wife Alice in England. He too begins 'Mine own sweet heart and entirely beloved bedfellow in as much as heart can desire' and rambles on about when would be the right moment to leave Calais and whether he will be able to sell his office there and obtain another one in England and whether he had not better wait until after the winter and, oh, he has sent her her toothpick by Robert Coke, and so on 'by your own loving husband both body and soul Thomas Rogers' – adding a postscript 'Bedfellow Will Terry my boy is run away from me.'[20]

Fifty years earlier, Elizabeth Stonor writes to her second husband, William, a year after their marriage, 'in good faith I thought never so long sith I see you, for in troth I had well hoped that your horses should have been here as this night . . . for in good faith I have not been merry at mine heart this sevennight day'. A few weeks later, she writes again with a host of domestic messages, inserting 'I long sore for you.'[21]

These happy marriages were also satisfactory from the property point of view. And it would of course be absurd to pretend that such harmonious arrangements of affection and property were ever typical. To gain some idea of the relative importance of and potential clash between the two factors we must look at other cases too, not simply at propertyless love matches (or misalliances) and loveless arranged marriages, both so notorious in folk memory, but also at the great number of proposed matches that broke down, either because the lovers were not determined enough to marry without their parents' consent, or because the two sets of relatives and guardians – or 'friends' as they were then called – could not agree on financial terms, or because the couple refused to go through with the match as they did not like each other enough, even though financial terms had been agreed.

What strikes us most nowadays on reading mediaeval correspondence is the extreme difficulty of getting yourself married at all. Even the matches made between upper-class adolescents as soon as possible after the age of consent – favoured by hard-boiled, ambitious parents as the chances of resistance were reduced – were constantly coming unstuck because one or other of the proposed couple did resist.

The letters of the upwardly mobile Pastons are littered with proposed matches that came to nothing; the *Lisle Letters*, being more concerned with politics and less with family advancement, rather less so. Yet both contain several examples of love matches, along with examples of arranged matches which were also love matches as well as arranged matches in which the views of the partners are unknown to us.

Thomas Leygh, a jovial English merchant, writes to his cousin Lady Lisle that he had not written earlier to inform her of his marriage because it was of 'so small a value' and 'in case I had not liked my wife better than the substance that I had with her I assure you I had returned unmarried again to Calais'.[22] Somewhat more romantic in tone is the misalliance between the young architect, Richard Lee, son of a mere stonemason, and Margaret, daughter of Sir Richard Grenville, who fiercely opposed the match. A letter to Lady Lisle from John Husee, the Lisles' man of business, says of Margaret's match, 'I cannot think but she hath well sped, for I know well that my Lord Privy Seal [Cromwell] thinketh that he is worthy to have as good as she.'[23]

What had happened here was that the couple had taken the matter into their own hands and *contracted themselves*. Neither Sir Richard nor anyone else could thereafter unmarry them. In this case, Lee was an up-and-coming man and no less a person than Cromwell thought he was worthy of Margaret. In the end, Grenville came round to his son-in-law, and Lee wrote to Cromwell thanking him for mediating between him and his father-in-law, adding, 'I do now find him right kind unto me, which every day appears more and more.'[24]

As late as 1537, the young couple still held the ultimate weapon –

the power to marry themselves, without the approval of parents or benefit of clergy. It was not only a legal but a moral weapon, since, although its use did contravene both the Tudor insistence on filial obedience and the Church's growing insistence that people should be properly married in church, it sprang from the principle of Christian canon law that true marriage depended on free consent and hence that it could not be separated from affection.

This ultimate weapon, the unassailable power of even the most downtrodden young woman to give or withhold her consent as she pleased, was a constant shadow over the ambitions of families such as the Pastons. Each generation had its share of setbacks.

For ten years, between 1449 and 1459, there had been negotiations to find a husband for John Paston's aunt, Elizabeth. They first tried to marry her to a rich man called Scrope, a widower aged nearly fifty who, he himself wrote, had 'suffered a sickness that kept me a thirteen or fourteen years ensuing; whereby I am disfigured in my person and shall be whilst I live.'[25] Elizabeth refused. Her mother Agnes shut her up and forbade her to speak to anyone and beat her cruelly 'sometimes twice in one day, and her head broke in two or three places'.[26] In the end, Elizabeth gave in, but the match failed for some unknown reason.

Worse still was the case of John's sister, another Margery, who had upped and married the Pastons' steward, Richard Calle. All the Pastons were furious. They hoped to get the betrothal annulled and laid the matter before the Bishop of Norwich, who examined both Margery and Richard separately and made her repeat the words she had used in pledging herself to Calle so that he might see whether they were sufficient and binding. Margery repeated the words, and more: 'If those words made it not sure, she said boldly that she would make it sure ere she went thence, for she thought in her conscience she was bound whatsoever the words were.'[27]

Calle himself had spoken in a letter to her of 'the great vow of matrimony that is made betwixt us, and also the great love that hath been and as I trust yet is betwixt us, and as on my part never greater'.[28] He was mystified by her parents' failure to understand that they were in effect married: 'This is a painful life that we lead. I suppose they think we be not betrothed together, and if they do so I marvel, for then they are not well advised, remembering the plainness that I broke [the matter] to my mistress at the beginning, and I suppose by you as well if you did as you ought to do of very right.'[29]

This is the heart of the problem. Every parent's carefully laid plan for advancing the family's fortune was at the mercy of two young people simply deciding to *marry themselves* by the exchange of vows. All England was a vast Gretna Green, with the Church courts desperately trying to regulate, register and make indissoluble these 'private marriages'.

And it is perhaps only from the records of these Church courts that we can distil some impression of the emotional character of mediaeval marriage *outside* the upper classes, and gain some insight into how young people such as Richard Calle looked on marriage.

Some remarkable pages from this huge volume of so far untapped official records are to be found in R. H. Helmholz's *Marriage Litigation in Medieval England*. Professor Helmholz examines the records of the Church courts, which describe, often very fully, the matrimonial disputes that came before them and show over the years the increasingly successful efforts of the Church to make marriage a public, officially ratified contract which was not to be dissolved. The records are naturally in Latin – a linguistic barrier which often seems to mislead modern readers who tend to look for evidence of intimate feeling to the scant fragments written in the vulgar tongue. In fact, some of the most passionate love lyrics, the most scabrous anecdotes and almost all the intimate touches in the biographies and autobiographies of princes, saints and scholars were written in Latin until well into the Renaissance.

We must also get rid of any idea that the argument in these courts was of an abstruse, theological nature. The courts' investigations were methodical and matter-of-fact; often they were brutally down-to-earth, much in the way that Victorian divorce courts shirked no unpleasant detail in order to establish whether there had been collusion between the parties. In mediaeval times, the most startling procedure was the manner in which the Church courts at York and Canterbury sought to establish whether a husband's alleged impotence was a genuine ground for granting a divorce.

The court would deputise a group of 'honest women', usually seven of them, to stir up the man's sexual desires. In Canterbury in 1433, for example:

The same witness exposed her naked breasts, and with her hands warmed at the said fire, she held and rubbed the penis and testicles of the said John. And she embraced and frequently kissed the same John, and stirred him up in so far as she could to show his virility and potency, admonishing him that for shame he should there and then prove and render himself a man. And she says, examined and diligently questioned, that the whole time aforesaid, the said penis was scarcely three inches long . . . remaining without any increase or decrease.[30]

The women then cursed the poor fellow for ever having presumed to marry a young woman whom he could not please.

In only one of the cases examined by Professor Helmholz did the man 'pass' such an examination. It happened in 1432; one of the worthy matrons there testified that 'the penis of the aforesaid William was bigger both in length and thickness than the penis of her own husband had ever been.'[31]

There is little sign here either of the modest, self-effacing sexless women supposedly produced by the male supremacism of the Church, or of the Church itself as an otherworldly body. Quite plainly, the Church courts should be seen more as an important arm of a bureaucracy attempting to control and regularise the sloppy habits of the laity.

But this intention constantly came up against the traditional popular view of marriage as a private affair which could be performed without benefit of clergy or without even any thought of going along to the parish church at a later date. The court records tell us of marriages contracted between 1292 and 1489 under an ash tree, in a bed, a garden, a small storehouse, in a field under a hawthorn, in a blacksmith's shop, near a hedge, in a kitchen, by an oak tree – even on the king's highway.

Helmholz quotes a not unusual example of such a 'private' marriage, from the diocese of York in 1372:

The witness says that 'one year ago on the feast day of the apostles Philip and James just past, he was present in the house of William Burton, tanner of York, about the third hour past the ninth, when and where John Beke, saddler, sitting down on a bench of that house, called in English "le Sidebynke", called the said Marjory to him and said to her, "Sit with me". Acquiescing in this, she sat down. John said to her, "Marjory, do you wish to be my wife?" And she replied, "I will if you wish". And taking at once the said Marjory's right hand, John said, "Marjory, here I take you as my wife, for better or worse, to have and to hold until the end of my life; and of this I give you my faith." The said Marjory replied to him, "Here I take you John as my husband, to have and to hold until the end of my life, and of this I give you my faith." And then the said John kissed the said Marjory through a wreath of flowers, in English "Garland".[32]

There is no mention of God as blessing, presiding over or instituting this joining-together. John and Marjory, like other couples in these cases, had, it seems, not thought it necessary to refer to the Almighty at all at the time – nor later, even when appearing in front of the bishop's court, which suggests that the Church authorities themselves expected no such show of piety.

What the Church objected to, not entirely without reason, was the uncertain character of these marriages. For the other notable absentee at these private weddings, apart from the Almighty, was the mediaeval crowd. We were taught that, in the Middle Ages, life took place in a seething throng of relatives and neighbours. Every action was public; village morality and village gossip were all-seeing and virtually all-powerful. Yet the court records indicate that often the marriage was not merely not registered at the church door, there were no witnesses to it either, apart from the couple themselves; even the supposedly authoritarian presence of the parents was not required; if there was a witness, it might equally be a brother, or a friend, or another young couple, or even a stranger.

The danger was that such a marriage would be unstable and all too easy to slide out of later for a spouse who had an eye on somebody else. And so it was that the great majority of cases in the Church courts were suits to enforce a marriage contract. The way to prove that a valid marriage had taken place was to establish that words similar to the conversation between John and Marjory had indeed taken place.

For the Church it was this exchange of words that counted, wherever they were said, in or out of church. And the words had to be *verba de presenti*, not *verba de futuro*. That is, 'I take you as my wife now,' not 'I promise to marry you at some time in the future.' The latter type of promise, however, was automatically converted into a full marriage according to canon law by sexual intercourse between the couple.

Naturally, it was often difficult to establish the tense with any certainty. But the real complication was that ordinary people often regarded even *verba de presenti* as merely a betrothal, an agreement to marry, not a marriage itself. Such a betrothed couple spoke of themselves as we do today, as an engaged couple, *affidati*, affianced, not married.

Take the case of John Astlott and Agnes Louth which came before the York court in 1422.[33] They had been in love for two years and meant to get married. He had to go abroad on business. She pressed him to marry her before he left, because her father had been pressing *her*. He agreed and married her by words of present consent before witnesses. Alas, John lost much of his fortune on the trip. When he returned, he found that Agnes had decided to break off what she regarded as only an engagement. John sued to enforce what he regarded as a marriage. The verdict is not preserved.

Ordinary people, then, believed that they had the right to change their minds up to the moment when the marriage was consummated and formally solemnised. A couple in Ely in 1377, asked if they could think of a reason why the court should not pronounce them married, replied, rather charmingly, that 'they knew none to put forward except for the reason that they had now changed their minds because they believed they did not love each other on account of the resistance put up by the said Johanna.'[34]

Couples and witnesses giving evidence seem to have regarded love as a prime factor for establishing consent to a marriage. Words of love were frequently quoted. From a Canterbury case of 1456: 'She said to him, "There is something I would like to say if it is not displeasing". And the man said "Speak". And then she said, "There is no man in the world whom I love more". And he said "I am grateful to you. And I love you." '[35] 'Love' here, as usual in mediaeval Latin, is 'diligo', or sometimes 'adamo' – meaning passionate love, not mere liking or esteem.

Nor could the canon lawyers rule out such evidence even had they so wished, for canon law based the validity of marriage on consent. In the case of those child marriages which have become so notorious to posterity, canon law prescribed that children who had contracted marriage could, on reaching puberty, either ratify or annul the original contract. Approval was shown by living together or consummating the match. Dissent was indicated by some public statement – before the bishop, or his court, or even a group of neighbours.

Here too there were naturally cases which fell somewhere between dissent and approval. Years might have passed without either party making any move, positive or negative. Such cases were liable to end up in the bishop's court if one party wanted the marriage to be dissolved and the other disagreed. Whatever canon law might say, it seems that teenagers often regarded themselves as merely betrothed, not married, even if they had taken no positive steps to disavow the contract.

William Aunger had been betrothed to Johanna Malcake at the age of eight. At the age of fourteen, at the urging of her family, he had been induced to spend a week with her. According to a witness, for one night he had even been persuaded to enter her bed and 'lie in one bed, just boy and girl alone, naked boy with naked girl'. But two days later, William went to the house of this witness in Swynflete village and said: 'I am sorry I ever came to know Johanna because she does not love me with lasting affection. And for that reason I never intend to consent that she should be my wife nor that I should live with her.' Consent for William was bound up with affection. Living together, even sleeping together did not equal consent. His disavowal convinced the York court in 1357–8, and he was pronounced free to marry another woman.[36]

Undeniably, throughout the Middle Ages people were married against their will and made to stay married. Among the better off, heiresses could be bestowed in marriage by the lord of the manor. Among the poor, many no doubt could not afford the fees to petition the courts, which might be forty shillings or more, a considerable sum (although a primitive form of legal aid was occasionally available). Many more must have silently complied with their parents' wishes, lacking the initiative to disavow at the right time the marriage that had been made for them.

But what the court records do show – and would doubtless show even more clearly with further research – is that popular tradition did place great emphasis upon the presence or absence of affection and that the canon law's criterion of consent meant that love was always a relevant factor.

Moreover, even among the upper classes whose commercial attitude to marriage seemed and seems so unattractive, there was a certain furtive respect paid to the notion that love was a desirable accompaniment to a good match. Thomas Betson, writing in 1476 to his thirteen-year-old fiancée, Katherine Ryche, not only instructs her to eat well and apologises in facetious terms for his habitual unpunctuality, but also addresses her as 'faithful and heartily beloved' and, with a wealth of awkward effusiveness, hopes she remembers him 'full womanly and like a lover'.[37] The letter is too delightful to have been dictated, but what is relevant to our purpose is that the sentiments expressed in it were obviously approved by parents as well as the betrothed couple. Even child brides had to be wooed.

The men and women who appeared before the Church courts were not usually as well off as Thomas Betson and Katherine Ryche. Most of them had surprisingly humble occupations in view of the substantial fees they might have to pay to prove that they were or were not married. But whatever canon law might say, they were not too frightened to express their feelings, nor too humble to regard those feelings as unimportant or irrelevant to the question of whether a true marriage had taken place.

For a fuller expression of those feelings we can only turn to our best literary source for the later Middle Ages – Geoffrey Chaucer – not only because he is the greatest writer in English before Shakespeare, but because he is the most realistic, down-to-earth and popular. Those adjectives immediately call to mind the *Canterbury Tales*, but almost more interesting for our purposes is Chaucer's *Troilus and Criseyde*.

That may seem surprising because surely *Troilus* is an epic of courtly love. For stanza after stanza, the hero languishes for the heroine and she for him; even when the verse reaches heights of emotional intensity and great beauty, we are still conscious of the artificiality of the conventions. Why don't they make love, since in this version of the story Criseyde has no husband living to bar the way?

This departure from the supposed conventions of the courtly epic may alert us; the adulterous, illicit element is absent; the tragedy is Criseyde's weakness in succumbing to Diomede's wooing after she has been taken from Troy to the Greek camp at her father's insistence. Although the courtly traditions are observed, it is more what we would regard as a love story than a drama of adulterous passion – more 'English' and less 'French'.

But more important, Chaucer insists throughout on the *foreignness* of the whole story; he poses as merely a translator and he apologises for the alien nature of the whole business in a remarkable preamble to Book II:

> And then, you know, the forms of language change
> Within a thousand years, and long ago
> Some words were valued that will now seem strange,
> Affected, even; yet they spoke them so,
> And fared as well in love, for all I know,
> As we do now; in various lands and ages
> Various are the ways to win love's wages.
>
> And therefore, should it happen by some chance
> That one of you, some lover, listening here
> To what I tell you of the slow advance
> Troilus made to gain his lady's ear,
> Thinks 'I would never buy my love so dear!'
> Or marvels at this phrase, or at that blunder,
> I do not know; to me it is no wonder.
>
> Not all who find their way to Rome will trace
> The self-same path, or wear the self-same gear,
> And in some lands they'd count it a disgrace
> Were they to act in love as we do here,
> With open doings, looks that make all clear,
> Visits, formalities and tricks of phrase;
> To every land its own peculiar ways.[38]

Chaucer teasingly attributes the difference in language and attitudes to the thousand years since the Trojan War. But of course the attitudes he is 'translating' were the *then* fashionable attitudes of courtly love. For his popular audience, the habits of upper-class wooing might seem as strange and distant as ancient Greece.

What was implied by 'to act in love as we do here'? What exactly was the 'open' method of wooing, so ironically contrasted with fancy foreign ways? Here we must turn to the *Canterbury Tales*, to consider the tactics of the luckless Absalon wooing Alison in 'The Miller's Tale':

> Up rose this jolly lover Absalon
> In gayest clothes, garnished with that and this;

> But first he chewed a grain of liquorice
> To charm his breath before he combed his hair.
> Under his tongue the comfit nestling there
> Would make him gracious. He began to roam
> Towards the carpenter's; he reached their home
> And by the casement window took his stand.
> Breast-high it stood, no higher than his hand.
> He gave a cough, it was a semi-sound;
> 'Alison, honey-comb, are you around?
> Sweet cinnamon, my little pretty bird,
> Sweetheart, wake up and say a little word!
> You seldom think of me in all my woe,
> I sweat for love of you wherever I go!
> No wonder if I do, I pine and bleat
> As any lambkin hungering for the treat,
> Believe me, darling, I'm so deep in love
> I croon with longing like a turtle-dove,
> I eat as little as a girl at school.'[39]

Absalon spruces himself up, makes sure his breath smells sweet and slicks down his hair before going out to woo Alison, borrowing the language of the popular love songs of his day. None of this seems to have changed much, but even if the style of rustic wooing sounds familiar, that might not necessarily mean that Chaucer shared our twentieth-century attitudes towards marriage and children. Certain wild statements have indeed been made over the years about what Chaucer did think – mostly by critics and biographers who failed to understand that the pilgrims are not the author's mouthpiece but fictional characters in their own right. John Masefield, for example, assumed that the poet's marriage was one 'of the utmost and liveliest horror'. There is, according to modern critics, not the slightest evidence for this. The most savage attack on women and marriage comes from the Merchant, who is a grasping, overbearing sort of man; the fact that he has married a shrew or complains that he has is clearly a piece of fitting fiction, not a passage of autobiography.

But there undoubtedly is an argument about marriage running through the *Tales*, and Chaucerian scholars such as G. L. Kittredge (1915) and W. W. Lawrence (1969) are agreed on what seems a reasonable interpretation: the argument corresponds to the popular debate at the time as to who was to have the 'mastery' in marriage – symbolised in song and story by a man and woman fighting over a pair of breeches. In the *Canterbury Tales*, the Host too suffers from being henpecked, and so presumably did the Wife of Bath's five husbands, all of whom she boasts of having kept well in hand, except the last one who beat her up:

> But in our bed he was so fresh and gay,
> So coaxing, so persuasive . . . Heaven knows
> Whenever he wanted it – my *belle chose* –
> Though he had beaten me in every bone
> He still could wheedle me to love, I own.
> I think I loved him best, I'll tell no lie.
> He was disdainful in his love, that's why.
> We women have a curious fantasy
> In such affairs, or so it seems to me.
> When something's difficult, or can't be had,
> We crave and cry for it all day like mad.[40]

When this violent husband spends the whole time reading out stories about the awful treacheries of women, the Wife of Bath grabs his book, tears out three pages and hits him so hard that he falls into the fireplace; he hits her back even harder, so that she lies unconscious; he is distraught.

> He came up close and kneeling gently down
> He said, 'My love, my dearest Alison,
> So help me God, I never again will hit
> You, love; and if I did, you asked for it.
> Forgive me!' But for all he was so meek,
> I up at once and smote him on the cheek
> And said, 'Take that to level up the score!
> Now let me die, I can't speak any more.'[41]

After that, they made it up and he conceded her the mastery of house and land and, from that day on, there was no argument. The Wife of Bath is one of the most vivid figures in all fiction. Neither her tale nor the rest of the *Canterbury Tales* suggests for one moment that women were unable to speak up for themselves or to assert certain rights over property, household management or the giving and withholding of sexual favours. Indeed, the first impression is the

83

opposite one: that in most households women were felt to be too powerful.

But it would be equally ludicrous to suggest that Chaucer is on the side of the grasping Merchant and the henpecked Host. If the author's view is presented at all, it is unmistakably through the benign, generous, practical figure of the Franklin who concludes the whole discussion.

According to the system of courtly love, marriage was supposed to be incompatible with true love, because marriage involves mastery on the husband's part and mastery inevitably drives out love.

The Franklin rejects this theory utterly. In true marriage, neither side can assert sovereignty. Love depends on equality and forbearance, and marriage depends on love.

Those who persist in asserting that Chaucer subscribed wholeheartedly to the rules of courtly love and that he did not believe in the possibility of love-in-marriage must reckon with the Franklin's lines. And those who still believe that the notion of love-in-marriage was unknown to the Middle Ages should tiptoe quietly away:

> Lovers must each be ready to obey
> The other, if they would long keep company.
> Love will not be constrained by mastery;
> When mastery comes the god of love anon
> Stretches his wings and farewell! he is gone.
> Love is a thing as any spirit free;
> Women by nature long for liberty
> And not to be constrained or made a thrall,
> And so do men, if I may speak for all.
> Whoever's the most patient under love
> Has the advantage and will rise above
> The other; patience is a conquering virtue.
> The learned say that, if it not desert you,
> It vanquishes what force can never reach;
> Why answer back at every angry speech?
> No, learn forbearance or, I'll tell you what,
> You will be taught it, whether you will or not.[42]

Taking up the tale of the devoted married couple, Arveragus and Dorigen, the Franklin explicitly answers the courtly-love argument that love depends on serving your lady-love and so you cannot love your wife:

> She took a servant when she took a lord,
> A lord in marriage in a love renewed
> By service, lordship set in servitude;
> In servitude? Why no, but far above
> Since he had both his lady and his love.
> His lady certainly, his wife no less,
> To which the law of love will answer 'yes'.
>
> So in the happiness that they had planned
> He took his wife home to his native land
> With joyful ease and reached his castle there
> By Penmarch Point, not far from Finisterre,
> And there they lived in amity unharried.
>
> Who can recount, unless he has been married,
> The ease, the prosperous joys of man and wife?[43]

It is no discourtesy to Professor Coghill's translation to repeat those last three lines in the original:

> Who coude telle, but he hadde wedded be,
> The ioye, the ese and the prosperitee
> That is bitwixe an housbonde and his wyf?

Can there be much doubt what Chaucer really thought? And can we doubt either that his audience understood him? It is sometimes argued that writers even as great as Chaucer might be presenting a heightened, romanticised picture of a reality which was much more brutal and commercial. Yet there is little romance in, say, the Wife of Bath's marital adventures. Chaucer certainly never pretends that all or even most marriages are happy and bound to last for ever.

Past centuries might not permit divorce in the modern sense, but poor men simply divorced themselves by running away.

Just how often marriages did break up at all levels of society is indicated by a unique and precious record of village life at the end of the seventeenth century, Richard Gough's *History of Myddle*. Myddle was and is a village in Shropshire near the Welsh border. It had a population then of about 600 persons, that is, not much more than 100 households – most of whose family histories are described, pew by pew, as they sat in the village church.

What is striking is how often Gough describes *the emotional charac-ter* of a marriage; of course, he is interested in who were so-and-so's parents and where they came from and whether he or she brought land or money to the marriage; but he is equally interested in how they got on together. Take this passage about Gough's own sister, Mrs Bradoke:

> After the death of Mr. Bradoke, my sister (against consent of friends), married Mr. Richard Glover, of Measbury. She had issue by him a son named Richard (who some while served as an attorney, and is unmarried), and a daughter named Dorothy. She is married to Mr. John Vaughan, of Lluin y Groise. This couple when they were married were so young, that they could not make passing thirty years between them, and yet neither of them were con-strained by parents to marry, but they going to school together fell in love with one another, and so married. They live lovingly together, and have many children.[44]

'Friends' here means 'relations', in particular those who might have been thought in traditional society to have some right to decide whom the widowed Mrs Bradoke should marry. In this case, their opposition did not prevail; the teenage marriage between her daughter and John Vaughan was also anything but an arranged match.

At the same time, Gough gives us a dozen examples from this one parish, not only of unhappy marriages but also of desertions and separations. Take Richard Cleaton, whose family occupied the second pew on the north side of the north aisle:

> . . . an untowardly person. He married Annie, the daughter of William Tyler, a woman as infamous as himself. The parents on both sides were displeased (or seemed so), with this match, and therefore allowed the new married couple no maintenance. Richard Cleaton soon out-run his wife, and left his wife big with child. She had a daughter, which was brought up by Allen Challoner (the smith) of Myddle; for his wife was related to William Tyler.[45]

The ups and downs of married life and the way in which strife runs in families are shown in the unhappy history of the wives of Rowland Muckleston:

> She was a quiet low-spirited woman, and suffered her husband to concern himself with all things both within doors and without, so

that their housekeeping was not commendable. She died, and left behind her one son named Edward, and two daughters.

Afterwards he married (a second wife), the daughter of Mr Cuthbert Hesketh of Kenwicke, commonly called Darter Hesketh; it was a hasty match and a small portion, but she was a very handsome gentlewoman and of a masculine spirit, and would not suffer him to intermeddle with her concerns within doors, and she endeavoured to keep a good house, but this caused them to keep an unquiet house, and many contests happened between them which ended not without blows. I think she never boasted of the victory for she had lost an eye in the battle. After that she had lived some few years with him she died and left no child behind her.

His third wife was widow to one Maddox of Astley. (Her son likewise married the eldest daughter of Rowland Muckleston). This wife is still living and I think she will not contest with her husband, for if she loses an eye she loseth all. They are both living but live not together, for he lives with his son at Meriton, and she with her son at Astley.[46]

The consequences of the collapse of a marriage were severe in the extreme for the wife and children if she had no family to take her in. In the sixteenth and seventeenth centuries, as before and since, children and deserted wives formed a great percentage of the poor. One in twelve of the indigent poor in Norwich in 1570 were deserted wives.

In London, John Howes tells us, the survey made throughout the wards of the City in the early 1550s showed a total of 2,160 persons in need of relief, of which 300 were 'fatherless children' and 350 'poore men overburdned with theire children'. In Norwich, a few years later, the census revealed some 2,000 people in need of relief out of a population of around 15,000; and of these nearly 1,000 were children, although a surprising number of them were shown to be at school.[47]

None of this fits in with the conventional historian's picture of marriage as an indissoluble but emotionally low-key arrangement for the begetting of children and the transmission of property. On the contrary, the emotional intensity of the relationship and the risks of failure leave an unmistakable impression. Marriage was a central experience in the life of every human being and the end of a marriage – whether caused by death or desertion – was likely to prove a desolating event.

In 1371, the Knight of La Tour Landry, a French provincial nobleman, wrote a highly successful book of instructive tales for his daughters. It was translated into German and a hundred years later into English by Caxton. The prologue begins:

In the yr of the incarnation of our Lord 1371, as I was in a garden, all heavy and full of thought, in the shadow, about the end of the month of April, but a little I rejoiced me of the melody and song of the wild birds; they sang there in their languages, as the throstle, the thrush, the nightingale and other birds, the which were full of mirth and joy; and their sweet song made my heart to lighten, and made me to think of the time that is past of my youth how love in great distress had held me, and how I was in her service many times, full of sorrow and gladness as many lovers be. But my sorrow was healed and my service well y-set and quit, for he gave me a fair wife, and . . . of all good she was bell and the flower; and I delighted me so much in her that I made for her love songs, ballades, rondelles, rivals and diverse new things in the best wise that I could. But death, that on all maketh war, took her from me the which hath made me have many a sorrowful thought and great heaviness. And so it is more than 20 year that I have been for her full of great sorrow. For a true lover's heart forgetteth never the woman that once he hath truly loved.

From the seventeenth century onwards at least, we have similar direct evidence from English letters and diaries of how middle-class people felt about their spouses.

The Rev. Ralph Josselin, an Essex clergyman and son of a small farmer, described the classic case of love at first sight when he preached his first sermon in 1639: 'the first Lord's day, being October 6, my eye fixed with love upon a maid, and her's upon me, who afterwards proved my wife.' Josselin's *Diary* recounts the life of a diligent parson and small farmer, but it is also the diary of an obsessive family man. Almost every entry contains some anxious reference to the health of his wife and children (who all chose their own spouses).

The Rev. Oliver Heywood, the son of a Lancashire yeoman and a non-conformist minister, wrote of his wife in a pious but nonetheless poignant memoir of her after her death in 1642:

She was as loving a wife as ever lay in any mans bosome, if she offended any way it was through vehemency of affection, the lord brought us together and continued our relation in abundance of mercy, for wch I haue cause to blesse him whiles I lieue; the circumstances about our closure are observable; her inclination towards me at the first view, a years interruption, or prevention of a motion, my disappointments otherways, her opposition to more probable motions, her constancy to me, my gradual complacency in her, every time more then other; – the review of these passages and many other is both pleasant and satisfying that the hand of the lord was in it, and the effects haue answered the promises, for never had couple so much comfort in each other and so little discontent, as we had in that sixe years we were togather.[48]

These texts from the seventeenth century are valuable because they antedate the supposed 'sentimental revolution' in the eighteenth century when it became the fashion to speak and write in affectionate, even gushing terms of your family and children. You need only look at the memorial tablets in any church or chapel to see marmoreal evidence of that.

But do we have similar direct evidence of what working-class attitudes were at that time? There is at least one such document and it is a remarkable one.

The *Diary* of Roger Lowe of Ashton-in-Makerfield, Lancashire, is the diary of a young apprentice, kept between 1663 and 1674. It is an enchanting document, open-hearted, brief, provincial, modest. Scarcely any famous people or great events are mentioned in it. Roger could read and write, but unlike Pepys, he did not rise far; at his death he was described as 'a husbandman' – a man of lower rank than a yeoman. In fact he was probably just a small trader. The record of his love life is unique and a few entries must be quoted:

19 Jenuery. – Tuesday. I went into Goleborne to James —— mith for to gett in some monys. From thence I went to Ann Barrowe's, and I supposd she hid her selfe. Att last I parted from house and she came after me, but I returned home with discomfort, tho I was very satisfied; for I went with a purpose to free my selfe and not to have nothinge to doe with her.

17. – I was to goe to Wiggin with Thomas Smith; Ales Lealand had promised me she would then and there answer my desire either

pro or con in a final ingagement to Thomas. Att this time Mary Naylor and I were solemnly agreed to be faithful to each other.

8. – Munday. I went to Roger Naylor and Mary cryd to me, said she would have nothinge to doe with me, was highly displeased att me; but in conclusion she was well pleased, would have me goe with her day after to Banfor longe, and she would goe before; and to signifie she was before, she would in such a place lay a bough in the way, which accordingly she did, and I found it upon.

8. – Wedensday. I was in a sad condition of mind, for Roger Naylor was from home and Mary would not assent to have me come thither, but I went and she was somethinge displeased. She went give calfe drinke; I followed her and there we speake to either, which was very satisfactory to both, and the other day after she came to shopp, and was very glad to see me. Said shee, 'Am not I a wise wench to ingage myselfe thus?' Att those times my effections ran out violently after her, so as that I was never contented one day to an end unles I had seene her, and cheefely my effections were sett upon her virtues and womenly qualities.

1. – Munday. Roger Naylor was gone to Chester, and I went downe and Mary and I went into parlour and talked 2 howres att least, and she cryd to me and seemed to be very sad, and the reason was because of fear of her friends, lest they would never respect her; so she would have us part. I was endifferant, tho sadly troubled, but ere we parted she was very mery because she had eased her spirit to me. So we parted, but it was with a further resolution of faithfull and constant effection.[49]

Ales or Elice Lealand had died two days earlier and Roger wrote a poem in her memory. The affair with Mary Naylor had its ups and downs. But soon he is off with Emm Potter, who eventually becomes his wife in 1668, after another stormy courtship:

[1664. August.] 8. – Munday. Being Ashton Wakes att this time I had a most ardent effection to Emm Potter, and she was in compeny att Tankerfield's with Henry Kenion, and it greeved me very much. Henry Low came to me and would have me to go to Tankerfeild's [to] spend 2d., so we went to the next chamber to

that they ware in. At last they came by us and I movd Emm to stay
to drinke with me, which she did, but would not stay with me,
neither there nor no where els; would not come to me, tho she
said she would; and I was in a very sad eflicted estate, and all by
reason of her.

14. – Lord's day. I went to Neawtowne and heard Mr. Balkeburne,
and he enjoined old William Hasleden and I to come to Roth-
well's, which we did and had 2 pints of wine, which he would
have payd for, but I would not suffer it. After I came home I went
to Elizebeth Rosbothome, and I spoke my mind to her concerneinge Emme, which I could not do without teares, and she did
pitie my state. I was very discomforted.

15. – Munday. The sun began to shine, for Elizebeth Rosbothom
had told Ellin my greefe, and she pitied my condition so as she
resolved she would never act against me so. I went to John
Rosbothome's and stayed awhile, and both Ellin and Emme came
downe, and Ellin went her way and Emme and I went into
chamber and there we professed each other's loves to each other;
so I was abundantly satisfied within my selfe and I promised this
night to come see her in her chamber. God will arise and show
pitie to his distressed servant.

16. – Old Mr. Woods came to towne and was all night att William
Hasleden's, and they would have had me to super, but Mr.
Woods ingagd me to come to be with hime. I was this afternoone
with William Chadocke and Thomas Heyes casting up their
accounts, and after I had done with them I came to shop and shutt
it up and went to William Hasleden's. They ware att prayer.
After prayer Mr. Woods' discourse was concerneinge wars and
troubles that he and old William had beene in togather, so att far
in night I came my way and came to the window that Emm Potter
lay in chamber, and I would gladly have come in, but she durst
not let me in; but she rise up to the windowe and we kisd, and so I
went to bed.

[1666. July.] 3. – Tusday. Em Potter had ecqueinted me that she
was told that my mother bore me a bastard . . .

> [August.] 16. – I was pensive and sad all day by reason I had heard some thing of Emm's unfaithfulness to me, and it greeved me very sore.[50]

Is there any reason to suppose Roger's attitudes were unusual for his time? Is there any reason to suppose his attitudes were new?

Over the five years before his marriage, he had love affairs with at least four young women – Ann Barrowe, Ales Lealand, Mary Naylor, Emm Potter. Yet Roger was not a libertine; on the contrary, he seems to have been a steady, rather serious young man. At times, these relationships are light-hearted and flirtatious; at other times, they cause Roger intense suffering. He seems free to woo any girl he comes across; and the girl is equally free to accept or reject him. The views of parents and the financial obstacles both have to be reckoned with, but neither seems decisive in relation to the outcome of the affair. How much difference in *emotional* attitudes is there between lower-middle-class romance in England in the 1660s and England in the 1960s or, if we think of the way Chaucer's Absalon wooed Alison, England in the 1360s?

6

THE
TROUBADOUR
MYTH

On our excursion into the past, we have now several times come across what is supposed to be a significant point. Some say it is one of the great turning points in history. According to the myth, there came a moment somewhere in the eleventh or possibly the twelfth century after Christ when, quite suddenly, romantic love was invented.

For nearly a century now, popular historical and literary thought has been dominated by a single, highly specific – and quite extraordinary – idea about the origin of love. Some scholars say the idea dates back to a little essay by Gaston Paris in 1883. Certainly by the following year Engels had taken hold of it and was vigorously brandishing it in *The Origin of the Family, Private Property and the State*. It may have been Stendhal in his *Essay on Love* (1822) who was the first writer to propose the troubadours of mediaeval Provence as the inventors of romantic love.

In English, the most celebrated exponent of the theory of courtly love was C. S. Lewis who, in *The Allegory of Love* (1936), breezily took for granted the date and the uniqueness of the phenomenon:

> Everyone has heard of courtly love, and everyone knows that it appears quite suddenly at the end of the eleventh century in Languedoc . . .

> French poets, in the eleventh century, discovered or invented, or were the first to express, that romantic species of passion which

93

English poets were still writing about in the nineteenth . . . Compared with this revolution the Renaissance is a mere ripple on the surface of literature.

Nobody could account for it. The invention of romantic love was a mysterious sudden thing. It struck the human race like lightning.

The new thing itself, I do not pretend to explain. Real changes in human sentiment are very rare – there are perhaps three or four on record – but I believe that they occur, and that this is one of them.[1]

An almost equally influential book was *L'Amour et l'occident* by Denis de Rougemont (Paris, 1939). At British universities since the war, along with *The Allegory of Love*, this has been the book first recommended to students as a guide to the whole subject of mediaeval romance. In Great Britain, the book was called *Passion and Society*, in the United States *Love in the Western World*; both these highly significant titles make explicit de Rougemont's claim that adulterous passion, dating from the Middle Ages, is both the driving principle and the destructive force behind emotional life in the West. Denis de Rougemont has, like Lewis, no doubts about the date and source: 'no one can doubt that the whole of European poetry issued from the poetry of the troubadours of the twelfth century.'

Above all, this poetry, we are told, celebrated *adultery*. C. S. Lewis listed four characteristics of this highly refined concept of love: humility, courtesy, adultery and the religion of love. But it is adultery – the only social as opposed to emotional condition among the four qualities – that absorbed him, and de Rougemont, and us. The chivalrous lover was paying court to a married lady; whether he won her love or sighed in vain, his love was essentially and crucially *illicit*. Her being married was both the barrier to their love and the mainspring of the whole poetic machinery; without the adulterous premise, there could be no tension and no passion.

Engels too had no doubt that the adulterous premise was highly significant:

The first historical form of sexual love as passion, a passion recognized as natural to all human beings (at least if they belonged to the ruling classes), and as the highest form of the sexual impulse – and that is what constitutes its specific character – this first form of individual sexual love, the chivalrous love of the Middle Ages, was by no means conjugal. Quite the contrary, in its classic form among the Provençals, it heads straight for adultery, and the poets of love celebrated adultery . . .

Before the Middle Ages we cannot speak of individual sex love . . . At the point where antiquity broke off its advance to sexual love, the Middle Ages took it up again – in adultery. We have already described the knightly love which gave rise to the songs of dawn. From the love which strives to break up marriage to the love which is to be its foundation there is still a long road, which chivalry never fully traversed.[2]

Nothing could be clearer.

Nothing could now be more emphatically or violently disputed. Most mediaevalists do not believe a word of the whole rigmarole. For the last twenty or thirty years, a stream of books and pamphlets have issued from the academic presses pouring the most acid scorn on C. S. Lewis, Denis de Rougemont and what is now called 'The Myth of Courtly Love'.[3] Professor D. N. Robertson of Princeton says bluntly: 'I have never been convinced that there was any such thing as what is usually called courtly love during the Middle Ages.'[4] At the same conference of mediaeval and early Renaissance studies, Professor John F. Benton remarked even more bluntly:

I have found the term 'courtly love' no advantage in trying to understand the theory and practice of love in mediaeval Europe. It is not a mediaeval technical term. It has no specific content. A reference to 'the rules of courtly love' is almost invariably a citation of Andreas' *De Amore*, a work which I think is intentionally and humorously ambiguous about love. The study of love in the middle ages would be far easier if we were not impeded by a term which now inevitably confuses the issue. As currently employed, 'courtly love' has no useful meaning, and it is not worth saving by redefinition. I would therefore like to propose that 'courtly love' be banned from all future conferences.[5]

Why have all these mediaevalists rejected so thumpingly the ideas which represented the conventional wisdom in their own student days – and which in the outside world are still largely taken for granted?

First, they are convinced, with good reason, that mediaeval poetry celebrates *married* love as much, or more than, illicit love. Professor D. S. Brewer claims that 'Chaucer nowhere celebrates illicit love,' and that there is always in Chaucer's serious love stories – as distinct from his comic pranks, japes and fables – 'an explicit connection between love and marriage'. Even in the notoriously licentious Boccaccio, many of the serious love stories end in marriage. Another mediaevalist, H. A. Kelly, asserts: 'Fiammetta's admonition against coveting other men's wives, "La maritata in niun modo è da disiderare" (4.52.1), seems to be in operation most of the time. Or, at least, if a man does desire a married woman, often enough she refuses him because of the love – or at least the loyalty – she bears towards her husband.'[6]

Even Chrétien de Troyes, whose romance of Lancelot and Guinevere is the classic instance of adulterous love, wrote five other romances with scarcely a hint of adultery in them.

One German scholar has gone so far as to argue:

Nowhere in the romances do we find a poet in love with his married patroness. The romances reflect every aspect of the life of their time, yet nowhere do they show us a troubadour of the kind Fauriel and Wechssler depicted . . . The troubadours' cult of their lady in the accepted (chivalric) sense is a legend. Women were loved and cherished in the Middle Ages in a way not very different from today's. But the forms of poetic expression were different, and that is what is important, and sets new problems for research. We must stop trying to explain all the particular qualities of this lyrical poetry by the social conditions in which the poets found themselves . . . it is useless to bring in feudal relationships to explain its spirit . . . it is a problem of *literary* history.[7]

It is, I think, this reluctance to understand the distinction between social history and literary history which explains why a handful of scholars still cling, in one way or another, to the myth of courtly love. Laurence Lerner in *Love and Marriage: Literature and Its Social Context* comes to the defence of C. S. Lewis and courtly love and argues strongly that 'the literature of love and marriage is drenched in ideology' and that 'literature is, in the end, the profoundest record we have of our real ideals.'[8]

He selects Tristan and Isolde, Lancelot and Guinevere and, 'especially for English readers', Troilus and Criseyde as 'representatives of courtly love: a sentiment that goes back to the troubadours, in which love is illegitimate and furtive'.[9] That is true of the Tristan and Lancelot stories, but the case of Troilus and Cressida – of which there were several English versions between Chaucer and Shakespeare – is quite different.

In the first mediaeval version of the story, Benoît de Sainte-Maure's *Roman de Troie* (c. 1160), Cressida is unmarried. In Boccaccio's *Filostrato*, and in Chaucer's *Troilus and Criseyde* written about fifty years later with the plot largely based on Boccaccio, she is a widow and so free to fall in love again. In all three versions, there are no real obstacles to the love affair between Troilus and Cressida. In both Boccaccio and Chaucer, it is the entirely legitimate courting which takes up most of the work. Criseyde's later surrender to the courting of Diomede is certainly a betrayal of her first and true love for Troilus, but it is partly to be explained, if not excused, by her position as a captive. Thus although the setting is pre-Christian and thus free of religious prohibitions, far from promoting adulterous love, these poems take it for granted that true love is moral and honourable, and depends on keeping faith.

Nor can the true-love-equals-adultery thesis be saved by the argument put forward by Laurence Lerner in *Love and Marriage*,[10] namely that, even where there is no husband to obstruct the course of true love, the love affairs described in these mediaeval romances are usually clandestine and so equivalent to adultery and hostile to the spirit of marriage, which is essentially a public ceremony.

The notion of love as a private affair, a shared secret, is far older than the troubadours and can be found everywhere, as far back as the love songs of ancient Egypt and Greece. Moreover, as we have seen from the mediaeval Church courts, even the Church accepted that marriage was a private contract which, however, ought to be publicly registered to cope with the social consequences and ought also to have the blessing of the Church. Churchmen no less than married couples in the Middle Ages would have been horrified at the idea that the modesty and decorous behaviour proper to young people in love was the same thing as the furtiveness of criminal adulterers. 'Aidos' or virtuous shame is one of the most ancient of virtues, common to both the Christian and classical traditions of ethics.

The fact that Criseyde is a respectable widow when Troilus pays court to her may diminish the dramatic tension to modern tastes, but we may presume that Chaucer did not think so and we may also presume that he was a tolerably good judge of his audience. That in itself may suggest to us that, in fourteenth-century England at any rate, adultery was not regarded as an indispensable dramatic mainspring.

Undoubtedly the stories of Lancelot and Tristan were popular in the Middle Ages because they were taken up, reworked and translated so often. But what modern literary critics tend to miss is that plenty of other, non-adulterous romances, both comic and serious, some with tragic endings of lovers dead or sundered, others with bourgeois happy endings of married couples reunited, were just as popular in the Middle Ages.

The unique and obsessive popularity of Lerner's chosen stories of illegitimate love belongs to a much later date. In particular, it is the Victorians who so enthusiastically embraced the adulterous mediaeval romance. If you were to trace an adultery-obsession curve, it would probably start at a fairly low level in the Middle Ages, rise steadily through the seventeenth and eighteenth centuries and reach a peak in the nineteenth century. In the section in chapter 8 on 'Muddling the evidence', I shall suggest why this might be so.

For the time being, what matters is to dispose of the idea that, in mediaeval romances, adultery was idealised as the unique obsession worth romancing about and also the idea that it was idealised as the only true expression of sexual love. It was not. Love was just as likely to be represented in chaste or comic or moral guise as it was in the form of illicit passion.

Literature is of course an uncertain guide to life. There is no reason to assume that the amount of adultery in fourteenth-century romances corresponded to the amount of adultery in fourteenth-century real life. But the troubadour myth is based on the evidence of the surviving mediaeval texts and on that evidence it can and must be refuted.

Besides, much of the evidence taken by Lewis and others to prove that true passion had to be adulterous comes from writers such as Andreas Capellanus and Chrétien de Troyes who made considerable use of *irony*. Their intention is to amuse and provoke, not to lay down serious views of whether or not love is incompatible with marriage. It is as though a modern man were to take comedians' wisecracks about mothers-in-law as guides to the correct treatment of his own wife's mother.

And, without doubt, the wider and deeper you delve, the less convincing becomes the theory that romantic love was *new*. Peter Dronke, in *Medieval Latin and the Rise of European Love-lyric*, believes:

(i) that 'the new feeling' of *amour courtois* is at least as old as Egypt of the second millennium B.C., and might indeed occur at any time or place: that it is, as Professor Marrou suspected, 'un secteur du coeur, un des aspects éternels de l'homme',

(ii) that the feeling of *amour courtois* is not confined to courtly or chivalric society, but is reflected even in the earliest recorded popular verse of Europe (which almost certainly had a long oral tradition behind it) . . .[11]

For those who need convincing of this, Dronke quotes a huge range of examples from Ancient Egypt, mediaeval Byzantium, the Caucasus, the Islamic world of the seventh and eighth centuries, Icelandic poetry of the tenth century – and other times and places which either predate the troubadours by centuries or could have had no knowledge of their songs.

For pleasure as well as argument, I cannot help quoting a few fragments from Mr Dronke's examples:

> I shall lie down at home
> and pretend to be ill.
> Then my neighbours will come in to see me
> and my beloved will be with them.
> She will make the doctors unnecessary
> for she knows my malady.
>
> (Egypt, about 1300 B.C.)[12]

> O that I were the negro girl
> Who is her companion!
> Then I should catch sight
> Of the whole of her body . . .
>
> (from a sherd in the Cairo Museum)[13]

> Sweet mother, I can no longer
> Work at the loom, stricken
> With love-longing for a boy
> By the slender Aphrodite.
>
> (Sappho, sixth century B.C.)[14]

99

This is one of the most beautiful of all, by Heinrich von Morungen, one of the great German poets of the late twelfth century:

> Alas, shall her body never again
> stream its light through the night for me?
> body whiter than snow,
> formed so perfectly;
> it deceived my eyes:
> I thought that it must be
> the bright moon's radiance.
> Then the day came.[15]

Let us allow Dronke to complete his case with a selection from the anonymous graffiti on the walls of Pompeii – scribbled by passers-by nearly 2,000 years ago:

Many of these Pompeian inscriptions are coarse, as one might expect. Others show tenderness, reverence, veneration:

> Cestilia, queen of all Pompeii,
> sweet spirit, farewell!

> May you be blessed, little love,
> may the Venus of Pompeii protect you.

> Whoever has not seen the Venus of Apelles,
> let him look at my love, for she is just as radiant.

> No one is beautiful unless he has loved when young.

> If there be any who reprove a lover, let him try
> to tame the winds or make waters cease to flow!

> Blessings on him who loves, let him who cannot love
> perish, a double death on him who forbids love![16]

The same ideas are to be found in Shakespeare and Burns and in a thousand popular songs, whether sung to Victorian piano or to modern electric guitar.

Nor are these celebrations of love confined to the Mediterranean world. Propagandists for Celtic and Anglo-Saxon civilisations often used to argue the opposite – that it was amid the Northern mists that love was first elevated as a noble emotion, while the shallow

Mediterraneans knew only mere sensual pleasures. This is moonshine too.

But certainly sexual passion and marital love do figure in the elegiac poetry of the Anglo-Saxon era, two or three centuries before the Norman Conquest – and moreover in terms far more passionate and poignant than the troubadours usually managed. Among the scanty fragments which have survived, we find in the Exeter Book three such poems, 'The Husband's Message', 'The Wife's Lament' and 'Wulf'.

These poems completely refute the belief that sex love or married love was somehow connected with the rise of the modern world, or the decay of feudalism or the Renaissance. For they come from the Dark Ages, the eighth or ninth centuries, and are to be found amid an assortment of heroic lays, sagas about blood feuds and the like.

The greatest of them, 'The Wife's Lament', concerns a woman separated from her husband, who has been exiled by the plotting of his kinsmen, 'that we might live in wretchedness apart'. Again and again, she refers to her distress at the separation, and to the time of their first love.

>   We have vowed
> Full many a time that nought should come between us
> But death alone, and nothing else at all.
> All that has changed, and it is now as though
> Our marriage and our love had never been,

Now for ever she is dragged into the feud of 'my beloved husband dear', confined in a cave in a wood:

>   Full often here
> The absence of my lord comes sharply to me.
> Dear lovers in this world lie in their beds,
> While I alone at crack of dawn must walk
> Under the oak-tree round this earthy cave,
> Where I must stay the length of summer days,
> Where I may weep my banishment and all
> My many hardships, for I never can
> Contrive to set at rest my careworn heart.

She thinks too of her husband's sufferings. Outcast in a distant land, frozen by storms, dwelling in some desolate abode:

> Beside the sea, my weary-hearted lord
> Must suffer pitiless anxiety.
> And all too often he will call to mind
> A happier dwelling. Grief must always be
> For him who yearning longs for his beloved.[17]

Nor is it possible to argue that the Anglo-Saxons were unique. In the earliest Irish literature, sexual love is lyrically celebrated. The surviving manuscripts of the 'Wooing of Étaín' and the 'Elopement of Grainne with Diarmait' may date from the ninth century or earlier. Very little of Welsh literature survives from this time, but by the twelfth century, romance is full-blown in Welsh poetry. The tone is fresh and popular and seems unconnected with the courtly style of Provence. I find it hard to imagine that the races inhabiting the British Isles were unique in their celebration of licit sexual love before and during marriage – as well as sharing the universal interest in adultery.

In the face of this endless stream of love songs, how can we cling to the view, which we learnt at school, that the ancient world regarded sexual passion as either a morbid disease or a mere sensual satisfaction? That may have been the line among statesmen, philosophers and intellectuals. It was never the popular view; even in high art, the lyric poetry of Sappho and Ovid accepts love as one of the great things in life.

A rather subtler version of the myth concedes that while the Middle Ages may not have invented sexual love, it was in the Middle Ages that sexual love was first expressed in literature with such frequency, intensity, eloquence and variety; and that this change in literary attitudes must imply a change in popular attitudes.

Unfortunately, there is no evidence for a huge change in either the quality or the quantity of love-poetry. On the contrary, over and over again, the same images, the same literary conceits, the same ideas are found all over the world, centuries before and after the time of the troubadours:

She whom I love has no equal. She is a queen. One moment with her is worth Paradise to me. I would gladly go to hell if she were there. She mirrors the divine light to the world. She puts the sun to shame. She is an angel, a goddess. She is the remedy for all my ills, my medicine, my balm. She is my salvation. She is the flower of flowers.

I wish I were the ring on her finger or the girdle on her dress or the mole on her cheek. To be separated from her is a torture worse than death. I am her slave, her vassal. I would die for her, go through fire for her. I *shall* die without her.

Love is good. God ordained love. Human love is the reflection of divine love.

These ideas are repeated ad infinitum, ad nauseam – and in popular and courtly love songs alike. In fact, as Peter Dronke points out, you continually come across the most complex and rarefied ideas and metaphors in the popular songs, just as you find the simple ones in the poems of great poets:

My love is like a red, red rose. She is my sunflower, my one flower, the flower of my heart. We must love one another or die. All you really need is love. Burns, Sinatra, Auden, the Beatles. 'I love you till the seas run dry'. Burns, yes, but the same words occur in an obscure Calabrian love-song of the early Middle Ages, perhaps as early as the tenth century, written in a Greek-Italian dialect in a manuscript not published until a century after Burns's death.[18]

And on and on too go the complaints about the vapid, slushy, sentimental, moral-fibre-sapping perniciousness of these ditties. Nothing is less historical than to assume that the 'puritanical' official disapproval of pop songs is a modern phenomenon, to be traced back to Oliver Cromwell at the earliest.

St Valerius, who lived in Spain between A.D. 630 and 695, mentions with horror an Ethiopian priest called Iustus, who was famous or infamous for his love-songs sung to a lute. From the sixth to the ninth century, churchmen and church councils all over Europe continually cried out against the apparently unstoppable flood of 'shameful and dissolute songs', 'songs about girls', and 'seductive songs and irreligious amusements'. As we shall see, it is from this chorus of complaints that we derive some of the evidence for the secret history of love.

7

THE MYTH
OF THE
INDIFFERENT
MOTHER

Now we come to the strangest myth of all. It is the myth about the relationship between parents and children in traditional society. The myth is fascinating in itself, but the reasons which caused the myth to be created may be even more important.

First, let us present this myth in its most assertive form. This, as usual, is to be found in Professor Shorter's *The Making of the Modern Family*: 'Good mothering is an invention of modernization. In traditional society, mothers viewed the development and happiness of infants younger than two with indifference. In modern society, they place the welfare of their small children above all else.'[1]

At first sight, Professor Shorter concedes, these are surprising statements:

> The little band of scholars which for some time now has been arguing that in traditional society mothers didn't love their children very much has met with stark incredulity. Mothers not attached to their babies? Indifferent to their welfare and resigned to their squalling, usually fatal 'convulsions' and 'fevers'? Impossible, says the twentieth-century spirit. But in fact, among the general populace, life was that way.[2]

Shorter derives support for this belief from a remarkable book, *L'Enfant et la vie familiale dans l'Ancien Régime* by Philippe Ariès, first published in 1960 and translated into English as *Centuries of Child-hood: A Social History of Family Life*:

> It was the pioneer social historian Philippe Ariès who first argued that maternal indifference to infants characterized traditional society. With the aid of portraits and family reference books, he concluded that small children were seen in the Middle Ages as creatures apart from people. Barely possessing souls of their own, they came at the will of God, departed at His behest, and in their brief mortal sojourn deserved little adult sympathy or compassion.[3]

This is not quite what Ariès himself says, but it is what a lot of people today believe about the Middle Ages. What justification is there for this belief and what kind of evidence can we legitimately use to defend it?

Professor Shorter infers his theories about maternal indifference 'from the way these mothers *acted* towards their children'. His basic criteria, perhaps showing a certain American bias, are essentially *hygienic*. Mothers in traditional society were always doing the wrong things; they left their babies in the care of wet-nurses and they swaddled them instead of allowing their limbs free play; they had no idea of the importance of breast-feeding or of keeping children clean.

There are a host of jumbled and conflicting accusations here. Swaddling, for example, was thought to be *good* for the child, as was rocking a child in his cradle – another practice objected to by Shorter. And other historians take a rather different view of wet-nursing, including Ariès himself who believes that, as cow's milk was un-hygienic, putting a child out to wet-nurse in the country

> can be interpreted as a protective measure – I hesitate as yet to call it a hygienic precaution – to be linked with the other phenomena in which we have recognized a special solicitude for children.
>
> In fact, despite the propaganda of the philosophers, well-to-do parents, of both the nobility and the middle class, went on putting their children out to nurse until the end of the nineteenth century, that is to say until the progress of hygiene and aseptic methods made it safe to use animal milk.[4]

These measures may or may not have been mistaken; but we cannot deduce from them, as Shorter says, that 'the point is that these mothers did not *care*, and that is why their children vanished in the

105

ghastly slaughter of the innocents that was traditional child-rearing.'
On the contrary, in many cases, mothers were simply following
standard medical practice.

Nor can we deduce maternal indifference from the thousands of
children left at the foundling hospital; if the choice lay between what
looked like certain starvation at home and a chance of survival –
though not always a very good one – at the foundling hospital, who
can say what was the right course of action?

But the principal grounds for saying that parents were indifferent –
at least the grounds advanced by Professor Ariès – are not drawn from
the hospital and the morgue, but from pictures and books. It is from
these artistic and literary sources that we are to deduce that parents
did not and could not attach themselves too passionately to children
who were all too likely to die in the first few years of life:

> This is the reason for certain remarks which shock our present-day
> sensibility, such as Montaigne's observation: 'I have lost two or
> three children in their infancy, not without regret, but without
> great sorrow', or Molière's comment on Louison in *Le Malade
> imaginaire*: 'The little girl doesn't count.' Most people probably felt
> like Montaigne, that children had 'neither mental activities nor
> recognizable bodily shape'. Mme de Sévigné (1671) records without
> any sign of surprise a similar remark made by Mme de Coetquen
> when the latter fainted on receiving the news of her little daughter's
> death: 'She is greatly distressed and says that she will never again
> have one so pretty.'
>
> Nobody thought, as we ordinarily think today, that every child
> already contained a man's personality. Too many of them died. 'All
> mine die in infancy', wrote Montaigne. This indifference was a
> direct and inevitable consequence of the demography of the
> period.[5]

Even here we are struck by something odd. *Why did Madame de
Coetquen faint?* If she cared so relatively little and could look forward
with equanimity to having other children, why should she have
reacted so dramatically to the news?

And the passage from Montaigne deserves rather closer inspection.
First of all, the passage occurs in his essay on 'The Affection of
Fathers for their Children'. The essay is dedicated to Madame
d'Estissac, and Montaigne begins by praising the way in which, after

being left a widow at such an early age, she brought up her children so well by her own 'unaided wisdom'. Montaigne says, 'We have no example of maternal affection more outstanding than yours in our time.'

This is not exactly the way you would expect an essay on parental indifference to commence. And the passage Ariès quotes has a rather different intention from that implied in *Centuries of Childhood*. It deserves reproducing in full:

> I, for my part, have a strange disgust for those propensities which arise within us without the control and intervention of our judgement. Touching my present subject, for instance, I cannot entertain that passion for caressing new-born infants, that have neither mental activities nor recognizable bodily shape by which to make themselves lovable; and I have never willingly suffered them to be fed in my presence.
>
> A true and regular affection should spring up and increase with our growing knowledge of them. Then if they are deserving of it, our natural inclination keeping step with our reason, we shall cherish them with a truly paternal regard; and we shall pass judgement on them also if they are unworthy, deferring always to reason, notwithstanding the force of nature. Very often it is quite the reverse; and we are generally more moved by our children's frolickings, games, and infantile nonsense than afterwards by their mature acts. It is as if we had loved them for our amusement, as monkeys, not as human beings.[6]

Montaigne is saying several things: first, many people like caressing babies, Montaigne does not happen to. He puts forward the humanist's rather starchy viewpoint, but then, in his usual charming way, throws up his hands and, half-contradicting himself, implies that he cannot help being diverted by the antics of children – not new-born infants. In modern terminology, we might say that he was a little repressed, perhaps even something of a male chauvinist in his distaste for dandling babies and watching breast-feeding, but he is certainly not unmoved by children, particularly when they are a little older – a preference shared by many twentieth-century men.

Nor does Montaigne speak of his own children in a tone which suggests indifference. In arguing that children should be educated by reason and tact and not by violence, he says:

That is how I was brought up. They tell me that in all my childhood I was only whipped twice, and then very mildly. I owed the same upbringing to my own children. They all died at nurse, except Leonor, my one daughter who escaped this unhappy fate. She has reached the age of more than 6 without anything but words, and very gentle words, being used to guide her and correct her childish faults. Her mother's indulgence readily concurred in this. And even if my hopes in her should be disappointed, there will be enough other causes for this without blaming my educational system, which I know to be both just and natural.[7]

Furthermore, Montaigne shows the greatest interest in the nature of the emotional link between parents and children. For example:

The late Maréchal de Monluc, whose son – a truly brave and most promising gentleman – died on the island of Madeira, when talking to me of his sorrow, greatly stressed, among his many regrets, the heartbroken grief that he felt at never having opened his heart to the boy. He had always put on the stern face of paternal gravity, and had thus lost the opportunity of really knowing and appreciating his son, also of revealing to him the deep love he bore him, and the deservedly high opinion he had of his virtues. 'And that poor lad', he said, 'never saw anything of me but a grim and scornful frown, and has died in the belief that I could neither love him nor value him at his proper worth. For whom was I saving the revelation of the singular affection that I felt for him in my soul? Was it not he who should have had all the pleasure and all the obligation? I constrained and tortured myself to keep on this foolish mask, thus losing the delight of his companionship, and of his affection too. For his feelings towards me cannot have been anything but cool, since all he had ever received from me was gruffness, and my bearing towards him was always tyrannical.'[8]

This is as far from indifference as any writer could get without indulging in the sentimental effusions of the eighteenth century. Curiously enough, it is from the eighteenth century that Professor Shorter chooses his examples of parental indifference:

Mothers would simply leave their dying babies 'lying in the gutters and rotting on the dung-heaps of London', a sight which horrified Thomas Coram, the patron of a hospital for foundlings. Dr.

Johnson's Mrs. Thrale was said to have 'regarded the death of various daughters at school with great equanimity'. And Sir John Verney 'cheerfully remarked when two of his fifteen children died that he still had left a baker's dozen'.[9]

But in Professor Stone's *The Family, Sex and Marriage*, it is the eighteenth century which is described as showing a 'trend towards a more affectionate and permissive handling of children'. Richard Costeker complained in 1732 that 'thousands are ruined by the very effect of maternal love'. Locke and Rousseau were the new guides to bringing up children. 'It is maternal rather than paternal affection which is most amply documented in the eighteenth century, and the intimate family groups of mothers depicted by Reynolds and Zoffany clearly had a firm basis in reality.'[10] And Professor Stone tells us that, far from being an indifferent mother, Mrs Thrale was 'a woman who directed all her driving ambition on to her children, for lack of any serious support from, or interest shown in her by her husband'. She expected far too much of her children and was disappointed with those who survived; they turned out not to be intellectual prodigies and they did not like her. Mrs Thrale wrote that for the twelve years which she spent bearing and bringing up children, she 'brought a baby once a year, lost some of them, and grew so anxious about the rest that I now fairly cared for nothing else but them and her' ('her' being Mrs Thrale's mother, whom she saw for several hours almost every day).[11]

There are, I think, several fallacies in the *interpretation* commonly offered of those remarks dredged up from past centuries which appear to show indifference to the death of new-born children. First, any sight which you see very frequently tends not to call forth language of the greatest intensity. This does not mean that you are unmoved by the spectacle of suffering. It is, however, hard to talk continuously in the language of high emotion. The spectacle of Bowery bums in the streets or of starving people in Indian cities are two obvious modern examples: visitors to New York and Calcutta are haunted by the sight of such misery; residents do not comment.

Second, we must always bear in mind that the mere recording of such apparently cold-hearted remarks suggests that these remarks struck the recorder as unusual. The remarks may indicate rather that the normal reaction was to be deeply upset by the death of a child.

Third – and this is perhaps the most difficult point to make – there

exists in all societies a certain hard-headed spirit of biological calculation. For a bereaved mother to be reminded that at least she has
other children may be highly insensitive. But even today, in discussing her bereavement, most people would make *some* distinction
between a mother who had lost her only child when she was past
childbearing and a bereaved younger mother who has other children
and may yet bear more.

Fourth – and this, I think, we do know from our own experience –
grief is very often dumb. Intentionally or unintentionally, it may look
like indifference; the inability or the reluctance to express extremities
of feeling is deceptive.

Even if we assume that there was at some point a revolution in
attitudes towards children, at what point in history are we to place it?
After all, foundling hospitals, orphanages, schools and institutions for
poor scholars in England – and other European countries – had been
founded at all times since records were first kept. The present author
was educated at a school founded for poor scholars in the 1440s, passes
every day a foundling hospital established in the 1740s and, when
necessary, takes his children to the out-patient department of a
hospital founded in the 1120s when he is not taking them to the
General Practitioner for free treatment under a National Health
Service founded in the 1940s. Does the founding of Coram's London
Foundling Hospital make the eighteenth century any more of 'a
child-oriented era' than the founding of the Hospital of the Innocents
in Florence in 1421? Does the term 'Innocents' suggest indifference
towards or moral disapproval of abandoned bastard children?

Some of the earliest reliable direct evidence comes from the Pyrenean village of Montaillou. Between 1318 and 1325 Jacques Fournier,
the Bishop of Pamiers and later to be Pope Benedict XII at Avignon,
carried out an inquisition of the villagers in order to stamp out the
Cathar heresy. His Register covered in graphic detail every aspect of
their lives – marriage and love no less than religion and farming.
Emmanuel Le Roy Ladurie's famous study of the village (*Montaillou*,
1978) concludes from Fournier's Register 'that there was not such an
enormous gap, as has sometimes been claimed, between our attitude
to children and the attitude of the people in fourteenth-century
Montaillou and upper Ariége.'[12]

Alicia and Serena were ladies of Chateauverdun. One of these ladies had a child in the cradle and she wanted to see it before leaving (she was going to join the heretics). When she saw it, she kissed it; then the child began to laugh. She had started to go out of the room where the infant lay, so she came back to it again. The child began to laugh again; and so on, several times, so that she could not bear to tear herself away from the child. Seeing this she said to her maidservant: 'Take him out of the house.'[13]

Nor did the women of Montaillou accept the loss of their children with equanimity.

Bartholomette d'Urs (she was the wife of Arnaud d'Urs, of Vicdessos) . . . had a young son, who slept with her in her own bed. One morning when she woke up she found him dead beside her. She started to weep and lament.

'Do not weep,' I said. 'God will give the soul of your dead son to the next child you conceive, male or female. Or else his soul will find a good home somewhere else.'[14]

Misplaced consolation perhaps, yet how difficult it is to find the right words. When Guillemette Benet lost a daughter and was weeping for her, Alazais Azema tried to console her with the words: 'Cheer up, you still have some daughters left; and anyhow you can't get the one that is dead back again.'

Quoted out of context, that could be made to sound unfeeling; in its context it was clearly meant sympathetically. Guillemette replied: 'I would mourn even more than I do for the death of my daughter; but, Deo gratias, I have had the consolation of seeing her hereticated on the night before her death by Guillaume Authié, who hurried here in a blizzard.'[15]

Another Montaillou mother was told by the Cathar holy man, Prades Tavernier, not to give her baby any milk or meat. But: 'When my husband and Prades Tavernier had left the house, I could not bear it any longer. I couldn't let my daughter die before my very eyes, so I put her to the breast.'[16]

Even among these French peasants of former times – who, we are told, were so unfeeling – maternal love appears to have been strong. What is the explanation of the discrepancy? Professor Shorter's evidence, for example, comes mostly from eighteenth- and nineteenth-century sources, very largely the reports of professional men – doctors, lawyers and folklore historians – who describe what they observed of peasant behaviour. The Inquisitor of Montaillou, 500 years earlier, collected the verbal statements of the *peasants themselves*. In the case of Montaillou, the evidence we have is the evidence of how the peasants themselves felt, not how their public behaviour – traditionally taciturn and inexpressive – may have appeared to articulate outsiders.

This interpretation gains strength if we collect references to marriage in the Inquisitor's Register. From the outside – that is, from official records or from the observations of middle-class visitors – peasant marriage may appear to have been almost entirely a matter of property. A woman is given in marriage by one man (her father) or by a group of her kinsmen to another man. There are negotiations about dowries and jointures; documents have to be drawn up. And yet these arrangements do not necessarily rule out love. Ladurie quotes Pierre Bourdieu's conclusion from his studies of the years 1900–1960 in Lesquire, a village in Béarn where the choice of marriage was just as limited as in Montaillou: 'happy love, i.e. love which is socially approved and thus likely to succeed, is nothing but that kind of *amor fati*, that love of one's own social destiny, which, by the apparently hazardous and arbitrary paths of free choice, unites partners already socially predestined for each other.'[17]

In Montaillou, too, marriages which could be said to have been arranged or at least were socially approved were often love matches as well. *Adamare* and *diligere*, the two verbs to describe 'passionate love' in the Inquisitor's Latin, are often applied to couples before and after marriage. Jean Maury, a heretic who had to take refuge in another village, *adamat* a local girl there, Marie. The marriage was a great success. His mother said: 'for our family, Marie is a daughter-in-law after our own heart. All that we want, Marie wants, and does it too.'[18]

Bernard Clergue, the rich *bayle* of the village, fell passionately in love with his future wife, Raymonde Belot – and she with him. His brother Pierre, the irrepressibly lecherous priest, made fun of him. Years later, Bernard recalled:

More than 12 years ago, during the summer, I was madly in love with Raymonde, who is now my wife: I wanted to go into the Belots' house . . . but I noticed, under the gateway of my house, my brother, the priest Pierre Clergue. At that, I did not like to go into the Belots' house, for my brother the priest laughed at me because I was madly in love with Raymonde 'Belote'.[19]

Erotic passion, both in and out of marriage, was taken as a natural thing; so was the intense mother love of children. I place the two varieties of love together here to emphasise how thoroughly saturated with the affections this fourteenth-century village seems to have been, according to the account of those who lived there. The notions of modern historians that sex was a mere bodily function carried out for socio-economic ends and that children were the socio-economic units produced by this function to provide agricultural labour would have seemed bizarre in the extreme to the villagers of Montaillou.

Nor do writers of an earlier time write as if their audience could be expected to be unfamiliar with parental love or parental grief for a dead child. King Lear mourning for the dead Cordelia in his arms and Macduff being told of the murder of his wife and children are two of the most intensely emotional passages in all literature. The description of Patient Griselda in 'The Clerk's Tale', hearing that her children are not dead after all, is scarcely less expressive:

> On hearing this Griselda fell aswoon
> In piteous joy, but made recovery
> And called her children to her and they soon
> Were folded in her arms. How tenderly
> She kissed them as the salt tears falling free
> Bathed them and glistened on their face and hair;
> How like a mother stood Griselda there!
>
> And Oh how pitiful it was to see
> Her fainting and to hear her humble tone!
> 'All thanks to you, my dearest lord,' said she,
> 'For you have saved my children, you alone!
> Were I to die this moment I have known
> Your love and have found favour in your sight,
> And death were nothing, though I died tonight.
>
> 'O dear, O tender ones, so long away,
> Your sorrowing mother steadfastly had thought
> That some foul vermin, hound or beast of prey
> Had eaten you. But God in mercy brought

> You back to me and your kind father sought
> In tender love to keep you safe and sound.'
> She suddenly swooned again and fell to ground.[20]

When his daughter Elizabeth died in 1528, at the age of ten months, Martin Luther, known to posterity as a father who believed in discipline and hard work for children, wrote to a friend: 'It is remarkable what a sorrowful, almost womanish heart her death has left me with, so very much am I filled with grief. I would never have thought beforehand that a fatherly heart could be so soft towards his children.'[21]

A few years earlier, in 1502, Henry VII's elder son Arthur died at Ludlow Castle. The news was conveyed to the King who was at Greenwich:

> When his grace understood that sorrowful heavy tidings, he sent for the queen, saying that he and his queen would take the painful sorrows together. After that she was come and saw the king her lord, and that natural and painful sorrow, as I have heard say, she with full great and constant comfortable words besought his grace that he would first after God remember the weal of his own noble person, the comfort of his realm and of her. She then said that my lady his mother had never no more children but him only, and that God by His grace had ever preserved him, and brought him where he was. Over that, how that God had left him yet a fair prince, two fair princesses, that God is where he was, and we are both young enough. And that the prudence and wisdom of his grace spread over all Christendom, so that it should please him to take this accordingly thereunto. Then the king thanked her of her good comfort. After that she departed and came to her own chamber, natural and motherly remembrance of that great loss smote her so sorrowful to the heart that those about her were feign to send for the king to comfort her. Then his grace of true gentle and faithful love, in good haste came and relieved her, and showed her how wise counsel she had given him before, and he for his part would thank God for his son, and would she should do in like wise.[22]

This anecdote comes from an unknown source and was first printed in 1715. But those who might doubt that the supposedly stern and miserly Henry VII should have shown such tenderness should not overlook the touching letter he wrote in his own hand to his mother in old age, giving thanks 'for the great and singular motherly love and affection that it hath pleased you at all times to bear me'.

Diaries and autobiographies, which turn up in increasing numbers from the seventeenth century onwards, indicate from the start that it was thought neither trivial nor unmanly to show grief for a dead child or a dead wife. Sir Henry Slingsby, who was beheaded as a royalist in 1658 and whose diary dates from the years 1638–48, wrote after the death of his wife: 'I had not been yet at my own house, not abiding to come where I should find a miss of my dear wife and where every room will call her to my memory and renew my grief I therefore staid at Alne at my sister Bethell's house until I had better digested my grief.'[23]

John Evelyn wrote on the death of his son Richard at the age of five in 1657: 'Here ends the joy of my life, and for which I go ever mourning to the grave.' He found the death of his daughter Mary from smallpox at the age of nineteen bitterer still: 'Never can I say enough, oh dear, my dear child, whose memory is so precious to me.'[24]

It will not do for critics to argue that these are merely conventional sentiments which demonstrate a sentimental revolution in literary taste. First of all, they don't sound conventional, but, even if they were, that convention could scarcely be described as new. Educated men of the time would have been familiar with, for example, Plutarch's *Letter of Consolation to His Wife on the Death of an Infant Daughter*. This letter does indeed contain some formal, schoolmaster-ish passages about the need to preserve dignity and moderation in grief. But what are we to say of passages like the following?

> You and I together have had many children and we have brought all of them up at home and looked after them ourselves. And I know how wonderfully happy we were when, after four sons, the daughter whom you had always longed to have was born and so made it possible for me to give your name to one of our children. Then too there is a very special kind of poignancy about the love we feel for such very young children; it is an absolutely pure pleasure . . . And our little girl had such a wonderfully good and kind nature . . . You remember how she would get her nurse to offer her breast and feed not only other small children but even the toys and playthings she was fond of . . . [25]

Not merely does that not sound formal, but Plutarch lets us know that he is conscious of the difficulties of writing a letter of condolence:

> Just as it was the sweetest thing in the world for us to hold her in our arms and look at her and listen to her, so now the thought of her must live with us and share our lives, and bring us more joy, much more joy than sorrow (if it is at all reasonable that the arguments which we have often used to other people should be of help to us too in our hour of need).[26]

Nor was this two-year-old daughter the first they had lost. Plutarch recalls the times 'When you lost your eldest child and then again when our lovely child Charon left us'. And yet the pain never grew easier to bear, even in the first century A.D.

And to use Ariès's own sources, how are we to explain the Marriage Capital on one of the columns holding up the Ducal Palace in Venice? The sculptures on the capital, which dates from about 1400 and is also known as the Capital of Human Love, show the engagement, the wedding ceremony, the couple naked in bed, then the birth of a child, then a family portrait with each parent holding the child by the hand. Then, in Ariès's own words, 'the story takes a dramatic turn: the family is in mourning, for the child has died; he is stretched out on his bed with his hands folded. The mother is wiping away her tears with one hand and touching the child's arm with the other; the father is praying.'[27] Indifference?

Moreover, this story represents the full panoply of the supposedly 'modern' attitudes towards marriage and the family, for what Ariès describes frigidly as the 'engagement' – which could signify merely an arranged match – is described by other writers rather more warmly as 'courtship' or even 'love at first sight', so that we have here all the elements – pre-marital love, post-marital sexual passion, nuclear family solidarity, maternal affection – and all in the early fifteenth century, or perhaps even the end of the fourteenth century, a dating by some scholars which Ariès shame-facedly describes as 'more surprising in view of the precocity of the subject'.[28]

But for us, looking back to Chaucer or to Anglo-Saxon poems such as 'The Wife's Lament', there is no surprise, because there is no question of the subject being precocious or retarded. It is simply a timeless, popular subject. I cannot resist quoting from dear old E. V. Lucas's *A Wanderer in Venice*: 'Many years ago, this column was shown to me by the captain of a tramp steamer, as the most interesting thing in Venice; and there are others who share his opinion.'[29]

Now this pillar is rather thicker than its neighbours (it bears the party wall of the great Council Hall above). It is in the middle. It has the medallion of the Queen of the Adriatic above it. It is surrounded on either side by capitals showing scenes of other aspects of earthly life – the months of the year, the fruits of the soil, the nations of the earth, the sun and planets, the crafts, the animals, the signs of the zodiac. And in the centre there is Marriage and the Family.

Perhaps the date does have a significance, though not the one Ariès attributes to it. For the Doge's Palace is a secular building, one of the first great municipal palaces, freed from any need to celebrate the religious pieties. Its decoration was directed not by bishops and abbots but by secular officials. And when they design a sequence of sculptures celebrating the earth we live in and the people who live on it, what do they put at the centre? Marriage and the family. This if you like is a proclamation of liberation from the religious dictatorship of the Middle Ages; it is a recovery of the earthly, fleshly core of human life.

Yet perhaps the most striking – because the most unintended – evidence against the myth comes from a recent book which is designed to reinforce the myth. Professor Lloyd de Mause is an American, an historian of progressive inclination and a scholar of psychoanalysis. His *History of Childhood* is, he claims, the first book to examine seriously the history of childhood in the West. It is designed to prove that 'the evolution of parent–child relations constitutes an independent source of historical change.' As in psychoanalysis, successive generations of parents 'regress' to the psychic age of their children and so, over the centuries, come to understand and sympathise with their children better and so gradually to treat them more kindly and thoughtfully.

In support of his thesis, de Mause produces a horrifying catalogue of child abuse in past times: killing, beating, torturing, neglect, sexual molestation, sale into slavery, swaddling and neglect of hygiene (although this last factor is more emphasised in Edward Shorter's *The Making of the Modern Family*). In all this evidence, de Mause discerns a pattern of historical improvement from brutal to tender, from the 'Infanticidal Mode' of antiquity, through the 'Abandonment Mode' of the Dark and Middle Ages to the 'Socialisation Mode' of the nineteenth and early twentieth centuries and finally the 'Helping Mode' which, de Mause says, 'results in a child who is gentle, sincere, never depressed, never imitative or group-oriented, strong-willed and unintimidated by authority'.[30]

This is a delightful picture of psychic progress. However, it has certain flaws. First the evidence which de Mause presents is of several different types of parental behaviour. He fails to distinguish between practices which parents, genuinely if mistakenly, thought were good for children, such as swaddling and corporal punishment, practices which were desperate last resorts of starving parents, such as abandoning their children and giving them to foundling hospitals, and practices which were in their own time, usually if not always, regarded by most people as criminal or wrong, such as pointless brutality or sexual ill-treatment.

In the nineteenth century, for example, which are we to see as typical of parents' psychic attitudes towards children: the new models of domesticity, the benevolent interest in education and the improvements in public health and child care; or the employment of children in factories, the thousands of child prostitutes roaming the streets, the squalor and disease of the slums, the stern Victorian paterfamilias? And if we concentrate, as de Mause does, on the improving philanthropic side of the nineteenth century, then in fairness we cannot overlook the philanthropic promptings which are to be found even in antiquity, in the age of the 'Infanticidal Mode'. Aristotle, Galen and many other sages of classical antiquity wrote treatises on paediatric medicine, nutrition, discipline and education. Juvenal condemned abortion and infanticide. Church fathers issued a stream of prohibitions against infanticide. These traditions continued throughout the Middle Ages. It simply is not possible to name a date at which people *began* to be interested in child care.

Nor, as far as I can see, is there any date which we can give for sure for the beginning of the supposed 'tenderness revolution' in the upbringing and education of children. Do we start with Rousseau? Or Locke? Or Commenius? Or St Anselm in the eleventh century? Anselm was celebrated for his sensitivity and compassion towards the young. He declared that he had always tried to behave to others with the same gentleness and understanding that his mother had shown him when he was a child. After her death when he was still a youth, he felt as though 'the ship of his heart had lost its anchor and drifted almost entirely among the waves of the world'.[31]

An abbot once described to Anselm his difficulties in controlling obstreperous boys in his charge, complaining that 'we never give over beating them day and night, and they only get worse and worse.' Anselm replied:

> Feeling no love or pity, good-will or tenderness in your attitude towards them, they have in future no faith in your goodness but believe that all your actions proceed from hatred and malice against them; they have been brought up in no true charity towards anyone, so they regard everyone with suspicion and jealousy . . . Are they not human? Are they not flesh and blood like you? Would you like to have been treated as you treat them, and to have become what they are now?[32]

Anselm was not alone and not the first in the mediaeval Church to take this line. In the days of Charlemagne two centuries earlier, scholars such as Alcuin had recommended patience and maternal affection as well as discipline in the education of children.

Peter the Venerable, Abbot of Cluny in the twelfth century, worshipped his mother almost as much as Anselm did. He described her as saintly, compassionate, happy and gay and so concerned for the welfare of her children that, even when she later became a nun after her husband's death and Peter visited her in the Cluniac priory, her concern about her children was so unceasing that the sisters thought it excessive. When Peter learnt of her death as he was returning from a journey to Italy, he felt as if he had been 'struck on the head with a stone'.[33]

St Hugh of Lincoln and his widowed father were supposed to have entered the same community of canons, and the child-saint, according to his hagiographer, would often relate with pleasure how 'for the rest of his father's life, he used to lead him and carry him about, dress and undress him, wash him, dry him and make his bed, and, when he grew feebler and weaker, prepare his food and even feed him.'[34]

These mediaeval biographies and autobiographies suggest both how normal and how admirable affection between parents and children was or was supposed to be. This impression is confirmed by the evidence of poetry and devotional literature both then and earlier. Eadmer of Canterbury in *Concerning the Excellence of the Most Glorious . . . Mother of God* (c. 1115) wrote:

Lo, brethren, let us try to understand the affection of this good Mother . . . the tenderness with which she beholds the Infant in her arms, sees him hang on her breast, hears him cry as children do at the little hurts of his little body, and hastens to forestall all evils which may happen to him . . .[35]

Similarly, the monk who wrote the life of the saintly Archbishop Anno of Cologne in about A.D. 1100 did not shrink from attributing motherly virtues to his hero:

Sometimes, when he passed by and saw that some of these starveling, half-naked children had fallen asleep because the long wait had made them so tired, he turned full of love to one of them that another man would not have deigned to notice and began to kiss the child tenderly like a mother. One or two women who had no children of their own would get hold of strange children in the safe assumption that Anno would take pity on them if they placed themselves before him with such little bundles.[36]

Nor was this tenderness a specifically mediaeval attitude. We can go back six centuries to St Augustine – and further:

Because the mother loves to nourish her little one, she does not on that account want him to remain little. She holds him in her lap, fondles him with her hands, soothes him with caresses, feeds him with her milk, does everything for the little one; but she wants him to grow, so that she may not always have to do these things. (St Augustine, Sermon XXIII, 4th–5th century A.D.)[37]

> No longer will you happily come home
> To a devoted wife, or children dear
> Running for your first kisses, while your heart
> Is filled with sweet unspoken gratitude.

(Lucretius describing a man contemplating his own death, 1st century B.C.)[38]

Now these passages are all quoted by de Mause and his colleagues to show the 'new' attitude of the relevant epoch and its 'contribution' to the development of 'modern' attitudes towards children. Sometimes, their contribution is so forceful and so lyrically articulate that the historian takes fright and tries to play the sentiments down as 'idealised' or 'conventional' and not accurately reflecting contemporary practice. But the ideals of the time are a central part of the history we are trying to discover and if at all times, whether classical or Christian, ancient or modern, we find fervent and explicit (and often beautiful) praise of love between parents and children, then we simply cannot go on assuming that parents and children did not care about each other and were not expected to care.

What the evidence suggests about family affection in times past and what progressive historians want it to suggest are often astonishingly far apart. James Bruce Ross, writing from the same 'psycho-historical' viewpoint as Professor de Mause, asks what he calls 'an historical question of absorbing interest: how could the deprived and neglected infants of the middle classes develop into the architects of a vigorous, productive and creative era which we call "the Renaissance"?'[39]

Yet he generously produces such a wealth of evidence against the premise that Italian children in the Renaissance were 'emotionally deprived' that the reader is baffled. We need quote here only Mr Ross's own epigraph, taken from the *Memoirs* of Giovanni Morelli (1398–1421):

> I called to mind when, the exact hour and moment, and where and how he was conceived by me, and how great a joy it was to me and his mother; and soon came his movements in the womb which I noted carefully with my hand, awaiting his birth with the greatest eagerness. And then when he was born, male, sound, well-proportioned, what happiness, what joy I experienced; and then as he grew from good to better, such satisfaction in his childish words, pleasing to all, loving towards me his father and his mother, precocious for his age.[40]

Here unmistakably we have the caring, sharing father of modern times; he follows conception, pregnancy, birth with poignant, often comic obsessiveness. Against such evidence of obsessive interest in children – and there is a good deal more of it – Mr Ross produces the practice of sending infants to the wet-nurse. Indeed, it is wet-nursing which for American Freudian or near-Freudian historians of child-hood constitutes the supremely interesting fact about the past, dwarfing even the boarding-school and the nanny as an unimaginable horror. Even where, as in Renaissance Italy, the danger of physical maltreatment or neglect seems to have been relatively modest, surely, we are told, the psychic damage caused by removing the child from his or her mother in infancy must have been huge and irreparable.

We are here in a still disputed realm about whether an infant can transfer affections from one exclusive parent to another and back again and how far this damage can be made up in later years. This is perhaps one point in the history of childhood which cannot be answered with certainty.

But because the question is difficult, we cannot therefore let logic or historical imagination idly lapse. Two points have to be made. The obsessive discussion in treatises and sermons on education about the choice of a wet-nurse and the right instructions to give her certainly do not suggest a lack of parental *concern*. And secondly, only a minority of the population – although the vast majority of the articulate – could afford a wet-nurse. It was an upper- and middle-class custom, like boarding schools in modern Britain, and attended by the same degree of anxiety – even if that anxiety does in its turn signify a degree of repressed feeling.

But it is not simply repressed feelings which historians such as Ariès and de Mause attribute in their different ways to parents in the old days. What is alleged is not merely, or not so much, that parents were unkind to their children as that parents were not really much interested in them: 'The density of society left no room for the family. Not that the family did not exist as a reality: it would be paradoxical to deny that it did. But it did not exist as a concept.'[41]

Now and then Ariès genially contradicts his allegations of indifference and concedes that 'we may conclude that these poor, badly housed people felt a commonplace love for little children – that elementary form of the concept of childhood – but were ignorant of the more complex and more modern forms of the concept of the family.'[42]

'The family fulfilled a function; it ensured the transmission of life, property and names; but it did not penetrate very far into human sensibility. Myths such as courtly and precious love denigrated marriage, while realities such as the apprenticeship of children loosened the emotional bond between parents and children.'[43]

What exactly is this concept of the family? And by what process does it penetrate into human sensibility? And by what sort of evidence would we be able to judge how far it had penetrated? If the concept of the family is, to some extent at least, distinct from loving your children in a commonplace way, in what does it show itself?

Here we are very close to the heart of the myth-making process.

8

WHERE DID THE HISTORIANS GO WRONG?

If it is true that most of what has been written until recently about the family in times past must now be dismissed or questioned, we have ourselves one large question to answer. Why should so many scholars – often of the greatest eminence, often too of unblemished integrity – have misled themselves and so misled others? Where did they go wrong? And why? How did these extraordinary myths ever gain credence?

No single historian – and I am not even a professional historian – could satisfactorily analyse and thoroughly dissect such a huge body of conventional wisdom. Such an undertaking would be a life's work, as well as being grotesquely immodest.

All that will be attempted here is to suggest a few of the main flaws that seem to crop up time and again when historians today – whether they be economic, social or literary – re-examine the works of their predecessors.

The Censor's Tale

At the end of the *Canterbury Tales*, Chaucer makes a Retraction. He apologises for his secular works, among them

The Tales of Canterbury, those that tend towards sin . . . and many a song and many a lecherous lay; that Christ in his great mercy forgive me the sin . . . But the translation of Boethius' *De Conso-latione*, and other books of Saints' legends, of homilies, and moral-ity and devotion, for them I thank our Lord Jesu Christ and His blissful Mother, and all the Saints of Heaven.[1]

Critics find it hard to agree whether Chaucer was sincerely stricken by repentance, or whether this Retraction was a formal device to keep out of trouble, or a mixture of both. Whichever it was, it shows the great psychological and institutional pressure exerted by the Church upon even so famous and so experienced a man of the world as Chaucer. One way or another, outwardly or inwardly, he needed to make a gesture to the pieties which forbade the glorification of sexual love and excessive concentration on earthly things.

The last tale is the Censor's Tale. And indeed for much of the Middle Ages, the information which we have about how people lived and talked comes in the form of censors' reports and acts.

Ecclesiastical decrees *against* dances with songs are the best evi-dence of the existence of such dance-songs on the continent long before the Norman Conquest. For Britain from the twelfth to the fourteenth century we have similar scraps of 'negative evidence' to suggest that there existed a whole range of popular poetry now almost entirely lost.

In his introduction to *Medieval English Lyrics*, R. T. Davies records how Giraldus Cambrensis in the twelfth century tells the story of a parish priest who, having heard dancers singing all night about his church a song including the refrain 'Swete lemman, thin are' (Sweetheart, have mercy), mistakenly incorporated the line in his mass next morning.[2]

Between 1317 and 1360, the Bishop of Ossory, in Ireland, dis-approving of the shameful songs the minor clergy of his cathedral were singing, composed for them some sixty pious lyrics in Latin to be sung, instead of the secular English and French words, to the same popular tunes. Several of these Latin poems are preceded by a line or two of the vernacular lyrics to indicate what tune is meant. These fragments are all we have left of what must have been a whole tradition of popular love poems.

Alas! how shold I singe?
Yloren [lost] is my playinge.
How shold I with that olde man
To leven, and let [leave] my lemman,
Swettist of all thinge?[3]

From the fourteenth century we begin to find ballads and lyric poems which reflect something of this popular tradition. For example, part of 'Alison', translated into modern English, runs roughly as follows:

> From all women my love is lent, and lights on Alison. Her hair is fair, her brow brown, her eye black; with lovely face she smiled on me, with middle small and well made . . . nights when I turn and wake and my cheeks wax wan, lady all for thine sake, this longing is come upon me. In all the world there is no man so wise who could tell all her bounty, her neck is whiter than the swan . . . [4]

This delightful love song dates from about 1300 – and there is no reason at all to assume that there had not been plenty like it throughout the preceding centuries.

The Church's censorship of such material and much that was a good deal bawdier has worked even more effectively on posterity than it did at the time. For in the days before printing, when the great bulk of scribes were monks, the Church had a virtual monopoly of production and distribution; and even after the invention of printing, since most libraries were ecclesiastical, popular literature, although produced in large quantities, was unlikely to survive. It is not until the sixteenth century that we have a few scraps of broadsheets and ballads to give us some idea of what popular taste was really like.

What sixteenth-century audiences enjoyed were tales such as 'How Howleglas set his hostess upon the hot ashes with her bare arse', printed in 1528. Many of these ballads were drawn from continental jest books of a century or more earlier, such as the *Liber Facetiarum* by Poggio Bracciolini (1380–1459). Caxton in his 1484 edition published eleven supplementary 'fables' by 'Poge the Florentyn'. And of course Chaucer took the plots of some of his *Canterbury Tales* from Boccaccio. Popular tales of adulterous friars, cuckolded husbands and faithless wives were among the first productions of the printing press.

In 1575, Robert Laneham, a London mercer, wrote in a letter to a friend a list of the books in the possession of a Captain Cox, described as a Coventry stonemason and of whom Laneham says 'great oversight hath he in matters of storie'. The list consisted of seven sorts of book: romances of chivalry which had survived from the Middle Ages, Renaissance fiction of the Boccaccio sort, jest books, a few plays, almanacs and prognostications, ballads, and a book about great rogues and imposters.[5]

This is a library which sounds not dissimilar from what you might see on the shelves of a small local library nowadays or a station bookstall. The onus of proof is very much on those who claim to discern a change, let alone a degeneration of popular taste over the years. All that has happened is that popular taste is now legally and economically able to satisfy itself.

Throughout the sixteenth century, romances were denounced as 'childish follye'. The ballad-mongers were not highly thought of. Henry Chettle spoke for respectable Elizabethan opinion:

A company of idle youths, loathing honest labour and dispising lawful trades, betake themselves to a vagrant and vicious life in every corner of Cities and market Townes of the Realme, singing and selling of ballads and pamphlets full of ribaudrie, and all scurrilous vanity . . . [6]

One of the best-known ballad men, Thomas Deloney, got into trouble with the law for writing a ballad complaining about the Scarcity of Corn, which showed the Queen 'speaking with her people Dialogue wise in very fond and undecent sort'. As I write, Mrs Mary Whitehouse has just complained about a television monologue by Alf Garnett, in which he imagines the Queen (Elizabeth II) telling Prince Philip, 'You're pissed.' Again, there seems no reason to imagine that popular taste has changed much, but what has changed is the ability of respectable opinion to enforce its preferences.

The history of sports and games is another instance of how wide-ranging were the activities which Church and State prohibited. There is scarcely any popular pastime which has not at one time or another been ferociously condemned if not actually made legally punishable: golf, football, archery (when its uses for military training were not appreciated), tennis. The mediaeval universities condemned the immorality of games of chance, the indecency of parlour games, the theatre and dancing and the brutality of physical sports – which did indeed often end in brawls. At Narbonne college in 1379 the regulations laid down, for example, that: 'Nobody in the house is to play tennis or hockey or other dangerous games under pain of a fine of six deniers; nobody is to play dice, or any other games played for money, or indulge in table amusements under pain of a fine of ten sous.'[7] The statutes also forbade pupils to invite any woman, however respectable, to lunch or dinner at the school.

What these condemnations show is the running campaign by the Church progressively to gain control of all educational institutions and stamp its own moral discipline upon them. Mediaeval colleges had been, for the most part, licentious, chaotic places. The teaching often took place in the street. Often the schools had only one room and one master teaching a rabble of children, adolescents and young men with no separation by age or educational attainment. Etienne Pasquier in the sixteenth century described in tones of horror the University of Paris in the old days of a hundred years earlier: 'Studies were in a jumble . . . the rooms on one side were leased to students and on the other to whores, so that under the same roof there was a school of learning together with a school of whoring.'[8]

Students were drunk and violent; duels were frequent; rebellions against authority were often terrifying; at English public schools particularly, the great mutinies went on breaking out until well into the nineteenth century.

But the point is that in the end the authorities, both religious and secular, did manage to impose order and discipline upon the schools, just as absolutist monarchs managed to impose order and discipline upon their whole realms by means of standing armies and standing bureaucracies. The mediaeval chaos was subdued and ordered; students were split up into classes and ages; the pox-ridden lodgings were turned into respectable boarding houses and eventually became either schools in their own right or 'houses' belonging to colleges and controlled by housemasters.

Yet the process had a bitter irony, at least from the point of view of the Church. This successful culmination of a campaign lasting six or seven centuries to impose discipline upon schools coincided with the final collapse of the Church's power to control the curriculum that was to be taught in those schools. Theology, Hebrew and even Latin gave way more and more to mathematics, science, history, modern languages and ultimately economics and sociology. Perhaps the

Church had been better off in the Middle Ages when the universities were chaotic and licentious, but at least the cathedral chapter had the right to prosecute priests who presumed to teach any books which went beyond the *De octo partibus orationis* of Donat, the fourth-century grammarian.

What matters here, though, is that we should appreciate the pattern of the Church's attempts to control thought and feeling: from strenuous and fiercely contested efforts in the Middle Ages to control intimate and social institutions such as marriage – as shown in disputes about divorce and the celibacy of the clergy – rising to a peak in the seventeenth century with the era of the Jesuits and the Puritans, who attempted to oversee every moment of a person's waking life, and then falling into a long and slow decline, of which the last twitches are gestures such as the prohibition of games on Sunday and the hostility of the Welsh chapels to the new pastime of Rugby football.

At one time or another, the Church (and often the State as well) has tried to discourage or suppress *all* occupations, diversions and attachments which might distract people from their religious and civic duties. And marriage, like golf or tennis, has always been a rival for the attention of hearts and minds.

Therefore when love – or gambling or Rugby football – surfaces in the historical evidence, we ought not necessarily to assume that it is a new pastime which has just been invented or suddenly become popular, but rather that the ability of Church and State to censor it has decayed.

Pressures and feelings

Censorship is not the only way in which the Church has made it hard to get at the history of the family. Nor is the Church the only source of pressure on the family.

The government, by laws of taxation or rules of inheritance, might considerably affect the size and structure of households and such crucial decisions as whether to marry or not to marry and whether to stay at home after growing up or not.

For example, folklorists used to describe it as a touching tradition of peasant family feeling that in certain parts of France so many adults should have continued to live in the household of their parents. Yet historians now incline to the view that this tradition was not a peasant one, but one imposed upon them by their seigneurs. By the right of *mortmain*, the lord in the Middle Ages took possession of the inheritance of the serf who, at the time of his death, was not living in the same household as his heirs. In such regions, therefore, the only way to be sure of your inheritance was to go on living with your parents. It seems that when the serfs were freed en masse in the Orléans and Paris regions, in the thirteenth century, all at once young adults began to leave home, and nuclear households became the rule. In the central provinces such as Auvergne and Burgundy, *mortmain* lasted until the eighteenth century, and so did large households. It was a purely artificial restraint on leaving the nest and had nothing to do with peasant *attitudes* to family ties.

The difficulty is that the evidence which has come down to us consists very largely of the pressures: ecclesiastical rulings, tax edicts, workhouse records, Blue Books on famine and poverty. And when we compare past with present, what we are often comparing are the relative strengths of the pressures. So what we are left with may well be not a 'sexual revolution' or a Great Transition in the history of the family but, simply and primarily, a change or diminution in the pressures.

The mistake made over and over again by historians, sociologists, moralists and journalists is to confuse two quite distinct things: the history of what people were compelled or expected to do and the history of what people liked doing. What people actually did do might belong to either sort of history, depending on the pressures. This mistake is made worse when historians confuse the history of art or of literature or of the Church with the history of the family. This confusion is like an historian five hundred years from now taking the novels of Agatha Christie as a guide to upper-class English behaviour in the first half of the twentieth century. Or, as Peter Laslett comments, 'a very similar distortion might come about if some future historian used *Lolita* or *West Side Story* as a source book for our own sexual habits, uncorrected by other evidence, unliterary and statistical.'[9]

What we can do is to use literary or any other kind of evidence to *disprove* theories about the past. If historians assert that affection was regarded as a foolish motive for marriage, then we are entitled to bring forward, say, the comedies of Shakespeare to demonstrate that in Elizabethan and Jacobean England it was, to say the least, not unknown for love to be regarded as a proper and moral motive for marriage and for loveless, arranged and child marriages to be regarded as wrong. To go further and argue positively that the Shakespearean attitude was the normal attitude, we would need strong unliterary evidence as well. The very late age of marriage – well into the twenties for both men and women – certainly suggests this. But it would be just as bad if we were to fall into the opposite myth and start claiming that true love triumphed invariably or even in a majority of cases.

The furthest we can reasonably go is, first, to point how often and how favourably the ideals of affection, mutuality and free choice in marriage and family life are mentioned in the surviving evidence of the last thousand years; and, second, to point out the strength of the pressures operating against the realisation of those ideals.

There was, above all, the pressure of *scarcity*. In the huge areas of old Europe in which almost everyone might be near the bread-line most of the time and in which the abyss of the workhouse or actual death by starvation was still daily visible, to stay alive might demand prudent calculation in marriage. A foolish marriage could ruin your life. A good marriage was one of the few routes to affluence.

At the level of the middle and upper classes, we are familiar with this problem from novels; the feckless curate marries a young woman without a dowry, they immediately have half a dozen children, and are condemned to permanent poverty by middle-class standards. Lower down the scale, the costs of a mistake were rather grimmer; the tiny patch of land which could support one or two might not support three or four or more; children might be abandoned or boarded out as soon as possible. To deduce from the sad fragments of evidence which come down to us from this harsh world that men and women had no feelings for one another or for their children is the most callous act of historical condescension.

The pressures of Church and State on the poor often combined with the pressure of scarcity; the combination of moral disapproval, legal penalty and wretched poverty produced the most horrible results of all. One of the most tragic and continually repeated spectacles in past centuries is the huge number of abandoned children. In France alone, Professor Shorter tells us, 33,000 children were abandoned each year throughout the nineteenth century.

We have often unthinkingly assumed that most if not all of these were illegitimate. We used to think that the stigma of bearing a love-child was the prime reason. But Professor Shorter suggests a different priority:

> What moved their parents to abandon them? In the first place, desperate poverty. Whenever grain prices rose in the eighteenth century, so did the number of foundlings, showing that the cost of living was forcing many parents to rid the household of a child or two. Moreover, the higher the prices, the higher was the age of the foundlings, which indicates that parents were ridding themselves not just of the new-born but of older siblings too.[10]

At all times it seems that a great number of foundlings were legitimate – and also illegitimate foundlings were often abandoned as much because their mothers could not support them as because they were ashamed of them.

The fiercest social condemnation of illegitimacy is now thought to have been relatively recent – and, in terms of centuries at least, mercifully short-lived. For here too, the Church did not succeed in imposing its grip on society until Elizabethan times:

> Until the sixteenth century, bastardy had not been thought any great shame. Men took care of their bastards, were indeed often proud of them and in many cases brought them home to their wives or mothers to be brought up. Children born out of wedlock were thus to be found growing up in their father's house with their half-brothers and sisters without a hint of disgrace either to them-selves or to their natural parents.[11]

There were of course legal distinctions and barriers which the bastard could overcome only with difficulty, if at all. But there seems to have been a certain charity in the treatment of unmarried mothers as well as of their children. Dick Whittington, as a benefaction to St Thomas's Hospital, 'made a new chambyre with viii beddys for young wemen that have done a-mysse, in trust for good mendement. And he commandyd that alle the thynges that had ben don in that chambyre shoulde be kepte secrete . . . for he wolde not shame no yonge woman in noo wyse.'[12]

According to Pinchbeck and Hewitt, 'There is little to suggest that, before the sixteenth century, it had been an overwhelming disaster for a girl to have an illegitimate baby and a great deal of evidence to show that until the sixteenth century, the illegitimate child itself, though legally underprivileged, was not socially stigmatised.'[13] As early as 1421, the foundling hospital in Florence was entitled the Hospital of the Innocents – and decorated with delightful ceramic plaques of children by Della Robbia.

Bastardy and Its Comparative History, edited by Peter Laslett and others, is the most comprehensive recent survey. Most of its authors confirm that the tolerance accorded to bastards only gradually evaporated somewhere between the Renaissance and the Victorians. Alan Macfarlane cautiously concludes:

> A brief survey of seventeenth-century English sources tends to give the impression that bastardy, though its ascription might be libellous, was not greatly disapproved of, as long as the child was maintained. Thus one vicar described how a neighbour had a maid who produced four successive bastards, 'yet because she was a good work woman he kept her still.' Gervase Holles recorded, more with fond indulgence than indignation or horror, that one of his uncles was very enamoured of women and begat several illegitimate children. It seems quite likely that sympathy with the plight of the mother and general tolerance of bastardy as a frailty, but not a sin, continued at least until the nineteenth century. Even in that century there are indications of such tolerance in two of the classical accounts of rural life at that time, *Lark Rise to Candleford* and *Forty Years in a Moorland Parish*. It is possible that the situation was similar to that observed in other societies, where there may be a scandal at the time, but afterwards the child, mother and father are accepted back into normal social relations and the affair does not cause shame.[14]

In France, the position of bastards was much the same, although the stigmatisation of unmarried mothers may have started rather earlier. In the Middle Ages, at any rate, according to Jean Meyer,

> No stigma attached to the word 'bastard' which was, on the contrary, a title to be proudly emblazoned on one's crest. In the mid-sixteenth century the lord of Gouberville, a country gentleman of Cotentin, thought it quite natural to bring up his bastards at home together with his legitimate children. Sexual licence outside

marriage was by no means confined to the nobility but was present in all sections of society, though it varied between classes, between regions and over the centuries. The religious laxity of the late middle ages was reflected in general moral laxity, but with the Reformation and the Catholic renaissance came a reaffirmation of the sanctity of marriage culminating in the austerity of the Jansenists and of the *Catéchisme de Nantes* (1689) in which Mesnard, its author, laid down that 'conjugal chastity must keep lust and passion within bounds'.[15]

It was the Puritans and their Catholic counterparts on the Continent who so ferociously condemned sexual irregularity and its results. There was a steadily intensifying official uncharitableness towards the unchaste and their children which, we may guess, probably reached its peak in the nineteenth century – and has since sharply declined, because it did not then and never really has accorded with popular feeling. Only in our own affluent time have we seen the unique spectacle of some orphanages closing for lack of custom and of adoption agencies running short of babies.

The Church of England Children's Society has recently closed its list of applicants wanting to adopt babies because of a sudden fall in the number of children available. In 1980 it received 2,500 applications, but only 156 babies were placed for adoption. In the mid-1960s the Society was still placing about 700 babies a year. The Society's Director attributed the change to 'the increased willingness of single girls to keep their babies'.[16] Nationally, the number of single women keeping their babies rose from 90,000 in 1971 to 130,000 in 1976.

A foundling discovered in a doorway wrapped in a bundle, perhaps with a pathetic message from a desperate mother, is now a rarity worth a newspaper headline instead of an appalling commonplace. This is no doubt the result of abortion and birth control reducing the proportion of unwanted children. It is also the result of the eagerness of so many childless couples to bring up other people's children for love, not money. But perhaps more significant still, it is the result of the new determination of unmarried mothers and *their* parents to keep and cherish their babies.

On the other hand, in Britain at least, the number of 'children in care' – that is, older children consigned to municipal institutions because their parents were adjudged, by a court of law, to be incapable of looking after them – has steadily risen, until at the time of writing the Department of Health and Social Security computes their number at 120,000. The London Borough of Greenwich has just opened an 'adoption shop' for some of the 600 children in its care. Dr Barnardo's Homes have already set up a similar institution in Colchester.[17]

The nature of official concern seems to have changed. Instead of newborn children being abandoned at birth because their parents cannot feed them or because their mothers are unmarried and ashamed, the State now removes children, usually older, from their homes, with or without the consent of their parents, on the grounds that the children are being neglected or brutally treated. Such parents are described as 'inadequate'; the blame is thus attributed to them individually rather than to general conditions of scarcity or poverty.

Parents who would be regarded as only averagely bad in, say, the eighteenth century might now be liable to have their children taken away from them and placed in care. This, I suspect, has more to do with changes in our attitude towards the rights and responsibilities of the State than with changes in our attitude towards the rights and responsibilities of parents.

All we can say for sure is that there are indisputably two new factors at work here: first, affluence and the ability of the Welfare State to provide a minimum standard of living for a woman to bring up a child whatever her marital circumstances. Second, the decline of the influence of the Church and of its power to make sexual irregularity appear horrific and sinful. Poverty and the power of the Church were essentially both *external* pressures on family life and only with their relaxation can we begin to enquire what ordinary people really think about marriage and motherhood; in previous centuries, their minds have been occupied by foreign forces laying down rules and conditions which may have often seemed not only harsh but *unnatural*.

To claim that working-class attitudes have changed on these topics is much like claiming that the working classes used to be indifferent to personal cleanliness but are now transformed into enthusiasts for hygiene. We cannot say what the working classes 'really' thought about baths when they did not possess them.

These alterations in official pressure have given rise to a variety of grandiose conceptions about changes in popular attitudes. Yet if you or your daughter would be ostracised and perhaps punished by law for having a child out of wedlock, and if the child might starve or have to be left at the door of an orphanage to have any chance of survival, you would be reckless not to think of the child as a misfortune and the result of a mistake. But that is not the same as saying that to bear a child out of wedlock is a *sin*. It would be difficult indeed to demonstrate that the poor had ever wholeheartedly endorsed the Church's fierce moral condemnation of sexual laxity. Nor would it be easy to prove that family feeling among the working class had either strengthened or weakened over the centuries. In pre-industrial England, children had to be sent away – into domestic service or as hired labour on another farm; now families can stay together until the children wish to move away. Shorter working hours and longer holidays mean more time spent together. More comfortable and roomier houses containing their own amusements lure the husband home from the bar.

These economic changes have so relaxed the divisive pressures on the family that it is not very helpful to talk of the present as 'a family-oriented age' – any more than it would be helpful to talk of it as a bath-oriented age. It would surely be simpler to say that in past times poor families clung together as best they could; now times are easier.

Muddling the evidence

The most obvious source of error is the fact that much of the evidence about the past concerns only the behaviour and attitudes of the nobility and upper classes. Historians themselves are uneasily familiar with this problem of sources.

The poor are silent and faceless. The rich have not only themselves, their houses, even their horses described and painted; their financial arrangements are written down, witnessed, preserved. We have their wills and their marriage contracts.

What passes for social history has a recurring tendency, even in describing quite recent times, to drift into being the history of upper-class behaviour and attitudes. And how difficult it is to remember always to compare like with like.

All too often, the marital customs of kings and noblemen in the Middle Ages are compared with those of merchants and other bourgeois in the eighteenth century, and then compared again with the customs of 'ordinary people' in the twentieth century. Those types of people who have *always* married for reason of public, financial and dynastic ambition are compared with those who never did.

Professor Lawrence Stone, for example, takes the dynastic obligations of Romeo and Juliet as typical of popular attitudes in 1600, while he relegates the private affections revealed in the *Merry Wives of Windsor* to a sort of parenthesis in the argument. Obviously, the audience at the Globe would have been familiar with what was expected of a Montague or a Capulet, just as a modern audience might be familiar with what is expected of Prince Charles in choosing a wife, but that is not to say that either audience would find such expectations at all relevant to their own lives; indeed, part of the charm of such spectacles is the knowledge that we are not burdened with such duties.

This failure to compare like with like often derives from a second error of method, which is the failure to recognise quite how unbalanced are the available sources. The further back you go, the scantier the material and the more likely it is to relate to royal, noble, and ecclesiastical life and the less to commercial, social and working-class life. For the early Middle Ages, we often have only the equivalent of the *Court Circular*, the *Tablet* or perhaps *The Times Literary Supplement* to go on. This imbalance of material continues until very recent times, certainly up to the founding of the popular press; even today, the history of industry and commerce is infinitely scanty compared with the history of government and politics. Of course, every historian pays some tribute to this imbalance, but few realise quite how crippling it is likely to be, especially in attempting to find out about intimate social practices such as marriage and the upbringing of children.

One of the most frequently used sources for the French attitudes to sex and child-rearing in the seventeenth century is the diary kept by Héroard, doctor to the infant Louis XIII. Philippe Ariès, for example, uses it to document his theory about the grown-upness of children in times past and the lack of any idea of childhood until relatively modern times. Yet you need only read modern memoirs and biographies of twentieth-century royalty to see that it appears to be an inescapable part of a prince's childhood to be treated much more as an adult than the rest of us. He tends to be surrounded by adult courtiers who have little else to do but join in his games or who may indeed be instructed to do so. Princes are different from us. They are at any rate scarcely typical.

Almost as common as the 'class muddle' in the use of evidence is what may be called 'tone muddle'. Here the historian takes some evidence which is clearly relevant and sometimes startling, but fails to understand the tone of that evidence.

The point of many proverbs and sayings resides in the *inversion* of the conventional view; the tone is essentially ironic, or even sarcastic; the purpose is to let off steam.

Edward Shorter, for example, in *The Making of the Modern Family* eagerly seizes on a handful of French popular proverbs to supplement the otherwise scanty historical evidence of how French peasants thought about their wives.

> The permanence of the peasant's affection for his property and the transience of his attachment to human life are revealed in several proverbs:
> 'Mort de femme et vie de cheval font l'homme riche.'
> (Brittany)
> (Rich is the man whose wife is dead and horse alive.)
> 'Deuil de femme morte dure jusqu'à la porte.'
> (Gascony)
> (Your late wife you so deplore until you enter your front door.)
> 'L'homme a deux beaux jours sur terre: lorsqu'il prend femme et lorsqu'il l'enterre.'
> (Anjou)
> (The two sweetest days of a fellow in life are the marriage and burial of his wife.)[18]

Now these are *jokes* and they can be jokes only because in general men thought more highly of their wives than of their cows and horses; otherwise, they would not be worth making. By Professor Shorter's logic, the popular Kipling line, 'A woman is only a woman but a good cigar is a smoke', would mean that Edwardian men thought more highly of cigars than of women. Of course, anti-wife jokes and, even more so, anti-mother-in-law jokes are intended to express the difficulties and resentments generated by almost every marriage, but they cannot be used as evidence of loveless marriage.

This kind of tone muddle shades into 'context muddle', in which the historian rightly notes an interesting complaint in his sources but makes a false deduction about the social conditions of the time from the fact of that complaint's having been voiced.

Take a present-day example. Popular newspapers now are full of stories of brutality towards children by parents, 'baby-battering'. Great indignation is worked up, particularly towards the social services which fail to notice the bruises until it is too late and the child is dead or permanently harmed.

It is not too hard for *us* to see that these stories reflect not an increase in general callousness but rather an increase in sensitivity and concern for the welfare of children; even statistics which purport to show an increase in baby-battering can almost certainly be put down to improvements in our methods of detecting it; we now have more doctors and social workers and they are trained to look out for bruises. But for a foreigner and still more for posterity, it might well look as if British parents were becoming more brutal. They would not stop to reflect that the newspapers a century ago may have paid less attention to baby-battering, not because there was less of it but because people did not expect to be able to prevent it or perhaps did not think it the State's job to try.

Context muddle is particularly difficult to spot and even more difficult to root out when the historian is trying to establish whether a practice in a certain historical period is new or not. For example, what does the outcry in Tudor times against child marriages and marriages for money mean exactly? One school of historians has assumed that the outcry is a sign of the new Renaissance individualism and the emergence of the new love-marriage; on this theory, the arranged marriage must have been on its last legs at that time. On the other hand, much the same outcry is to be found a century or even two centuries earlier; equally, the arranged marriage – among the upper classes – is still to be found two centuries later. Neither the rising trend nor the retreating trend seems to be quite as new as was supposed.

All these muddles are aided and abetted by the historian's desire to use (or abuse) the material for his own present-day purposes. It is at this stage that we move from the realm of honest error to an area where the historian's intentions are a little more dubious.

Consider, for example, the extraordinary idea that romantic love was invented by the troubadours of mediaeval Provence. How did that ever gain credence?

I think the fallacy is based on two circumstances: first, the fact that Provençal love-poetry survived in such copious quantities, and second, the fact that adultery was a theme of such supreme interest to nineteenth-century readers. It was in fact The Theme, so much so that some people, even now, think of the novel – the great nineteenth-century art-form – as essentially and at its best concerned with adultery. The reasons for this obsession are not far to seek: the continued near-impossibility of divorce and the entrance into public discussion of the idea that life was a project for the realisation of Happiness – 'a new idea in Europe', according to Saint-Just, and one enshrined in the American Declaration of Independence. For the nineteenth century, adultery was both the great crime and the great act of liberation.

The proof that these were the reasons for the total misreading of mediaevel attitudes is very simple: stories of and hymns to adultery form a remarkably small part of the troubadours' output.

It was Wagner and Engels and Tennyson who invented the mediaeval obsession with adultery. And later literary historians who have still clung to the old myths have, I fear, been reading mediaeval texts through Victorian eyes.

The historicising of everything

The Victorians did not invent history-as-story but theirs was the first era to be obsessed by it. I mean the concept of history which regards the past as a story with a plot possessing a beginning, a middle and if not an end, at least a future. The notion that modern times had not fallen away from the classical era or the golden age but on the contrary had developed from and would or could improve on the past is an essential part of what we call the Renaissance. Advances in scientific knowledge strengthened the belief that this development was on the whole progressive. More and more educated people came to think, like Bacon, that we could see further than our ancestors, even if they had been giants, simply because we were 'sitting on their shoulders'. To have the benefit of hindsight was also to possess the capacity of foresight. In the eighteenth century, history as written by the

philosophes, by Voltaire and Condorcet, became increasingly opti-
mistic and also increasingly sweeping in its territorial claims; history,
Montesquieu and others argued, should embrace not only the doings
of armies and kings but also cultural and social history.

But it was only in the nineteenth century that the growing pace of
technical invention drove on the scholarly world to historicise everything. Every human institution and relationship, every molecule of
blood and skin and earth and air was *developing*. The fact that the
time-scale of development in these various different fields of study
might vary between days and millions of years was of trivial importance beside the overwhelming, inescapable ubiquity of the law of
development. Marx and Darwin and Morgan and Macaulay and
Maine and Mill were all enthusiastic workers in their own departments of this huge development project.

Most of the myths we have been discussing originate in the second
half of the nineteenth century. They are essentially *Victorian* myths,
even if in some cases their full academic elaboration has been delayed
until much more recent times. And the view of history that underlies
each myth is a straightforwardly progressive one; social institutions
such as marriage and the family progress from a simple, 'primitive'
form to a higher, more complex form – not necessarily more productive of happiness, but certainly more civilised.

Love-in-marriage *had* to be a modern development; the further you
went back, the more commercial and eventually the more barbaric
marriage customs you were likely to find. The civil position of women
had to have been gradually improving throughout history from an
abysmally low starting point; the protests from mediaeval historians
such as Maitland that this was not necessarily so were brushed aside.[19]
The campaign for relaxation of the divorce laws was another obvious
modern development; in traditional society, women *must* have been so
enslaved and brutalised that no question of divorce could have arisen.
The possibility that popular resistance to the Church's view on
divorce had never ceased, and the further possibility that at least until
the seventeenth century people looked *back* to an Anglo-Saxon golden
age before the Church had imposed its power on people's lives, were
ideas not to be thought of; they were unprogressive.[20]

Such simple-minded progressivism has not died out, even now,
particularly in the United States. De Mause's *History of Childhood* is a
prime example. But in most specialities it is being reluctantly but

radically revised. Feminist historians are now torn between, on the one hand, the desire to show that women in times past were mercilessly trodden down and, on the other, like Mary Beard in *Woman as Force in History*, the desire to show that women have contributed far more to human history than is commonly recognised. In their introduction to *Becoming Visible: Women in European History*, Renate Bridenthal and Claudia Koonz say that:

> These notions of linear improvement or decline are too simple. A highly technological capitalist society differs so fundamentally from a nonliterate, communal one that relations of power, family and the economy defy simple comparisons. Yesterday's abbess is not today's woman priest; the mediaeval alewife is not the modern barmaid; and the preindustrial wife is not the alienated drudge described by Betty Friedan.[21]

This post-Victorian open-mindedness about the past is certainly a gain but we are still left with a subtler legacy from the Victorian historicism. This is the idea that everything still has a significant history to be told, even if it is not a straightforward one of steady progress or decline. In the literal sense, this must of course be true; traditional pre-Victorian history – 'annals' as we used to call them – used simply to say, 'This happened, then that happened, then another thing happened.' The Book of Chronicles would say: 'And Ram begat Amminadab; and Amminadab begat Nahshon, prince of the children of Judah; And Nahshon begat Salma, and Salma begat Boaz.'[22]

Everything relevant and important had to be put in, but that did not mean that everything necessarily was *related* to everything else in a significant and pregnant fashion. The belief that everything *is* significantly related is one of the principal working assumptions of Marxist economics, sociology, semiology and half a dozen other 'human sciences' which have been invented by the modern era. In particular, these human sciences are addicted to a relentless *plaiting* of distinct strands of human activity which happen to brush against each other. If the history of something unmistakably shows a pattern of development, then the history of something else which comes into contact with it must show a comparable pattern. Indeed, you can deduce the history of the one *through* the history of the other. I think this is a highly dangerous type of deduction.

In *Centuries of Childhood* Philippe Ariès follows a distinct and straightforward method. It is to trace the history of childhood, not through what people have directly said or written about children, nor even through the available evidence of how children have been treated, but through the history of other things. Ariès tells us, for example, that, 'An analysis of iconography leads us to conclude that the concept of the family was unknown in the Middle Ages, that it originated in the fifteenth and sixteenth centuries, and that it reached its full expression in the seventeenth century.'[23] Iconography, then, is to be our key to unlock the secrets of the family. The scholarly study of *images* is the way to discover how people thought and felt about marriage and children. In fact, there are four separate fields of historical study which Ariès uses to find support for his general theory: pictures and sculpture, dress, games and pastimes, and lastly education. It is from each of these that he deduces an absence of the idea of childhood, a lack of awareness in the Middle Ages of 'the particular nature of childhood that distinguishes the child from the adult, even the young adult'.[24]

These four topics are each worth brief inspection, not just because they are the props of the Ariès theory but because each in its own right represents an important element in our general impression of life in times past. They are part of our mental furniture and influence many people who have never read or heard of *Centuries of Childhood*.

First, pictures and sculpture. The theory here is that in mediaeval art children are represented as little adults, mere scaled-down versions of grown-ups, without any of the softness or roundness of the childish body. From this we are to infer that people at that time were in some sense unable to *see* children as they really were, because they had no idea of childhood.

This undoubtedly means that men of the tenth and eleventh centuries did not dwell on the image of childhood, and that that image had neither interest nor even reality for them. It suggests too that in that realm of life, and not simply in that aesthetic transposition, childhood was a period of transition which passed quickly and which was just as quickly forgotten.[25]

On the other hand, Ariès has to recognise an awkward fact:

The evolution towards a more realistic and more sentimental representation of childhood begins very early on in painting: in a miniature of the second half of the twelfth century, Jesus is shown wearing a thin, almost transparent shift and standing with His arms round His mother's neck, nestling against her, cheek to cheek.[26]

The discovery of childhood, we are told, began as early as the thirteenth century. Indeed, if we adopt Ariès's own theory, that is certainly true. There are, for example, three Duccio Madonnas in the National Gallery, London, dating from the early fourteenth century; in all of them, it is clear that an effort has been made to depict the roundness of the Christ-child's limbs and face and the unformed nature of His features as distinct from the angular adult figures with their aquiline features. The child is also naked, or virtually so but for a decently placed part of the Virgin's robe – again a mark of the realistic representation of childhood.

Now all this is somewhat inconvenient for Ariès's thesis. If the concept of childhood depends on improved expectation of life and on the sense of each person's individuality, then indeed 'there are grounds for surprise in the earliness of the idea of childhood, seeing that conditions were so unfavourable to it. Statistically and objectively speaking, this idea should have appeared much later.'[27]

So it should, but in practice the representation of children in pictorial art is entirely realistic by the time we reach the beginnings of the supposed age of individualism, the Renaissance. And what is more, as it is not until then that we see artists begin to aim wholeheartedly for *likeness* in portraiture – an important index of individuality which Ariès neglects – we should expect to see a long time-lag before children are as realistically represented as adults. But do we? In the National Portrait Gallery, London, the portrait of the eight-year-old King Edward VI seems just as realistic as the portraits of his father King Henry VIII or those of his young half-sisters. Those portraitists who represent children in stiff conventional poses represent adults in stiff conventional poses too.

Is it possible that the changes we are examining have nothing much to do with the history of childhood but a great deal to do with the history of art? The difference between Margaritone and Cimabue, like the difference between Cimabue and Duccio and the difference between Duccio and Giotto, consists in an advance towards realism on *all* fronts. The stiff stylisation of Byzantine art gradually gives place to softer, more fluid, more lively treatment both in line and colour of everything – drapery, limbs, faces. Not only do children cease to be represented as tiny men, but women cease to be represented as indistinguishable from men except for their head-dress. To isolate the change in the representation of children alone is wrongly to deduce a social change from a purely aesthetic revolution.

Byzantine art, like many other schools of art of various times and places, happens to place a low value on individuality. The inextricable mingling of religious and aesthetic purpose is precisely what we mean by the word 'icon'. Figures in such works of art need to be differentiated from each other only in so far as it is necessary for the story; the Virgin has a blue mantle, St Joseph a beard, the Child is reduced in size; any further characterisation to portray differences of age or sex would be a distraction.

If Ariès was right, we would have to assume that the Russians had no 'idea of childhood' until the most recent times; for the Russian icon-painters have continued to work in the ancient tradition, virtually undisturbed by the changes in the West. Yet what seems to strike visitors to the Soviet Union with particular force is the way Russians lavish love and attention upon their children.

Next, dress. 'Nothing in mediaeval dress distinguished the child from the adult.' Not until the seventeenth century did children have an outfit reserved for their age group which set them apart from the adults. That seems clear enough, except that once again we need to enquire more generally what people, both young and old, wore in the Middle Ages. Ariès himself tells us:

> The child's robe is simply the long coat of the Middle Ages, of the twelfth and thirteenth centuries, before the revolution which in the case of men banished it in favour of the short coat and visible breeches, the ancestors of our present-day masculine costume. Until the fourteenth century everybody wore the robe or tunic; the men's robe was not the same as the women's – often it was a shorter tunic, or else it opened down the front.[28]

Everyone then wore the robe or tunic, and the women's form of dress was not much different from men's. What happened in the fourteenth century is that men abandoned the robe for the short coat – although lawyers, churchmen and others continued to wear it – while children, at least children of good family, continued to wear the robe. And so did women, for whom various fashions developed, such as hanging sleeves. What we have is a gradual evolution and differentiation of clothing *not only by age but also by sex and by class*. Almost unconscious of what he is saying, Ariès points out: 'Every social nuance had its corresponding sign in clothing. At the end of the sixteenth century, custom dictated that childhood, henceforth recognized as a separate entity, should also have its special costume.'[29]

But that does not mean that *childhood* has emerged as a separate entity; otherwise we would have to claim that sex and class had emerged as separate entities too and that the Middle Ages really could not tell men from women and had no idea of class.

There seems to be a conflict here with another generally held idea about the Middle Ages – an idea which has coloured mediaevalists' nostalgia ever since the Gothic Revival in the early years of the nineteenth century. This is the idea that, far from mediaeval life being an undifferentiated blur, to be alive in the Middle Ages was a particularly *sharp* experience. This inherently romantic view is most floridly put in the famous opening words of an even more influential book on times past, perhaps the most influential of all such books, Johan Huizinga's *The Waning of the Middle Ages*:

> To the world when it was half a thousand years younger, the outlines of all things seemed more clearly marked than to us. The contrast between suffering and joy, between adversity and happiness, appeared more striking. All experience had yet to the minds of men the directness and absoluteness of the pleasure and pain of child-life. Every event, every action, was still embodied in expressive and solemn forms, which raised them to the dignity of a ritual. For it was not merely the great facts of birth, marriage, and death which, by the sacredness of the sacrament, were raised to the rank of mysteries; incidents of less importance, like a journey, a task, a visit, were equally attended by a thousand formalities: benedictions, ceremonies, formulas . . .
>
> We, at the present day, can hardly understand the keenness with which a fur coat, a good fire on the hearth, a soft bed, a glass of wine, were formerly enjoyed . . .
>
> All things presenting themselves to the mind in violent contrasts and impressive forms, lent a tone of excitement and of passion to everyday life and tended to produce that perpetual oscillation

between despair and distracted joy, between cruelty and pious tenderness which characterizes life in the Middle Ages.[30]

Whatever you may think about all this – which may say more about Western attitudes in the 1920s than about what life was really like in the Middle Ages – it hardly squares with the Ariès theory about childhood. For if all experience was so much more keenly savoured, then seeing that life was both so precarious and so uncluttered, how could childbirth and childhood alone remain a numb, mute, trivial, routine business?

What reason is there to suppose that differentiation in dress accompanies a keener perception of difference of age? To Western eyes, Chinese costume – particularly since the Communist revolution – appears singularly undifferentiated. Yet the Chinese are famous for their love of children and their obsessive interest in and concern for them.

In the case of dress (as of pictures and sculpture), what we are confronting is not a crucial episode in the history of childhood but a crucial episode in the history of dress.

> On the one hand the children were separated from their elders, on the other hand the rich were separated from the poor. There exists, in my opinion, a connection between these two phenomena. They were the manifestations of a general tendency towards distinguishing and separating; a tendency which was not unconnected with the Cartesian revolution of clear ideas.[31]

No, that is not Ariès talking about dress, but Ariès talking about education. Once again, we can see the confusion of categories. Mediaeval education was a chaos, a jumble; pedagogues had no idea of pupils progressing from the easy to the difficult, no idea of separating children according to age. But then is that so surprising when they had no clear idea of how to separate *subjects*? If what we now think of as distinct subjects were all jumbled together under the (to us) mysterious and misleading titles of rhetoric, grammar, dialectics and philosophy, is it so surprising that the pupils were all jammed together too? We need assume no particular preconception about the nature of childhood; the more natural conclusion is that the Middle Ages had little analytic grasp of how to organise education – and, as far as the Church usually went, not much purpose beyond training competent choir-school men. It is not their conception of childhood that is foreign; it is their conception of education.

To English readers, however, it is Ariès's chapter on 'Games and Pastimes' that reads most oddly:

> In every case the same evolution takes place with repetitious monotony. At first some games were common to all ages and all classes. The phenomenon which needs to be emphasized is the abandonment of these games by the adults of the upper classes and their survival among both the lower classes and the children of the upper classes.[32]

True, Ariès does modify this by conceding that in England the upper classes have not abandoned the old games as they have in France, but they have completely transformed them, and it is in unrecognisable modern forms that the games have been adopted by the middle-class sportsman. This hugely understates the truth. For while the French nobility may indeed have forsaken tennis and taken up hunting, in England the popular sports of cricket and football have increasingly been played by all classes and ages, although they were often restricted by the authorities. In Scotland, the same was true of golf. Nor is it the case, as Ariès claims, that games have always tended to originate with adults and were to be passed on to children only when adults wearied of them. On the contrary, some of the earliest mentions of most ball games ridicule them as suitable only for children. And it is children who are just as frequently depicted at an early date holding bat and ball or club. Some games we know for sure were invented by children, such as Eton fives, played by idle boys hitting a ball against a wall between two buttresses of Eton College Chapel. The shape of the fives court with its awkward nooks and angles is religiously reproduced in each expensively built modern fives court. The handful of schoolmasters who ran the school at the time naturally discouraged the game.

The earliest mention of football in mediaeval England comes from FitzStephen in the twelfth century. He says that London *boys* 'annually upon Shrove Tuesday go into the fields and play at the well-known game of ball'[33] (Shrove Tuesday was a great football day up until the nineteenth century) – and the *adults* went out to watch them play. Football was so popular in the fourteenth century that Edward II issued a proclamation forbidding the game as likely to cause a breach of the peace: 'Forasmuch as there is great noise in the city caused by scrimmaging over large balls . . . ' Edward II further objected to the game as likely to distract young men from their archery; he wrote to the Sheriffs of London complaining that 'the skill at shooting with arrows was almost totally laid aside for the purpose of various useless and unlawful games'. To no avail, for forty years later Richard II had to pass a similar statute forbidding throughout the kingdom 'all playing at tennise, football and other games called corts, dice, casting of the stone, kailes, and other such importune games'. In Scotland, kings had the same trouble. In 1457 James III decreed that 'footballe and golfe be utterly cryed down and not to be used'.[34]

Nor was football confined to the urban lower classes. In 1508, Barclay in his fifth eclogue shows that it was popular in the country too:

> The sturdie plowman, lustie, strong and bold,
> Overcometh the winter with driving the foote-ball,
> Forgetting labour and many a grievous fall.[35]

The Church was just as hostile as the State – though for different reasons. In the 1580s Stubbes, in the *Anatomie of Abuses in the Realme of England*, decries 'football playing and other develishe pastimes' – in addition to 'cards, dice, tennise and bowles, and such like fooleries' – and not just on Sunday either:

> Any exercise which withdraweth from godliness either upon the Sabaoth or any other day, is wicked and to be forbidden. Now who is so grosly blind that seeth not that these aforesaid exercises not only withdraw us from godliness and virtue, but also haile and allure us to wickednesse and sin?[36]

This is exactly the same reason for which Welsh ministers three centuries later strongly disapproved of the craze for the new game of Rugby football.

Now clearly from the beginning football was a game for boys and for young men of the lower classes. There is no suggestion that upper-class adults played it. Indeed, I find no such suggestion until the old boys of several leading public schools revived and organised the game in the middle of the nineteenth century.

Even cricket, now widely regarded as an upper-class English game, seems to have taken its origin as a game for children and young men. It seems to have evolved out of one of the dozens of mediaeval variants of ball-and-stick games: stool ball, trap-ball, pell-mell, cat-and-dog, the game often called 'hot rice' (though it has a hundred other names) and so on. Even in the early eighteenth century, the poet Gray still refers to it in a letter to his friend as a pastime of their adolescence; it was only in the mid-eighteenth century that grown gentlemen seem to have taken up or kept on playing the game.

Golf, it is true, had quite early on attracted noble and even royal enthusiasts in Scotland; Montrose, for example, was a keen golfer. There is a report of an Anglo-Scottish money match in the reign of James V in which John Paterson, the Scottish champion, a poor tradesman, was given half the stake money, as a reward – the first example of a professional's fee. But here too there is no question of the game having originated as a young nobleman's pursuit; most players, then and now, were humble folk.

One or two games, for obvious reasons, were essentially upper class, such as tennis; only noblemen could afford a royal tennis court. But other games had less grand origins. Racquets is said to have originated in the Fleet Prison.

The history of sports, in England at least, tends to suggest precisely the opposite of the Ariès thesis. In the Middle Ages, children seem to have played a huge variety of games, some organised, some casual. Some of these, such as football, were played by young men as well; one or two were also popular among the upper classes, who had in addition their own knightly pursuits which were too expensive for the lower classes – the mediaeval equivalents of foxhunting, game-shooting and fly-fishing. In other words, children *can* be distinguished from adults by the games they played. Perhaps adults did join in some of these games, just as adults today fly kites and play beach cricket and Monopoly with –and often without – their children. Ariès is excited by mediaeval pictures of grown men bowling hoops; but there are modern newspaper photographs of grown men and women wiggling their bottoms inside hula-hoops. New crazes may be enjoyed by all ages for a time; it is a matter of historical accident – or perhaps of the inherent potential of a game, or of economic circumstances – which age group or groups continue to play it. It is hard to see any constant pattern of historical development.

Certainly most sports are more organised than they once were: rules are drawn up, equipment and venue are standardised, coaches and coaching manuals appear, the game becomes codified, regularised – and eventually professionalised. This applies just as much, and rather earlier, to such field sports as fox-hunting and hare-coursing as it does to football, cricket and lawn tennis – although real or royal tennis is the best surviving example of what complicated rules mediaeval sportsmen could draw up. It is often forgotten how early on such professionalism happened; Hazlitt's essays on Cavanagh, the great fives-player, and on prize-fighting offer a useful corrective.

Once again, all this has nothing to do with 'an idea of childhood'. Children indulged in any games or sports which were available to them, from bowling a hoop to gambling. But what the histories of most sports and games do have in common – and share with the histories of pictures, dress and schools – is a growing rationalisation and differentiation.

It is this growing application of the 'scientific spirit' which Ariès and his admirers have mistaken for a history of childhood. And the intellectual sources of this mistake are not far to seek. The trouble derives basically from the Victorian belief that everything passes through stages of development. Our scientific knowledge of nature advances by stages; so has the evolution of the human species. Why then should man's emotional attitudes not pass through a similar linear development moving from lower to higher levels of 'affect' – to use Professor Stone's word? Why should not all these feelings of sexual love and maternal affection develop socially?

Ariès asks: 'Are not we ourselves unconsciously impressed by the part the family has played in our society for several centuries, and are we not tempted to exaggerate its scope and even to attribute to it an almost absolute sort of historical authority?'[37]

Perhaps we are. And yet there is another and opposite temptation, far stronger in our own day, which is to try to force the family into a historical pattern in order to prove that it is a freakish and fleeting phenomenon.

And so we must finally ask: what makes intellectuals want to destroy the family or at least to obliterate its credentials? What is the emotional force which pushes clever men and women into so much intellectual muddle and even dishonesty? Why do they devote so much energy to discrediting the circumstances in which they were born and bred? Why, finally, do they hate the family so much?

PART TWO

THE FAMILY THEN AND NOW

9

THE
FAMILY-HATERS

The family is not an historical freak. If the evidence we have put together is correctly interpreted, the family as we know it today – small, two-generation, nuclear, based on choice and affection (or as near as we can manage in the face of Church and State and scarcity) – is neither a novelty nor the product of unique historical forces. The way most people live today is the way most people have always preferred to live when they had the chance.

But, as we look at the historical arguments, we become more and more aware of the other criticism of the family, which is far older than the historical one. Indeed, we begin to get the impression that the historical arguments have been dredged up only in the past hundred years, partly in order to support these other, older criticisms (although the two critiques cannot both be true together).

The older criticism is a *moral* objection. The family is said to be selfish and materialistic, inward-looking, indifferent to the sufferings and struggles of the outside world. People devote to their families the ardour and effort that ought more properly to be showered on God or nation or community or class.

What a long way back this complaint goes. In Plato's *Republic*, as we have seen, all citizens are to be taught to regard one another as brothers.[1] The community of wives and children is said to be the source of the greatest good. It is the natural complement to the community of property. The guardians will not tear the city in pieces

by differing about 'mine' and 'not mine'; the citizen will not drag his
private property off into a separate house of his own, where he has a
separate wife and children and private pleasures and pains.[2]

Over and over again, we find repeated the view that communism
and free love are more delightful and/or morally superior to family
life. In the second century B.C., the Greek historian Diodorus Siculus
described the Isles of the Blessed:

> All citizens have the same perfectly healthy constitution and the
> same perfectly beautiful features. Each takes his turn to perform
> every necessary task as hunter or fisherman or in the service of the
> state. All land, livestock and tools are thus used in turn by every
> citizen and therefore belong to nobody in particular. Marriage is
> unknown and sexual promiscuity complete; the tribe is responsible
> for bringing up the children, and this is done in such a way that
> mothers cannot recognize their own.[3]

In the *Recognitions of Clement*, a curious kind of travelogue of the
third century A.D., the following opinions are recorded:

> . . . a very wise Greek, knowing these things to be so, says that all
> things should be in common amongst friends. And unquestionably
> amongst 'all things' spouses are included. He also says, just as the air
> cannot be divided up, nor the splendour of the sun, so the other
> things which are given in this world to be held in common ought not
> to be divided up, but really ought to be held in common.[4]

These views surfaced again in the Middle Ages, but this time
mistakenly attributed to Pope Clement I himself. Thus in the twelfth
century, this praise of free love came to be included in Gratian's
Decretals, the basic text for the study of canon law in the universities.

Such ideas began to appear in literature, in the *Roman de la Rose*,
for example. In the 1300s, the Brethren of the Free Spirit were said,
though mostly by their enemies, to practise communism, nudism and
free love in an effort to re-create the conditions of the Garden of Eden.
And when the first great millenarian sects began to crop up, free love
of one sort or another was an essential part of the lost Eden that was
to be regained; the Adamites of Bohemia in the 1420s declared that
the chaste were unworthy to enter their kingdom. In 1534, the Ana-
baptists established polygamy in Münster; all women under a certain
age had to marry; since there were few unmarried men, this meant

that many women had to accept the role of second, third or fourth wife; disobedience was made a capital offence; but the quarrels between the women were so great that

> in the end, divorce had to be permitted and this in turn changed polygamy into something not very different from free love. The religious ceremony of marriage was dispensed with and marriages were contracted and dissolved with great facility. Even if much in the hostile accounts which we possess is discounted as exaggeration, it seems certain that norms of sexual behaviour in the Kingdom of the Saints traversed the whole arc from a rigorous puritanism to near-promiscuity.[5]

In seventeenth-century England, extreme puritan sects such as the Ranters were constantly being accused of denouncing marriage. Thomas Webbe, the Rector of Langley Burhill, who was put on trial for adultery but acquitted, was alleged to have said 'there's no heaven but women, nor no hell save marriage.' John Pordage, the Rector of Bradfield, was accused in 1655 of having said that marriage was a very wicked thing. Pordage defended the most notorious of Ranters, Abiezer Coppe, who in his second *Fiery Flying Roll* launched one of the most famous assaults on chastity, marriage and the family:

> Hear one word more (whom it hitteth it hitteth) give over thy base nasty stinking, formall grace before meat, and after meat (I call it so, though thou hast rebaptized it –) give over thy stinking family duties, and thy Gospell Ordinances as thou callest them; for under them all there lies snapping, snarling, biting, besides covetousnesse, horrid hypocrisie, envy, malice, evill surmising.
>
> Give over, give over, or if nothing els will do it, I'l at a time, when thou least of all thinkest of it, make thine own child, the fruit of thy loines, in whom thy soul delighted, lie with a whore – before thine eyes: That that plaguy holinesse and righteousnesse of thine might be confounded by that base thing.[6]

For Coppe, sex was the salvation:

> . . . by base impudent kisses (as I then accounted them) my plaguy holinesse has been confounded, and thrown into the lake of fire and brimstone.

155

> And then again, by wanton kisses, kissing hath been con-
> founded; and externall kisses, have been made the fiery chariots, to
> mount me swiftly into the bosom of him whom my soul loves, (his
> excellent Majesty, the King of glory.)[7]

The French utopians of the eighteenth century continued to attack
the hypocrisies of marriage and to invent rather stilted little utopias
where love was less constrained; travellers' tales developed a taste for
supposed real-life utopias such as Tahiti. By the nineteenth century,
the hypocrisy of marriage and the need for political freedom to extend
to the love-bond were commonplace themes in progressive circles.
There is, in short, no break in the utopian tradition.

Coming nearer our own time, we find no slackening in the quantity
of venom spewed out against the family as a selfish, secretive organism
subversive of true affection and liberty. This venom is the reverse side
of the sweet vision of philadelphia. Sir Edmund Leach rightly pleads
that the celebrated assertion in his Reith Lecture – 'Far from being
the basis of the good society, the family, with its narrow privacy and
tawdry secrets, is the source of all discontents'[8] – is by no means
original. He prays in aid Jesus's insistence that his disciples should
hate their families and the denunciations of the Ranters such as
Abiezer Coppe. Sir Edmund could also have invoked as allies André
Gide – *'familles, je vous hais!'* – or Engels's searing indictment of the
hypocrisy and 'moral contradictions' of bourgeois monogamy, 'with
its eternal attendants of hetaerism and adultery'. The bourgeois wife

> only differs from the ordinary courtesan in that she does not let out
> her body on piecework as a wage worker, but sells it once and for all
> into slavery. And of all marriages of convenience Fourier's words
> hold true: 'As in grammar two negatives make an affirmative, so in
> matrimonial morality two prostitutions pass for a virtue.'[9]

As the power of priests and preachers to command public attention
has declined, so their role as denouncers of the selfishness of the family
has been seized by artists – in particular, by modernist and futurist
artists.

Marinetti, the founder of the Futurists, wrote in *Futurist Democracy*
(1919):

> Family feeling is an inferior sentiment, almost animal, created by
> fear of the great free beasts, by fear of nights bursting with

adventure and ambush. It comes to birth with the first signs of old age that crack the metal of youth.

. . . The family dining room is the twice-daily sewer drain of bile, irritation, prejudice, and gossip.

. . . Hallways of idiot wranglings, litanies of reproaches, impossibility of thought or creation on one's own. One mucks around in the daily swamp of dirty domestic economy and dull vulgarities . . .

The family functions badly, being a hell of plots, arguments, betrayals, contempts, basenesses, and a relative desire on everyone's part for escape and revolt.[10]

The solution was to 'Put the artists in power! They will solve the problem of well-being in the only way it can be solved – spiritually. They will multiply a hundredfold the capacity to dream. Every man will live his best possible romance.'

How precisely Marinetti's attack on the family mirrors the description of 'thy stinking family duties' in the *Fiery Flying Roll* of Abiezer Coppe nearly three centuries earlier!

The novelist William Gerhardie, a militant celibate, described the family as 'that ungodly unit of pernicious preferential loyalty' and said of Tolstoy: 'The bane of Tolstoy's life, as the bane of most writers' lives, was his family. Having made the initial error of marrying, he multiplied the error by multiplying himself through his children.'[11]

Marriage is said to be disastrous for artists. Cyril Connolly included marriage high on his list of 'Enemies of Promise': 'If Dr Johnson said, a man who is not married is only half a man, so a man who is very much married is only half a writer.' And if marrying is bad for a writer, having children is fatal: 'There is no more sombre enemy of good art than the pram in the hall.'[12]

The artistic vocation is said to be a lonely one. Artists simply cannot afford to dissipate on spouse and children their scant resources of time, emotion and concentration, which must be exclusively devoted to their art. Now this theory in itself might be little more than the equivalent of saying that sailors make bad husbands because they are married to the sea. And it can be justified by pointing to the number of great English writers who have indeed been unhappily married: Shakespeare, Milton, Dr Johnson, Byron, Thackeray, Dickens, T. S. Eliot. Among great women writers, we notice that many never married, or married only towards the end of their lives, and very few have had children: Jane Austen, the Brontës, George Eliot, George Sand, Virginia Woolf. In earlier times, many literary men were celibates in holy orders; more recently, many have been homosexuals.

Whether people are enabled to become great writers by the accident of a celibate nature or an unhappy marriage, or whether their ambition to create great works helps to make them celibate or unhappily married does not matter much for our purposes. What has to be admitted is that, in modern times at least, the creation of great art and happy families do not often seem to go together.

Besides, artists have before them two daunting races of celibates, rivals for public reverence: on the one hand, the religious – hermits, priests, missionaries, monks and nuns; on the other hand, philosophers, mathematicians and physicists, dwellers in the purest realms of speculation. Newton, Descartes, Locke, Pascal, Spinoza, Kant, Leibniz, Schopenhauer, Nietzsche, Kierkegaard and Wittgenstein, all were unhampered by family ties. 'Perhaps', as Dr Anthony Storr suggests, 'the capacity for the higher flights of abstract thought only occurs in those who find continuing intimate relationships difficult of attainment. Perhaps, also, intense concentration upon difficult problems is easily interrupted by emotional demands and the patter of tiny feet.'[13]

Whatever the precise mixture of psychological and practical pressures, artists cannot afford to let their vocation seem less vital, less demanding of time and concentration than these rival priesthoods. They must be as lonely as priests, as totally absorbed in creation as a philosopher is absorbed in thought.

But the attack on the family does not stop there. Perhaps we could not expect artists to leave the family alone, to regard it as merely another form of human enterprise and one for which they do not happen to be suited. After all, what draws us to them in the first place, what excites our praise, is their huge capacity for absorbing common human experience and transforming it into works of art. We admire them precisely because they will not leave things alone. That is what gives them licence to intrude, to wander through our lives and our homes, and to dissect them and condemn them as hypocritical, humdrum and second-rate.

Nor can they help taking their own lives as models of the sort of life that ought to be attempted. When they say, as they may say now and then, as Auden and Eliot used to say, that art is ultimately inferior to life, we do not really believe that they believe it. Nor do we expect them to act as if they believed it; on the contrary, we expect them to sacrifice their lives to their art, if need be. And we are certainly not surprised to find them criticising marriage and the family as comfortable evasions of the real challenges that life offers, any more than we would be surprised to hear a sailor talk pityingly of landlubbers.

To become an artist is to join a company of separated brethren, like monks or sailors. It can sometimes be a cold and cheerless life, lonely and unconnected, deprived of biological narrative by the absence or refusal of children and grandchildren. Artists have no given duties, no programme defined by age. They do not become parents and then grandparents. They have only before them at all times the same duty, which is the duty to go on creating masterpieces, as Connolly put it, although he himself was much married and in middle age became a fond papa.

This isolation gives a curious tone to much high art of the past century: cold, even a little clammy, suspicious of sentiment, solitary. We do our best to find excuses for the artist's personality as revealed by the eager biographer, but undeniably there is something repulsive about it. Indeed, as soon as we do find some genial, warm characteristic, we begin to suspect that the artist's work may not be quite first-rate, after all, and that there may lurk within him or her some soft patch.

The male artist, even when in fact surrounded by wife and children, writes as if he was on his own, as if he remained quite indifferent to his biological luggage. He conducts a *public* dialogue, with other artists, with the public. He talks in large, cold terms of Sex, and Violence, and Death. He prefers to set himself and his characters in public places: bars, cafés, hotels, campuses, parties, bullfights, demonstrations, meetings. He does not write much of what daily and most nearly surrounds him: his family.

There is in all this an element of bad faith. For serious artists, the family has taken the place of sex as the great not-to-be-spoken-of.

The result is that, just as we used to be bullied by unmarried priests, now we are bullied by artists who pretend to be unmarried or pretend to think that being married is not important. High culture, like high religion, like ideologies of all kinds, always tries to monopolise the high ground so that it can look down with contempt on the smoky shacks of the lower orders, with their smell of cooking fat and nappies.

10

PRIVACY
AND THE
WORKING CLASS

The real trouble with the working class, we are told, is that they do not know what has happened to them. They are the helpless, passive, *unconscious* victims of huge economic and social processes.

Karl Marx, for example, believed that 'modern industry, in over-turning the economical foundation on which was based the traditional family, and the family labour corresponding to it, had also unloosened all traditional family ties.'[1] This meant great suffering for those involved; men were brutalised, women degraded, children deprived if not actually starved – yet for the long-term workings of history, this unloosening represented progress:

> However terrible and disgusting the dissolution, under the capital-ist system, of the old family ties may appear, nevertheless, modern industry, by assigning as it does an important part in the process of production, outside the domestic sphere, to women, to young persons, and to children of both sexes, creates a new economic foundation for a higher form of the family and of the relations between the sexes.[2]

Now, as we have seen, it is highly dubious whether modern industry did have such an effect. The evidence from the first industrial towns often suggests the opposite: that far from loosening family ties, factory work strengthened them. The extra incomes earned by the women and children enabled the family to stay together until the children had grown up. By contrast, on the traditional farm girls would have to go away into domestic service and boys would have to go away as labourers on another farm or as apprentices to another trade. Moreover, what strikes us most forcibly is how these new industrial working classes spent their combined incomes, when they had any surplus after paying for rent, food and clothing. They spent the money on *family* holidays. The great Northern resorts such as Blackpool are to this day a living refutation of Marx; and so are the newer resorts along all the coasts of Europe.

D. H. Lawrence and other English pastoralists have argued that smoke and concrete robbed the working class of direct experience of nature. According to F. R. Leavis, commercial relationships and commerical media stunt relationships and pollute language. People have become incapable of using their private power to create or enjoy true and lasting things.

Such complaints appear to be slightly at odds with the complaints of other more modern pastoralists that the working classes are ruining nature by insisting on plonking themselves in the middle of it; they crowd beauty spots, trample down and erode cliff paths, and spoil the sea view by building bungalows in order to enjoy the view.

But all high critics – whether aesthetic or economic – agree that the working classes are ignorant victims of social forces. And because they are not aware of the pitiful, subhuman, shrivelled state to which they have been reduced, they cannot be capable of estimating their true wants and needs. They do not know what they lack. At the most immediate level, they are constantly *bamboozled* by advertising, which creates false wants, by politicians and political systems pretending to 'minister' to their needs. At a deeper level, they are unaware of the shallowness of their lives. The family – and we are talking here about the broad generality of families of which the majority are working class or lower-middle class – is not an independent, self-moving social entity. It is, we are told, a greedy little monster which has no understanding of its own plight.

Now this is not how 'ordinary people' naturally think of the family in industrial society. Indeed they do not tend to think at all of 'industrial society' as being different from previous societies in any large, general way. I mean humanly different; everyone is well aware of the invention of electricity and motor cars. For ordinary people, industrial society has presented certain advantages – less hard manual labour, more leisure, better medical care – offset by certain disadvantages; life sometimes seems to be moving too fast, children are more rebellious and may exercise their independence too soon for their own good, the motor car may divide families as much as it unites them. But most people do not regard these disadvantages as constituting a change in kind, let alone as amounting to a theft of personality.

To the elitist, however – and here I take a huge sweep including not only Lenin, Marx, Sartre and Marcuse but also Eliot, Ortega and most theologians – the ordinary man's views of the world are of relatively little interest and certainly not to be seriously considered as a system of thought worthy of theoretical discussion. For the ordinary man's 'verbal gestures' are inauthentic; to imagine that there is much to be learned from them is to begin to fall into his own bamboozlement.

This condescending attitude provokes the ordinary family to a kind of underground *rebellion*. For the working classes refuse and for the most part have always refused to accept the dogmas of the official orthodoxy. Centuries later, historians have begun to show us how little interest the poor ever took in the Christian religion and how purely formal their allegiance often was; they went to church on Sundays only when forced and were baptised, wed and buried by the priest for reasons of social conformity and *family* solemnity. The same lack of popular faith is now evident in the Communist world; yet only recently representatives of other public ideologies – often conflicting ideologies – were admiring the Chinese masses' supposed devotion to 'permanent revolution', just as ideologues in the 1930s – again many either non- or anti-Communist – had been stirred by the Russian masses' devotion to Communism. It was all cant and humbug. It still is.

That is why I speak of the family's permanent revolution against the State, and of the working-class family as the only true revolutionary class. For the working-class family provides, every day, its own living refutation of the accusation of passivity and manipulation. The simplest way to demonstrate this is to refer to talk in public houses – the working-class equivalent of parliamentary debate or the talk of Left Bank cafés – and regarded by its practitioners with just the same sentimentality. What are the characteristics of pub talk – crass, tedious, repetitive and vulgar as elevated persons may find it?

First, pub talk is critical and sceptical. These two features, which find high praise in academic circles, are in fact rarely practised in academe. It is the intelligentsia which provides suckers for each New Dawn and which buys ideologies wholesale. The working class regards all ideologies as pretentious claptrap which has little to do with real life.

Second, pub talk is habitually discontented. It is not the case that people believe that consumer society is marvellous, or flawless or the best of all possible worlds. To put forward such a view would provoke instant derision. Nor is it the case that people accept the claims of television advertisements, let alone of politicians. I do not pretend that this discontent is 'divine', any more than I pretend that working-class scepticism radiates intellectual energy. But it is difficult to argue that it is either complacent or credulous.

Third, pub talk is prosy. Ordinary people are markedly free of *serious* utopian sentiments. Working-class utopias are playful and sensual – Big Rock Candy Mountain, Lubberland, Cockaigne, places of leisure and plenty. They do not aspire to replace or intensify the known pleasures of earthly life. Plato's *Republic* and More's *Utopia* – the dreams of middle-class intellectuals – have little appeal to ordinary people, reproducing as they do the regimes of army barracks and English boarding-schools, with the added drawback that the inmates are expected to be happy.

Now these characteristics – criticism, scepticism, discontent, prosiness – are all in direct contradiction to the more elevated attitudes which bishops, politicians and academic ideologues wish to instil. You may find working-class conversation dull or limiting. You may not wish to hear endless talk about football and pay-slips and booze. But you can scarcely deny the *independence* of the attitudes.

And when it comes to the family, you can scarcely overlook the *rebellious* quality of popular attitudes. For ordinary people are quite capable of describing their position and defending it. The car-worker refuses to accept that he is 'spiritually stunted' – even if he were to accept the legitimacy of such language – simply because he works 46 hours a week on an assembly line. Nor would he dream of denying that the work is very boring. But he would and does strongly assert that he makes a deliberate choice, fully conscious of what he is sacrificing, in order to *provide a better life for his family*.

That last phrase, hurried over with impatience by the intellectual obsessed with self-realisation, constitutes the heart of the argument.

For working men do not tamely register contentment with their car, their washing-machine, their extra weeks of holiday and their warm, dry houses. And they do not passively accept these consumer durables in the way that a hard-worked carthorse munches its oats. They will argue, strongly if pressed, that these are, simply, good things because they make life easier *for one another*; wives are not worn out at the age of thirty-five, children are educated, husbands pay more attention to their wives, go out to pubs together. What is strongly contested by the working class is the definition of these goods as *materialist*; on the contrary, they are aggressively defined as of potential social and spiritual value and capable of altruistic uses.

Seen from outside and above, from some Olympian spectators' stand, these goods may seem to be greedily devoured by materialist families; seen from ground level and *from inside the family*, the goods are seen as gifts and transfers between one member and another, charitable gifts which express affection and repay filial, parental and marital debts, thus blessing both the giver and the receiver.

I am compelled to use these questionable terms such as 'working-class families' and 'the car-worker', because I fear there is no other way to explain these things to the intellectual audience. For this working-class way of looking at a fridge or washing-machine is the most alien of all to the intellectual critics of industrial society, because they cannot understand that the family is in permanent rebellion against the public ideology of the Establishment.

Above all – and this common feature is so widely shared among intellectuals that most of them are scarcely aware of it – they regard human life and human society as primarily and optimally *public* matters, to be measured in public benefits, discussed at public meetings, celebrated by public performances of public masterpieces. This assumption is such common ground in public debate that few intellectuals appear to understand not only how much is being taken for granted but how strongly the assumption colours the rival pictures of the ideal society proposed in critical debate. From Plato onwards, the characteristic intellectual demand has been for society to be transparent, permeable, harmonious, integrated, organ-ised – that is, given an organic structure so that each human being may be a limb of a great body or, if you prefer the mechanical analogy, an instrument in one great process. The New Testament may be quoted as one among many expressions of this organising will (Marx or Rousseau would do just as well):

> Neither pray I for these alone, but for them also which shall believe on me through their word;
>
> That they all may be one; as thou, Father, art in me, and I in thee, that they also may be one in us: that the world may believe that thou hast sent me.
>
> And the glory which thou gavest me I have given them; that they may be one, even as we are one.
>
> I in them, and thou in me, that they may be made perfect in one.[3]

Public goods are supposed to be better, higher, nobler, grander than private goods; a man who has dedicated himself to the public welfare is 'greater' than one who has dedicated himself to his family. He is greater because he has contributed towards the making-one of society. He is a servant of holism. It is fitting in a tribute to a public man to lay stress on his integrating work. Even in an obituary of a party politician who has spent most of his life keeping alive the spirit of faction and class conflict, it is thought more appropriate to commemorate even minor episodes in which he promoted oneness.

We cannot overlook personal case studies here. Public life often seems to attract people who either do not like or cannot manage private life. By its remorseless pressure it shrivels the capacity for love, friendship or even interest in other people as individuals.

What could be sadder and more pathetic than the private lives of Napoleon, Stalin and Hitler? How dismal and mechanical the ruthless couplings of Mussolini and President Kennedy. When divorce became respectable for British politicians, for the first time outsiders began to see how totally public-ised most politicians had become and how few enjoyed or wanted or were capable of ordinary family life.

Private persons regard this characteristic as the 'hollowness' of public men. Naturally, public persons prefer to think of it as 'self-sacrifice' and 'dedication to the public weal'. It is a question of the viewpoint from which you look at the matter. But there can be no doubt that public life imposes its own demands upon its servants and chooses them accordingly. There is equally no doubt – and this is what puzzles public persons who cannot quite understand why they are so unpopular – that private persons are highly sensitive to the difference.

In meeting many politicians, you cannot help noticing their *detachment* from private feelings and concerns, their obsession with struggles and issues which seem to private people little more than games and quibbles. I stress that this does not of itself mean that public work does not have to be done by someone, still less that private people are either obtuse or superior. But the difference exists. It partly explains the baffled and irritated language which we use to describe politicians – 'creep', 'crook', 'on the make'. And it explains why politicians seem so insensitive and why they cannot understand how dry and odd their public priorities appear to us.

The most striking proof of all is how public persons *neglect* those questions of marriage and the family which seem most crucial and valuable to ordinary people, how little space in political or theological debate is taken up by the family, how it is dealt with as an afterthought forced upon public attention by practical difficulties.

There is something lowering about the way in which priests too tend to see family life as primarily 'problematic'. Their eyes are the eyes of spiritual policemen; they tend to range somewhat coldly over family relationships; their participation in family rites of birth, marriage and death hovers between embarrassment and condescension. It is embarrassing because the best priests – I mean the nicest men – are aware of the pretentious detachment of the role allotted to their calling; they know the contradiction between the humility which they are supposed to aim for and the dedication which is to set them apart from ordinary men. That rather serpentine coldness of manner which ordinary people complain of is all too often the result. When priests talk of 'the joy we experience' at a birth or a wedding, in many cases it is hard to resist the suspicion that what they mean is 'the joy you experience'.

Nor is this surprising, for the Christian profession is to renounce not only the devil but also the world and the flesh: 'Solid joys and lasting treasure none but Zion's children know.' A priest cannot and must not lose himself in earthly pleasure, any more than a policeman in uniform can lose himself in pub revelry on a Saturday night; he must stand outside and above the proceedings, for there is always the chance of a breach of the law. Public service still comes first.

Now the working class instructively rejects these priorities. The features of industrial society it likes best are those which serve private purposes.

Planners, socialists, fascists and anarchists too, all those who dream of public things, mourn the passing of the old 'sense of community' in, say, the East End of London; they mourn the loss of the 'old ideals' which are assumed to be exclusively communal. *What Went Wrong: Working People and the Ideals of the Labour Movement*, by Jeremy Seabrook, is the clearest and most eloquent recent exposition of this nostalgia.

Mr Seabrook travelled round Britain in the 1970s. Everywhere he found 'the desolation of ruined communities and broken human associations'. Consumer capitalism had eroded 'working-class identity'. Capitalist plenty has subjugated and cheated us:

> The chance to abolish poverty, one of the great scourges of mankind, should have given rise to a spontaneous and sustained cry of joy; but instead, there is nothing but discord and violence, ruined human relationships, the contamination, not only of work, but of neighbourhood, kinship and comradeliness, division between the generations, distrust within families.[4]

The breakdown of community has dehumanised working-class people, 'who have become more like things . . . dispensable, disposable, interchangeable, arbitrary . . . A vast pall of unhappiness hangs over these working-class communities.'[5]

At Christmas time especially,

> The ghosts of the extended family that we have failed to renew become too insistent, that seemingly irreducible throng which none the less disappeared so swiftly; it is at these times that we can measure the extent of our loss; and the material consolations seem at their most oppressive and lifeless. Between us all there is a sense of shame that we should all have gone our separate ways in search of individual fulfilment.[6]

This passionate response to the way we live now is based partly on Mr Seabrook's own reaction to the physical sights and sounds of modern life – essentially, *outdoor* street life – shopping centres, motorways, noise, ugly buildings. His own sensitivity is bolstered and given political authority by interviews with veterans of the Labour movement: for example, 84-year-old Jessie Stevens, suffragette and I.L.P. activist, daughter of a staunch republican father who himself had been an early member of the Independent Labour Party. She laments that 'there aren't people like me now . . . I shall carry on as long as I can. Only I sometimes wish there was some of the generosity, the self-sacrifice there was when I was young.'⁷

Not all the elderly interviewees who lament the selfishness and laziness of the younger generation were militants, though a good many were. In part, the complaints are those that you could hear from an elderly member of any class at any time; it is the right, perhaps the duty of the elderly to criticise the young and to offer lessons and parallels. But by choosing Labour Party activists, Mr Seabrook, like so many nostalgic for a collective past, assumes what he sets out to demonstrate.

'Under the dominion of consumer capitalism', we are told, 'all sense of place, function and class is weakened, the characteristics of region or clan, neighbourhood or kindred.'⁸ If this is so, Labour activists are not the people to prove it; they are not reliable witnesses because their function is to animate and aggravate precisely those sentiments of place and class which compose 'working-class solidarity'. They are double-glazing salesmen trying to convince you that your house is draughty and noisy.

When they and Mr Seabrook bemoan 'materialism', they are bemoaning the lack of followers and activists to march, write letters, knock on doors, attend meetings and all the other duties of collective action. Mr Seabrook contrasts the sloth of the people who lie in bed on Sunday mornings and the gallant handful who turn out for the meeting of the Rent Action Group; and we are assured that 'the effect of communal action on people can be very positive and exciting.'⁹ That is no doubt true, just as it is also true that the effect of communal action on people can be to make them intolerant, domineering and unpleasant.

But we must examine the assumptions of Mr Seabrook and his activists a little more closely. The extended family, as we have already seen, is an historical fiction, in Britain at least. All the evidence, from Young and Willmott's study of Bethnal Green onwards, suggests that people see *more* of their non-resident kin – parents, aunts and uncles – not less than they used to; and this for the obvious reasons that they have more leisure and can get about more.

And the gaping absence in Mr Seabrook's description of modern life is his reluctance to discuss the quality of modern family life in detail – except in his personal epilogue where he movingly describes how little he sees of his family nowadays, because they are so scattered, and how awkward they are when they meet. Yet, again, the evidence suggests that in most families there is more, not less, contact than there used to be.

Nor is the complaint of the decline in public spirit in the working class in any way new. Thomas Cooper, the old Chartist, touring the North of England in 1869 and 1870,

> noticed with pain that their moral and intellectual condition had deteriorated . . . In our old Chartist time, it is true, Lancashire working men were in rags by thousands; and many of them lacked food. But their intelligence was demonstrated wherever you went. You would see them in groups discussing the great doctrine of political justice . . . or they were in earnest dispute respecting the teachings of socialism. *Now*, you will see no such groups in Lancashire. But you will hear well-dressed working men talking of co-operative stores, and their shares in them, or in building societies. And you will see others, like idiots, leading small greyhound dogs, covered with cloth, in a string! They are about to race, and they are betting money as they go! . . . Working men had ceased to think, and wanted to hear no thoughtful talk; at least it was with the greater number of them. To one who has striven, the greater part of his life, to instruct and elevate them, and who has suffered and borne imprisonment for them, all this was more painful than I care to tell.[10]

As in the case of Jessie Stevens, we cannot help noticing the personal resentment. After all Thomas Cooper had done for them, the workers had abandoned the good old cause and reverted to their private concerns. All the golden years of his youth which he had devoted to chivvying, rallying, marching and agitating on their behalf had been wantonly and ungratefully cast away. The workers had not proved worthy of him.

In all such political animals there is a mixture of idealism and busy-ness, of self-sacrifice and self-dramatisation, of renunciation and egotism. Their personal virtues bring with them personal defects; and they must not be judged too unkindly. But what we cannot accept is that other men and women who refused to accept these priorities and who preferred to live differently – in a private, family sphere –

should thereby be judged morally inferior. And we do not have to accept the historical pattern of the myth either.

In 1870, Thomas Cooper locates the Golden Age of collective militancy in the Chartist years – 1840–5, the Hungry Forties. Jessie Stevens, talking in the 1970s, locates the Golden Age in the Edwardian era when she was a suffragette. If you were born at other times, you could no doubt have chosen other moments of high exhilaration – in the twentieth century the General Strike, in the Napoleonic wars the Luddite risings. I do not undervalue either the importance or the excitement of any of these events, but to imagine that they represent either the peak or the sum of human moral experience is a sad delusion.

This myth-making is possible only on one supposition: that public action is morally superior to private action. And this supposition can be held only by confusing the family with the individual and pretending that all non-public motives are equally selfish and 'individualistic'.

Yet as Anthony Crosland points out in *The Future of Socialism*:

> Membership of a group can also stunt the individual personality, since groups themselves often develop distinctly undemocratic and selfish characteristics. In any case, we surely do not want a world in which everyone is fussing around in an interfering and responsible manner, and no one peacefully cultivating his garden.[11]

Quoting Thomas Cooper's lament, he argues that there is no reason why working men should not be well dressed and have shares in co-operative stores and race greyhounds.

> If one believes in socialism not on paternalistic grounds, but as a means of increasing personal freedom and the range of choice, one does not necessarily want a busy, bustling society in which everyone is politically active, and spends his evenings in group discussions, and feels responsible for all the burdens of the world. As Bertrand Russell once wrote, 'the sphere of individual action is not to be regarded as ethically inferior to that of social duty. On the contrary, some of the best human activities are, at least in feeling, rather personal than social . . .'[12]

And what Crosland called 'a full family life' is a prime source of such enrichment of personal life – for most people, *the* prime source. To include it simply under the heading of 'individualism' is to narrow the scope of the moral life to collective actions only – a narrowing which runs the risk of narrowing human sympathies in a way now all too familiar to us: people's courts, enemies of the people, people being 'sent to Coventry' and so on.

Moreover, even when it *is* possible to speak of 'a loss of community', who is usually responsible? What causes the loss of familiar faces and places? Who uproots people to new towns and boxes them away in high-rise flats and throws motorways past their bedroom windows? The loss of nearest and dearest people and things is almost always due to the initiatives of *public* bodies – slum clearance, overspill housing, by-passes and motorways, and worst of all, wars. It is not industrialisation or capitalism which is primarily responsible for these latest upheavals. The architects of the modern Clearances and Enclosures are less often dukes and mill-owners than idealistic public servants. It is the reach and power of the public domain which today are the prime uprooting and alienating factors, not the dehumanising nature of factory work or the cash nexus – for the family has managed triumphantly to overcome these.

This seems obvious enough. Public-minded people can shrug off their own responsibility for what has happened only by setting as the ultimate goal, not the fulfilment of the family but the achievement of 'community spirit' – or, in some versions, the recapture of the old community spirit said to have existed in some imprecisely specified golden age.

Community spirit is not a chimaera. It is an observable phenomenon. And what you cannot help observing about it is that community spirit is like happiness. It is not an end which may be directly and deliberately planned. It is a fragrance given off by successful social arrangements. And success is not hard to define. It means simply those arrangements which fit in with the wishes and serve the private ends of the individuals concerned.

For ordinary people, the purpose of a local cricket club is not to 'create community spirit'. It is to play cricket and talk and drink afterwards. Such community spirit as may be created is a natural by-product – certainly a valid way of describing why one prefers this cricket club to that one, but not an accurate or full definition of the purpose of the enterprise.

Loyalties to faith, class, trade union, race or country are natural by-products of living somewhere and being someone living among other someones and so inevitably belonging to this faith, class, trade union, race or country, rather than that. This belonging may, again naturally, engender certain affections and loyalties; in the course of time, it may come to be thought that the belonging entails and exacts these affections and loyalties. Tricky moral and juridical questions arise: is disaffection or treachery to be punished by social disapproval or legal penalties and, if so, when? But however far affection and loyalty may crystallise and even fossilise into duties prescribed by custom and law, it remains true that to describe these duties as *the* purpose of life is to misunderstand what it is to be a human being.

Being human does not *exclude* or forbid public life. People may choose to devote their lives to public works or derive their satisfactions from public activity; if the world is to run properly, such people are essential. But the question – as seen by the working class – is not only one of practical usefulness but also one of personal liberty. To exclude the possibility of a public life would be to prevent someone from doing what he or she wanted and so conflict with the general rule of vulgar tolerance: people should be allowed to do what they wish as long as they cause no harm to others. But by the same rule of vulgar tolerance, public busybodies do not have the right to enforce their personal scale of priorities on the rest of us.

This vulgar view fits in little better with traditional conservatism – which is potentially just as holist as Marxism or Christianity. Burke, for example:

> To be attached to the subdivision, to love the little platoon we belong to in society, is the first principle, the germ as it were, of public affections. It is the first link in the series by which we proceed towards a love to our country and to mankind . . .

> No man ever was attached by a sense of pride, partiality, or real affection, to a description of square measurement. He never will glory in belonging to the Chequer no. 71, or to any other badge-ticket. We begin our public affections in our families. No cold relation is a zealous citizen. We pass on to our neighbours and our habitual provincial connections. These are inns and resting places. Such divisions of our country as have been forced by habit and not by a sudden jerk of authority, are so many little images of the great country in which the heart found something which it could fill. The

love to the whole is not extinguished by this subordinate partiality. Perhaps it is a sort of elemental training to those higher and more large regards, by which alone men come to be affected, as with their own concern, in the prosperity of a kingdom . . .[13]

Burke too has in mind a grand structure whose purpose and crowning glory are 'those higher and more large regards'. Traditional conservatism of this sort is scarcely less public-oriented than socialist or fascist ideologies; indeed, in one sense you could say that it was more so, because the Burkean conservative is aware of the existence of private affections and encourages them as useful foundations of a stable society. Private affections are thus to be enlisted and integrated rather than simply to be ignored or destroyed; whereas Maoism at least *acknowledges the autonomy* of private affections by regarding them as enemies of the good state, Burkean conservatism sweeps them up in one grand public embrace. That private space which even the most brutal persecution cannot invade is here denied; far from love enabling you to escape Big Brother, Big Brother looks benignly on, like a chairman at a staff outing.

Burke's formulation here seems more suspect the more closely you look at it. Cold relations often *are* zealous citizens; that, after all, is the point of Burke's gibe at Rousseau – for putting his children in an orphanage – 'lover of mankind, hater of his kindred'. The *opposition* between private and public affections cannot be so blandly blanketed. It may be true that *happiness* depends on an 'elemental training' in the giving and receiving of affection in childhood. But happiness is not the same as good citizenship.

The family's most dangerous enemies may not turn out to be those who have openly declared war. It is so easy to muster resistance against the blatant cruelty of collectivist dictators, even if the resistance is only silent and inward. It is less easy to fight against the armies of those who are 'only here to help' – those who claim to come with the best intentions but come armed, all the same, with statutory powers and administrative instruments: education officers, children's officers, housing officers, architects, planners, welfare workers, and all the other councils, agencies and task forces which claim to know best how to manage our private concerns, and which declare that they are only acting out the principle that 'we are all members one of another'.

What is objectionable is not merely that these public officials are frequently wrong – though they are. Nor is it that for the most part we have no means of controlling or challenging their activities – though that is often true too. What is always affronting, offensive and distressing is the simple fact of their *intrusion* into our private space.

Our feelings are mixed even in the case of the most helpful of all public visitors. The District Health Visitor who visits mothers with babies is often sweet and sensitive and genuinely useful. Frantic women with their first child do often look forward to her calming and informative advice. But – and it remains an inescapable, embarrassing But – they cannot help being continuously aware that she is there as an inspector as well as an adviser. Her eye roams the room and the baby for evidence of dirt, neglect, even brutality. This kindly, middle-aged body has at her ultimate disposal a Stalinist array of powers – to remove the baby temporarily or permanently from the mother, to have the house cleared, condemned as unfit for human habitation or even demolished, to clap the mother and father in jail. All these powers are miles away from her mind as she dandles the baby and boosts the mother's confidence by praising and encouraging her; and yet that potential hostility inherent in her inquisitorial role never ceases to mark the relationship with unease which may flare into resentment at a tactless word.

The Visitor – grim, symbolic title – remains an Intruder. Many Visitors – I use the term here to embrace all official intruders – have in recent years come dimly to grasp the resentment which they cause. Welfare workers talk increasingly of 'consultation' and 'participation' and of encouraging people to help themselves. But in many cases these efforts to make their own activities more popular and acceptable contain a measure of bad faith; for many welfare workers do not appear to believe that their clients are capable of helping themselves. A more general belief in the essential helplessness – the 'inadequacy' – of the working class is at least one element in that justification for existing which every profession must possess.

There is then an undeclared war between the two domains, somewhat like the class war described by Marx. On the one hand, an overclass, bossy, acquisitive of power and security, intermittently guilty about both; on the other, an underclass, bossed, gulled and harried, intermittently aware of its situation and resentful. In all the revolts against big government and high taxes – which have swept the

Western world in the past couple of years – this resentment has played its part. Domain-consciousness – the feeling that the State is intruding into private space more and more and ought to be stopped – is growing. The Visitor is being made to feel unwelcome. His or her claim to moral superiority is being disputed.

What few have yet grasped is that the working class is the true defender of liberty and *privacy*, because it has no ulterior motive. The material triumph of the masses – the access they have finally gained to a decent standard of living – is not to be used for making society more public and collective. On the contrary, it is to be used for dispersing the delights of privacy to all. Naturally, this *redistribution of privacy* has much annoyed elitists: bungalows, ribbon development, millions of little private cars clogging national parks, worst of all, Los Angeles – as Mr Reyner Banham observed, the only city in history deliberately designed by the people who live in it. All these elements reduce the privacy of the professional man living in the Georgian rectory who almost overnight finds the old paddock filled with Wates houses. How much more agreeable it would be if the masses would stay massed in architecturally stimulating flats and travel to work in charming trains.

This invasion is certainly an egalitarian act, a gesture of levelling down. But it is also a moral gesture of sorts – an implied declaration of the moral independence and individuality of each family, of its right to adopt its own territory and its own values. The other domain, the domain of home and family, here asserts its primacy over the public domain and its tired old quarrels of class and race.

11

THE DILUTION OF FRATERNITY

The family's demands are clear and consistent: subsistence, privacy, liberty. These demands are denounced by public ideologues as selfish and inward-looking. But what do the public ideologues – the priests, the artists, the generals – offer as replacements? What are the out-ward-looking, unselfish loyalties which are to replace the family?

Intellectuals, monks and soldiers no longer acknowledge fathers and mothers. What they all invent for themselves or have invented for them are *brothers*. It is remarkable how universally fraternity is chosen as the image of the alternative family.

Why brotherhood? Why, out of all the images, metaphors, models, paradigms that might have been chosen to express community and goodwill between men, has the ideal of brotherhood taken such pre-eminent hold? Fraternalists have also used the flock, the phalanx, the tribe, the village, and the family as metaphors of community. But none of these has begun to take the place of brotherhood in the language of utopia. The theory that men are, or ought to be, or could be made to be brothers has reverberated so long and deep in the Western mind that to analyse its origins, nature and implications seems almost pedantic, like analysing a joke or a sunrise.

Fraternity permeates both the Christian and the Marxist hope, lends warmth to liberalism and dogma to the anarchist. The ideal is passionately invoked in religious, poetic, and political prescription and prophecy. Yet hardly ever do men ask themselves or anybody else exactly what it means to love as *brothers*. Wilson Carey McWilliams, for example, in his massive *The Idea of Fraternity in America* can dredge up only a handful of previous discussions of the subject, and those mostly glancing, peripheral. He himself skimps analysis of the concept of fraternity and concentrates on its historical development. Even the formidable James Fitzjames Stephen tackled the subject somewhat timidly in *Liberty, Equality and Fraternity* (1873). He could understand men wanting justice and respect – but brotherly love? . . . Well, that was a little outside the brief of a criminal lawyer. Yet fraternity presents exactly the same ambiguity, the same awkward angles, as the other legs of the revolutionary triad. Are men in some absolute and enduring sense Free, or Equal, or Brothers? Or is it rather that they ought to be or could be made so? And what would that process of making entail? Is it possible to be both free and equal, free and fraternal, equal and fraternal – or all three at once?

The juxtaposition of these three ideals provokes such pressing and difficult questions that the neglect of the third leg is curious, even disturbing. It can hardly be accidental, in view of the prodigious quantity of time and thought expended on the other two.

The Marxist historian E. J. Hobsbawm, puzzled by 'this remarkable gap in the literature', suggests three reasons:[1] that the ideal of Fraternity is less conveniently translated into practice by the processes of law and politics than are Freedom and Equality; that 'middle class liberal political thought' is essentially individualist and unfraternal; and that those 'who have used and needed fraternity most in modern societies are least likely to write books about it' (namely, the poor and oppressed). I find these reasons unconvincing. After all, they would apply just as well, *mutatis mutandis*, to the Kingdom of Heaven, which has never lacked students and critics. There remains something oddly inaccessible about the ideal of fraternity, something which daunts enquiry.

Hobsbawm himself describes fraternity as 'a type of social cooperation' which implies 'a relationship between a group of equals for the utmost mutual help and aid, given both voluntarily and as of right, but *not measured in terms of money or mechanical equality or reciprocal exchange*'. He equates it with the ideal, common to R. H. Tawney and William Morris, of 'fellowship' and asserts that it has 'a built-in collectivist or communist tendency' – wherein lies the cause of its neglect. For it was too 'passionate and imprecise' a concept to describe or bring to birth a socialist society. Hence 'most socialists since Marx have no longer given it an important place in their theory', which is where we came in.

Fraternity is essentially a socialist ideal. Yet socialists, it seems, find it somehow unfruitful. It is easy enough to describe the practical implications of a fraternal relationship, as Hobsbawm does, but apparently not so easy to describe exactly what that relationship is like. Hobsbawm's string of synonyms would do well enough to describe almost any kind of friendly co-operation between equals. But they are no more adequate to describe what it is *to love as brothers* than the promised endowment of all my worldly goods is adequate to define marriage. Fraternity continues to elude us.

It is significant how often the ideal is presented in terms which are negative. This quirk is striking in Shelley's famous description of the new man who will 'make the earth one brotherhood':

> Sceptreless, free, uncircumscribed, but man
> Equal, unclassed, tribeless, and nationless,
> Exempt from awe, worship, degree, the king
> Over himself; just, gentle, wise: but man
> Passionless? – no, yet free from guilt or pain . . .[2]

To be master of oneself has been the goal of all philosophers from the earliest times. 'Just, gentle, wise' – that we should always be, utopia or no. But of the characteristically utopian qualities mentioned, only freedom and equality stand out as positive virtues – and they are already separately blazoned on the revolutionary shield. It is *absence* (of pressures, constraints, obligations, loyalties) which is the common feature of the others. Above all, there is something very odd about Shelley's assertion that the new man will not be passionless. It is a defensive, lukewarm sort of assertion; he leaves it hanging, a quizzical unsupported double negative in a cluster of plain negatives. Not exactly a passionate affirmation of man's continuing ability to love and feel intensely when released from his chains.

The same uneasy, lukewarm, negative tone runs through Edward Bond's vision of a new society:

> How do we make freedom?
> There is only one way:
> When no man uses another for profit

He will not need force: he will make no enemies
He can be guided by sense: not fear or advantage
He can call all men brothers: for then love will not be
    made sentimental by fraud
But passionate by reason . . . [3]

Again, the negative is strongly marked in St Paul's great universalist promise to the Galatians: 'There is neither Jew nor Greek, there is neither bond nor free, there is neither male nor female: for ye are all one in Christ Jesus.'[4]

As soon as we do start thinking about the positive nature of fraternity, the case becomes more curious still. Brothers, after all, are not notorious for loving one another. Herzen said: 'Most men interpret brotherhood in the spirit of Cain and Abel.' He presumably intended a crack against the shortcomings of fellow revolutionaries. But the remark serves also as a reminder that our myths usually present brothers as *enemies*, riven by jealousy and greed, and ready to resort to theft, deceit, and murder to gain the upper hand, the family inheritance, the throne. If Cain and Abel were the first pair of brothers, the second great story of brotherhood is that of Esau and Jacob. In myths when men show 'fraternal' affection to each other, they usually turn out to be not brothers, but cousins, father and son, uncle and nephew, or no kin at all. David and 'Jonathan my brother' are no relation. Classical myth observes the same paradox. Damon and Pythias are no relation. Achilles and Patroclus are cousins. Eteocles and Polynices really are brothers, the sons of Oedipus, and the one kills the other in single combat. The tragedy of the house of Atreus begins and ends with fratricide. Castor and Pollux are exceptions to the rule, but twins may be held to represent a different principle, that of identity and fusion rather than of fraternity.

This mythical presentation of brotherhood in the Western tradition accords on the whole well enough with our own experience. Brothers *are* jealous of each other, do drift apart and lose touch, live on non-speaking terms for years, have at best stiff and short-lived reconciliations – and much more so than other immediate family relations. Even in families where the fraternal link is warm and enduring, the links between parents and children and between brother and sister are likely to be just as close, if not closer. I know no family where *only* the brothers are close, the other relationships within

179

the immediate family being marked by indifference or dislike. Of course there must be exceptions to these generalisations, but, I wager, not so many as to lead us to think of brotherhood as the family relationship which most typified affection and closeness.

But then why should the metaphor of community be plucked from the *family* anyway? After all, the fraternalist tradition is imbued with distaste for, or at best indifference towards, the family. The promoters of universal brotherhood have found it remarkably difficult to accommodate the family in their scheme of things.

If they do not care for the family, and if brotherhood is the most frigid relationship within the family, why choose brothers as the image of community? It is no help to say that true brotherhood would be a transformed, purged version of the shoddy present reality. Of course it would. But what exactly would be *brotherly* about it? What are the advantages that brotherhood typically possesses that other family relationships do not? How do brothers differ from father-and-son or brother-and-sister or even grandparent-and-grandchild?

The most prominent special characteristics of brotherhood are: *equality, non-responsibility,* and *dilution*.

Brothers are *equal*. Their relationship is reciprocal. *A* is *B*'s brother. *B* is *A*'s brother. Neither has any right to tell the other what to do. The answer to Cain's sullen rhetorical question 'Am I my brother's keeper?' was, of course, *No*. Mr Enoch Powell rightly points out in his reply to the Rev. Paul Oestreicher (the latest in a long line of clergymen to misinterpret this passage) that:

> if I am to be 'my brother's keeper', I must literally have my brother in charge. No one can be responsible for what he does not control. Therefore, if I am to be held responsible for my brother's welfare, safety, and standard of living, I must be given control over him, as a parent or guardian has control over a minor. The misconceived ordinance is thus a prescription for paternalist tyranny . . . [5]

A father is responsible for his son precisely because they are unequal. Of course, an eighteen-year-old boy taking his five-year-old brother for a walk is responsible for him, but his responsibility inevitably diminishes as the younger brother grows up. That is the consequence of the younger brother's freedom as an adult.

This adult freedom is the nub of John Locke's attack on Filmer's *Patriarcha* in his first *Treatise of Government*. In this polemic against the patriarchal tradition, Locke lays not only the essential ground of his own teaching but also the ground of the modern atomic political world. The temporary and limited nature of filial subjection may be 'obvious' to us, as Peter Laslett claims in his edition of Locke's *Two Treatises of Government* (Cambridge, 1960), but that is because Locke has prevailed: 'The power, then, that Parents have over their children, arises from that duty which is incumbent on them to take care of their offspring, during the imperfect state of Childhood.'[6] After the son has come of age,

> The Father and Son are equally free as much as Tutor and Pupil after Nonage; equally subjects of the same Law together, without any Dominion left in the Father over the Life, Liberty, or Estate of his Son . . .[7]

> Nay, this power so little belongs to the Father by any peculiar right of Nature, but only as he is Guardian of his Children, that when he quits his care of them, he loses his power over them, which goes along with their nourishment and education, to which it is inseparably annexed, and it belongs as much to the Foster-Father of an exposed Child, as to the Natural Father of another.[8]

On Locke's view, the son's majority transforms the relation utterly: father and son become *brothers*, equals, neither responsible for the other, both free, *separate*. Their freedom is a freedom from responsibility. To have someone responsible for you is just as much a limitation on your freedom as to be responsible for someone else. Such responsibility is the defining characteristic of a family. A blood-family which does not acknowledge or exercise responsibility has ceased to be more than a family in name. Conversely, a group of persons not related by blood who do exercise such responsibilities can come to be described as a family.

The responsibilities implicit in fraternal relations are much less marked than in other relationships within the immediate family; they therefore tend to give rise to less tenacious affections. That is why brotherhood is the most *diluted* of immediate family relationships. It mimics most nearly the way of the outside world in which particular responsibilities are spread thinly across society and so transmuted into general civic duty. *Brotherhood has been selected as the image of perfection not because it represents the family at its best but because it is the family at its least familial.*

Blood is thicker than water. Blood is also stickier; it clots, coagulates, congeals. Water is thin, neutral, constant, ever-flowing; it leaves no stain. Aristotle was the first to criticise the kind of political brotherhood sketched in Plato's *Republic* as 'watery'. He argues:

> As a little sweet wine mingled with a great deal of water is imperceptible in the mixture, so, in this sort of community, the idea of relationship which is based upon these names will be lost; there is no reason why the so-called father should care about the son, or the son about the father, or brothers about one another. Of the two qualities which chiefly inspire regard and affection – that a thing is your own and that you love it – neither can exist in such a state as this.[9]

This objection is often misunderstood (by Bertrand Russell and by Wilson McWilliams, for example). Aristotle is saying not that Plato's ideal state could not generate any kind of affection (though he is sceptical about that too), but rather that such love as it does generate will be of a new, diluted kind and that Plato is being dishonest in giving it the old name. Dilution is not an unintended defect in the Platonic scheme; it is its essential purpose. In the interests of general political concord Plato aims to destroy the particular private attachments and affections which obtain within the family in order that the love so selfishly concentrated should be spread throughout the community. Shelley describes the intended process:

> Soon as the sound had ceased whose thunder filled
> The abysses of the sky and the wide earth,
> There was a change: the impalpable thin air
> And the all-circling sunlight were transformed,
> As if the sense of love dissolved in them
> Had folded itself round the spherèd world.[10]

Aristotle says that such a process could not happen, because family love is generated by the social reality of the family. If the family is destroyed, that kind of love ceases to be generated. Perhaps the ideal Republic will generate its own watery kind of affection, but we must not use the language of the family to describe it. It will be diluted beyond recognition. If you insist on *equality, freedom, separation*, you must accept the consequences, and recognise that you have created an entirely new world which cannot be kept warm by the old love.

We are getting close here to the cause of the evasiveness which surrounds the idea of brotherhood. It is not that people are reluctant to discuss dilution. On the contrary, dilution is the commonplace of modern Western thought. It is familiar to us as a historical thesis, a therapy, and a political and social programme. But only rarely do its proponents have either the clarity of mind or the courage to accept the consequences.

Dilution is most generally put forward in the guise of a theory of history. In one form or another, that theory runs: in the old days – variously identified as the Middle Ages, feudalism, pre-industrial or pre-capitalist society – society was a network of communities. Despite poverty, disease, oppression, man was essentially at ease with himself, reposing in a kind of hammock of kinship which both protected and defined his identity. This slumbrous security was disturbed by the incursion of a new and irresistible force – variously described as the Reformation, the Calvinist or Puritan ethic, capitalism, technological rationality, the Industrial Revolution. This dry, hard, calculating force destroyed the old sense of community. No longer was man to be defined as the sum of his connections to family, clan, guild and village. He became a naked, calculating, independent, rational, individual atom, shorn of relationship. No longer could he find solace in the warmth and close mesh of his hammock and the protection it afforded him against the cold indifference of the outside world. All at once everywhere was outside him. He was alone, equally separate from all men.

This view is implicit or explicit in Marx, Weber, Tönnies, Tawney, Sombart and a hundred others. Disraeli wrote: 'There is no community in England; there is aggregation, but aggregation under circumstances which make it rather a dissociating than a uniting principle.' D. H. Lawrence echoes this in *Lady Chatterley's Lover*: 'Even in him [Mellors] there was no fellowship left. It was dead. The fellowship was dead. There was only apartness and hopelessness.'[11] *Gemeinschaft* gives way to *Gesellschaft*, community to association. In the words of the Mike Nichols–Elaine May sketch, there is 'proximity but no relating'.

Sir Henry Maine states the thesis with majestic precision. In primitive society, every tribe is perpetually at war with its neighbour. But within the tribe, there is amity, equality, fraternity.

> The men who composed the primitive communities believed themselves to be kinsmen in the most literal sense of the word; and, surprising as it may seem, there are a multitude of indications that in one stage of thought they must have regarded themselves as equals.

But modern society has changed all that.

> Just as the conceptions of human brotherhood and (in a less degree) of human equality appear to have passed beyond the limits of the primitive communities and to have spread themselves in a highly diluted form over the mass of mankind, so, on the other hand, competition in exchange seems to be the universal belligerency of the ancient world which has penetrated into the interior of the ancient groups of blood-relatives. It is the regulated private war of ancient society gradually broken up into indistinguishable atoms.[12]

By ceasing to cling to the company and prefer the interests of our own family, village, trade, class, race, religion, nation to those of others, we may make all men equally our brothers, but we must make that restricted group whom we formerly called our brothers that much less so. We have diluted the quality of brotherhood. Or, as Benjamin Nelson incapsulates it, 'all men have been becoming brothers by becoming equally others.'[13]

This great change from tribal brotherhood to universal otherhood is usually said to be irreversible. To toy with the idea of returning to the warmth of clan and family is said to be escapist, utopian, reactionary, fascist, in bad faith – for tribal solidarity was based on a myth, on the illusion of blood. There can be no going back from rational atomism. And on balance, it is said, a good thing too. As Nelson says: 'Better the abhorred "atomized individualism of bourgeois liberalism" than conflicting "Brotherhoods of Blood and Soil". Better still the Brotherhood of Man.'[14]

For psychiatrists of the R. D. Laing school it is the obligations and oppressions of the family that set up inside us those terrible tensions which break out into neurosis, bitterness, and violence. Laing himself says melodramatically: 'the initial act of brutality against the average child is the mother's first kiss . . . ' And, though he concedes that some families, including his own, provide happy and rewarding experiences, these benefits are accidental; they do not flow from the nature of the family as an institution. Even so-called happy families, where nobody has openly broken down, conceal terror and oppression. The family has an inherent tendency to turn people into things, into pieces of private property. The politics of the family are the dirtiest politics of all. Just as oppression in society at large is mirrored by oppression within the family, so repression within the family is mirrored by repression within the individual personality. Just as psychiatrists are ready to resort to recommendations in the interests of the patient which would have the effect of dissolving the patient's family, so some of them are now talking in terms of working towards a less 'dense' personality. They set up as their ideal a less 'imploded' psyche, a more neutral, open-ended, fluid kind of person – 'watery' as Aristotle would have put it, or less knotted or twisted or hung-up, as common speech describes it.

Of course, we do not want to overdo this process of dilution; at the other extreme, there is a danger of the personality fading away altogether, a sort of *anorexia psychologica*. Those people who find life empty and pointless, who have no friends and who neither feel nor awaken love are said to suffer from 'a thinning of affect'. Their personalities need density, contact, relationship. Such is the confused state of the art that some therapies, such as the 'Encounter group', are attempting to rectify both extremes at the same time, not only breaking down tensions and simplifying complexes but also trying to build up relationships – to move at one jump from the blood-family to the universal family. The results are, not surprisingly, ambiguous.

The Encounter group, for example, often claims to be neutral in its attitude towards the blood-family. Some marriages and families, we are told, are worth keeping together and strengthening. In other cases, the therapist and the group are delighted when the subject develops the strength needed to break away. This sort of independence is often the criterion of 'growing as a person'. Carl R. Rogers speaks with just as much satisfaction of former patients who have since divorced as of those whose marriages are now more securely based as a result of his ministrations.[15] This neutrality towards the blood-family is in reality a pose which is made possible only by the refusal of most Encounter group leaders to engage in debate on the presuppositions of their practice. The truth is that in essence the

Encounter group is antagonistic to the blood-family. For the group concentrates exclusively on the here-and-now of feeling. The essence of the blood-family, on the other hand, is that it is historically continuous. The shared experience of its past engenders loyalties, obligations, and affections – hatreds and resentments too, for that matter. Its future demands planning, discussion, sacrifice. Encounter groups, consciously and unconsciously, try to shrug off the weight of this future no less than of this past, regarding both as forms of repression. For the group, authenticity is to be attained only in the free expression of passing emotion as it passes: '*Now* I feel this, *now* I feel that.'

The new universal family has no future and no past. There is no necessity shaping its future development, no fetters imposed by its history. It is free because it is fluid, provisional, impermanent. Permanence is fossilisation. In the new family there are no relationships of which permanence is a defining feature. Love, marriage, parenthood, friendship – all are contingent, open-ended. Nothing in the new family is *given*, by God, morality, or even biology – nothing except its fluidity.

The marks of the New Family are that you both join and leave it of your own free will and that all its members are equal. Engels says:

> What will quite certainly disappear from monogamy are all the features stamped upon it through its origin in property relations; these are, in the first place, supremacy of the man and secondly, the indissolubility of marriage. The supremacy of the man in marriage is the simple consequence of his economic supremacy, and with the abolition of the latter will disappear of itself. The indissolubility is partly a consequence of the economic situation in which monogamy arose, partly tradition from the period when the connection between this economic situation and monogamy was not yet fully understood and was carried to extremes under a religious form.[16]

Women's liberation, divorce at will, marriage solely for love – all these follow naturally upon the abolition of capitalism and the property relations that go with it. But what exactly becomes of love? According to Engels, before the Middle Ages we cannot speak of 'individual sex love'. It is the invention and the glory of the bourgeois age. Of course, this new standard has fared no better in feudal or bourgeois practice than all the other standards of morality. It is ignored; but none the less, there it is. Monogamous marriage is a great step forward in the direction of civilisation and a truly human world, and despite the fact that it is also a step back in that it is founded upon the oppression of women, we must recognise the grandeur of the bourgeois achievement.

How was it done? Christopher Caudwell, the young Communist writer who was killed in the Spanish Civil War, argued that

> In their early stages bourgeois relations, by intensifying individualism, give a special heightening to sexual love. Before they crystallise out as relations to cash, bourgeois social relations simply seem to express man's demand for freedom from obsolete social bonds, and this demand for individuality is then a progressive force. Sexual love now takes on, as clearly seen in art, a special value as the expression *par excellence* of individuality. We have the emergence of that characteristic achievement of bourgeois culture, passionate love, conceived as both romantic and sensual, whereas neither Greek nor mediaeval culture could conceive romantic and sensual love except as exclusive opposites. Passionate love contributes new overtones to feeling and conscious life. Moreover, this demand for individuality was also enriching other forms of love, as long as it was revolutionary and creative. It gave men a new tenderness towards each other, conceived as a tenderness of each other's liberty, of each other's personal worth. Thus bourgeois culture in its springtime gave birth to passionate sexual love, and a tenderness for the 'liberty' – the individual outline – of other members of society. Both these are genuine enrichments, which civilisation cannot now lose.[17]

That's good news, but wait a moment, a few lines later Caudwell tells us that 'With the exhaustion of bourgeois social relations, bourgeois passionate love begins also to wither before the economic blast.'[18] If passionate love is rooted in bourgeois property relations and flowers with their flowering, how can it survive their decay and exhaustion? Why can't civilisation 'lose' these enrichments? What the historical process gave, surely the historical process can take away or, at least, transform beyond recognition.

Well, says Caudwell, a little evasively, the 'ugly possessive features of bourgeois social relations always gave bourgeois love a selfish jealous undertone'.

Passionate bourgeois love really prepared its own death . . . Today it is as if love and economic relations have gathered at two opposite poles . . . This polar segregation is the source of a terrific tension, and will give rise to a vast transformation of bourgeois society. They must, in a revolutionary destruction and construction, return in on each other and fuse in a new synthesis. That is communism.[19]

But what does this bewildering mixture of botanical, electrical, and chemical metaphors actually mean? Is communist love the same as bourgeois love minus the 'selfish jealous undertone'? But Engels himself points out that 'sexual love is by its nature exclusive'. Engels, showing the cunning of the old campaigner, avoids going into the problem too deeply by the usual Marxist cop-out: we can't know what it will be like till we get there. He says (p. 145):

What we can now conjecture about the way in which sexual relations will be ordered after the impending overthrow of capitalist production is mainly of a negative character, limited for the most part to what will disappear. But what will there be new? That will be answered when a new generation has grown up.[20]

But even Engels cannot really escape the dilemma. It is the essence of marriage that it is private and apart from the rest of society. Its 'selfishness' or 'exclusiveness' is not its undertone but its heart and soul.

Whether passionate love is to be described as Christian or bourgeois, it remains unalterably a matter of concentration, of privacy, of exclusivity. Whatever kind of love a society based on co-operation and solidarity is likely to engender, it cannot be the same sort of love as bourgeois marriage. What sort of love will it be? The answer is unmistakable: in the new society passionate love can be directed only towards the collective abstraction, towards God or Big Brother, towards the State or Society. For your individual fellow-citizens, pair-bond-partners, and offspring, you are to feel a diluted emotion, best called 'comradeship' or 'fellowship'. This is frankly recognised by Maoists and monks. It is their profession to root out attachments to particular persons with the same zeal as they try to root out the attachment to material goods. In the austerity of the enclosed order, there is no distinction drawn between the two. Both are of the world, worldly.

With endearing simplicity the Spanish anarchists resolved: 'for the illness of love, which is a sickness that can become blind and obstinate, a change of commune will be recommended.'[21] Other commune-promoters have exacted more complicated punishments for any deviation from solidarity.

Now, in fact, we have a fair idea of what this feeling of comradeship or fellowship is like. Most people have tasted the pleasures of solidarity at some time in their lives. The shared project of union, club, team, class, movement or regiment provides an adequate taste of that exhilaration and satisfaction which, it is hoped, the larger fraternity will engender. Olof Palme, the former Swedish Prime Minister, quoted with enthusiasm the lines of a Swedish poet:

> Solidarity is a wealth
> of untried possibilities.
> The future is adventure
> and there is freedom:
> to find release through fellowship.[22]

But this is not really true. Solidarity is not an entirely new adventure. It is as old as mankind, and the essence of the genuine and satisfying feelings it engenders is that they are *subordinate*. The fellow-feeling arises from the project – which may be to express, realise, make concrete the love of God or State or nation or humanity. The fellow-feeling is, therefore, subordinate to that project, whereas private sensual love between two persons has no purpose beyond itself. In so far as fellow-feeling grows out of its subordinate role, it threatens the project and thereby becomes the less fraternal. The officer who lets his affection for the men who compose his little platoon blind him to the needs of the whole army has failed in his duty. This threat of emotional *insubordination* is a constant anxiety to the promoters of fraternity. As we have seen, St Paul warns us against 'inordinate affection'.[23] At least, that is the King James Version. The Revised has 'passion'; J. B. Phillips has 'uncontrolled passion'; the New English Bible has 'lust'; the Greek is *pathos*. This prohibition has always puzzled me, and I am relieved to see that it divides not only translators but commentators. Bloomfield (1841) says it is confined to unnatural lust. Alford (1871) says it just means the erotic passion generally, as in Plato (*Phaedrus*, 265b). While the *NEB* translation may well be the best, there is no doubt that the Authorised Version is

189

more revealing. Passion is to be avoided essentially not because lust is bestial, but because its insubordination may prevent us from loving God as we ought.

The subordinate and diluted nature of comradeship permeates all fraternities from the Boy Scouts to Red Chinese communes. In fact, the tepid exhortations of Chairman Mao's *Little Red Book* have struck resonant chords in many of those who still remember Baden-Powell's *Scouting for Boys*. It lays exactly the same stress on practicality, toughness, and endurance, channelling the life of the heart into the single theme of self-sacrifice in the interests of the collective. Once the project – overriding, imperious, all-embracing, superb, terrible – has been adopted, the inter-relationships of those engaged upon it become merely instrumental. It matters not whether it is God or History or Conscience which has called us to this work. Once we have answered the call, we are committed, *engagé* like cogs in a gear. And yet there is surely something strange in committing ourselves to a project in the belief that our experience will thereby be enriched, illuminated, intensified – only to discover that this commitment asks of us first that we dilute what has been for us the most solid, innermost substance of experience. It is a distressing thought that solidarity might not itself be solid.

In fact this commitment is more than strange; it is a desolating demand. The call for a revolutionary to be 'hard' in order that fraternal love may eventually triumph is one of the most paradoxical and searching demands that men have ever made upon themselves and one another. How does this demand come to be made? The *Oxford Dictionary* gives two meanings for the verb 'to fraternise': *intransitive*, to associate or sympathise with as a brother or as brothers, and *transitive, now rare*, to bring into fraternal association or sympathy. How does the intransitive become transformed into the transitive? At what point do we cross that divide which separates the voluntary fraternisation from the forced fraternisation? The well-known German refrain put it with most brutal clarity:

> Willst du nicht mein Bruder sein,
> dann schlag ich Dir dein Schädel ein . . .

(If you won't be my brother, I'll smash your skull in.)

Old-fashioned English slang includes an affable shortening of the verb, namely, 'to frat', meaning to make friendly overtures, usually to persons or groups coming from a different class or nation. It is a far cry from this usage to the concept of class warfare elaborated by the most thorough-going fraternalist. Where and why does English fratting stop and Leninist fraternalism take over?

There is above all a difference in *tone* between the voluntary fraternisers on the one hand and the forced fraternisers on the other, between the apostles of spontaneity and the believers in revolutionary dictatorship, between Mensheviks (or revisionists or social democrats) and Bolsheviks. This difference in tone strikes one forcibly at the outset of the argument and lingers in the mind long after the ideological and tactical minutiae of the debate have faded. The true revolutionary is marked out by his ruthlessness, his sincere contempt for established law and morality, his lack of bourgeois scruple about violence or coercion. Only a person who has freed himself from the sentimental chains of existing society can really possess this hardness; he cannot achieve it without having first achieved an *intellectual* liberation. He must work through the fraternal argument to its logical conclusion.

Voluntary fraternity, it has to be argued, can never be more than partial. Because of the conflicts of economic interest which are bred by the existing social order, there will always remain enemies, strangers, backsliders, and traitors. Only in an utterly transformed social order is universal fraternity possible. The test of the true fraternalist is whether he is ready to start completely afresh, whether he has the strength of intellect and will to go through with the transformation process to the end.

The decisive moment in the making of a revolutionary occurs when he *breaks free* of the social assumptions into which he was born. This moment is lyrically celebrated in Marxist myth as the first moment of true freedom. At this point the consciousness slips its tether and hovers like a hawk over the surface of social reality, able at will both to map its true shape and to swoop down and participate in the process of changing it.

Now this may indeed be a freedom both to understand and to act but it is also a freedom *from* something which we may hesitantly describe as 'a shared creatureliness', a freedom from 'compassion' in the robust sense of that word. Nothing is more remarkable on the individual level than the conscious striving for dryness of the 'hard' revolutionary, and the contrast this aridity makes with the sometimes overpoweringly generous characters of many great labour leaders and social democrats – generous both in the sense of moral nobility and in the sense of personal abundance (convivial, emotional, sensual). They are tethered to the earth, the voluntary fraternisers. Only the believers in imposed fraternisation want or manage to break away to that empyrean where the divine interpreter resides. If we are to hasten the dawn of a truly human history, we must, it seems, leave our own humanity behind, including our families.

Yet if the family in its present form is a recent and fleeting by-product of capitalism, it is odd that both the attacks upon it and the vision of an alternative society should have altered so little in two millennia and more. The theologies and cosmologies of past ages may seem primitive and outdated to us; but the tussle between Family and Fraternity appears timeless.

For instance, in Godwin's rational society just as in Plato's Republic nobody is to know who is the father of any child. And now here comes Clem Gorman to advise us on *Making Communes*: 'In a group family, if group marriage is also being practiced, it is not desirable to know which male member was the father of which child, as this might encourage distinctions and possessiveness.'[24] The chilly, abstract tone of the fraternal vision, its negative phrasing and its lack of intensity are curiously unchanging too. The modern Counter-Culture's phrases of approval – 'spaced out', 'far out', 'cool', 'sent' – convey an almost Platonic absence of passion, closeness and tension. Meanwhile, the family continues to be denounced as 'up-tight', suffocating, inward-looking, oppressive, and selfish. Far from linking the family and the revolt against the family to stages in the rise and fall of bourgeois society, the surviving visionary and polemical literature of Western civilisation tends to suggest that the family and the fraternal ideal were social realities from the start. It also tends to suggest that the quarrels between passion and reason, between the social and the individual, between commitment and detachment are an enduring and unavoidable part of being human – and not to be easily resolved by the facile projection of philadelphia or by fabricating historical myths of a Golden Age.

No verbose and cloudy fusions of Eros and History, as attempted by Herbert Marcuse or anyone else, can hide the internal logic of the thesis. If the nuclear family is an historical aberration, then so is the passionate love which it generated. For we are not speaking here of some bourgeois invention or enrichment of thought which might survive the passing of the bourgeoisie. We are talking about the spiritual essence of the bourgeois age, the core of its social reality. Private love cannot survive the Revolution any more than private property. The destruction of privacy cannot perfect love; it can only diffuse it. To proclaim community is to condemn particularity. To seek fraternity is to flee from intimacy.

The fraternalist, of course, passionately denies that he is fleeing from intimacy. He dreams of managing to reconcile freedom and intimacy. The difficulty of achieving this is betrayed by the uneasy defensiveness which often characterises commune-dwellers. Outsiders, we are told, will not understand the pure and unconstrained nature of relations within the commune. Yet the ambivalence is often too painful to be entirely covered up.

In *The Children of the Dream*, his trenchant study of communal child-rearing in an Israeli kibbutz, Bruno Bettelheim records the agonisingly split attitude of kibbutz mothers towards their children. On the one hand,

> The founding generation knew they had no wish to replicate the family as they knew it, and of this they were entirely conscious . . . part of the ghetto existence to which kibbutz founders reacted, and possibly over-reacted, was a closeness in family life that to them seemed devoid of freedom.[25]

Private emotions, no less than private dining arrangements or private property, threatened to destroy the comradeship of the group and to re-impose the ancient tyranny of the family. They wanted the best for their children but not if it cost them their freedom.

From the practical point of view, conveniently enough, their freedom and their children's freedom were interrelated. The children live in a separate children's house, looked after by trained nurses and teachers. The parents are not bothered by screaming babies in the middle of the night; at the same time, the children are free from the jealous interference and control of parental authority. Nor are the parents supplanted in their children's affections by anybody else. The turnover of nurses and teachers is rapid; and within the peer group of children, as within the peer group of adults, close friendships between two persons are severely discouraged 'as something alien, as an effort to escape from the group'. All this is part, an indispensable part, of any *conscious* plan to build a society whose emotional satisfactions are founded on solidarity alone.

The trouble is that in such a society, however highly praised intimacy may be in theory, in practice it has to be fearfully avoided. As Dr Bettelheim says:

> Kibbutz founders hoped that by removing all external impediments to human relations they would flower most fully. What they did not recognise was that it was the shared worries about those impediments, and all the fighting in the ghetto family, that revealed its members to each other and eventually to themselves.
>
> Intimacy thrived because people depended on each other, not only for security, but also for being the only ones on whom they could safely discharge their aggressions and frustrations . . . Only inside the family – both the immediate, and the larger ghetto family – did their crying meet with empathy and compassion. Only there could one safely get rid of one's negative feelings without risking steadfast relations . . .
>
> What was overlooked [in the kibbutz system] was that one cannot really cry with some thirty people. One cannot fight with them and avoid getting badly bruised, because it is hard to make up with so many when the fighting is over, however close one's relationship with them. Two or three dozen people can sing and dance together, can laugh together, and this they did in early kibbutz days. But to satisfy the good feelings is not enough to bring about true intimacy. For that one must also feel free to vent one's anger and fear and disappointment without its having bad effects.[26]

Yet to acknowledge this difficulty would be to undermine the whole basis of the kibbutz – for it would involve nothing less than the admission that a vast scheme of social engineering designed to promote freedom and openness in human relationships had in practice tended to develop new forms of constraint and repression. Any disappointment with the degree of emotional intensity experienced in kibbutz relations cannot be admitted, even to oneself. As a result, the fraternal community often throws up in diffused form all the familiar hypocrisies of bourgeois marriage.

Bettelheim's arguments have been challenged (though supported in large measure by previous observers such as Spiro); but his description of how the kibbutz dwellers mask the superficiality of their relationships by the heartiness of their greetings rings true enough. It corresponds strikingly with the only comparable experiences most of us have: in pubs, clubs, camps, institutions, and places of work. Friendships contracted in such places tend to remain superficial. They cannot be pushed too far within the limits of the group without a certain falsity.

It is in fact the sign of a genuinely growing friendship that it should tend to set the twosome or threesome apart from the rest of the group, to draw them into a private place, both geographically and emotionally. For the converse proposition is also true: to establish intimacy is to flee from fraternity.

Intimacy always entails personal authority. In a truly intimate relationship one person makes unique claims upon another, claims for services, affection, respect and attention which can be supplied only by that other person. This body of claims, when acknowledged both 'voluntarily and as of right' (to borrow Hobsbawm's phrase), constitutes authority but not domination, because the authority is both partial and reciprocal, whereas domination is by definition one-sided. The claims of a child for care and love, even if unspoken by child or mother, are just as much a moral authority over his father as the father's claims for filial affection and/or obedience and respect. The fact that the claims may be different for the two sides of the relationship, 'asymmetrical' in the modern jargon, does not alter the fact that there *are* two sides. Nor do more symmetrical relationships (those, let us say, of ancient friendship or modern marriage) exclude the element of authority. For authority in this sense does not depend upon inequality nor does it wither away under the beneficent rays of equality. It depends solely upon one person acknowledging another person's right to make claims on him.

The authority of intimacy always has certain features from which it derives its strength. It is assumed to be personal, irreplaceable and permanent. Lacking these features, the authority is weakened just as the authority of a lame-duck President is weakened because we are already beginning to picture another man in his shoes and to make our dispositions accordingly.

In passionate love there can be no replacement envisaged. The Beloved is The One, The Only, forever. Intimacy is particular in every sense of the word. Fraternity is indifferent: fraternity makes no distinction of persons.

The suggestion that belief in the brotherhood of humanity may hide a chilling indifference to people as individuals is a familiar one. It is the criticism that Burke made of Rousseau for prating of brotherhood while dumping his children in an orphanage. It is unforgettably expressed in Dickens's picture of Mrs Jellyby, absorbed with her 'telescopic philanthropy' while completely neglecting her own under-nourished and ill-clothed family. Experience confirms the justice of such portraits, but do they represent the *perversion* of the fraternal ideal or its *logical extension*?

Mrs Jellyby, it must be remembered, is genuinely devoted to her cause. She neglects her own appearance as well as her husband. And, after all, 'the natives of Borrioboola-Gha, on the left bank of the Niger' must be a good deal worse off than even the Jellyby children. If 'her handsome eyes had a curious habit of seeming to look a long way off as if . . . they could see nothing nearer than Africa', that is because Africa was the place where her help was most needed. Might some people not approve of her philanthropy – so long as it was effective – precisely because it was telescopic? To live among the natives, to become intimate with them, is always to run the risk of paternalism. There was a revulsion against Albert Schweitzer when it was alleged simultaneously that his leper hospital was insanitary and that he behaved as a rather bad-tempered and bossy father to the lepers. Was Schweitzer perhaps less of a Good Samaritan than Mrs Jellyby?

At first sight the question seems grotesque. After all, the Samaritan 'had compassion' on the man who fell among thieves 'and went to him, and bound up his wounds, pouring in oil and wine, and set him on his own beast, and brought him to an inn, and took care of him.'[27] Surely that is just what Schweitzer did. Mrs Jellyby never left Holborn. But the matter is not quite so simple. The parable does not end there: 'And on the morrow when he departed, he took out two pence, and gave them to the host, and said unto him, Take care of him; and whatsoever thou spendest more, when I come again, I will repay thee.'[28] After the Samaritan had done his fraternal duty, having completed the formalities required by the cash nexus, he went on his way. His charity was above all effective and practical; it ceased as soon as his usefulness was at an end. And it is by the standards of the Samaritan that charitable acts are judged in the modern world.

Efficacity is the criterion. It is not the depth of feeling behind the act but its practical results which count. The scope of our duties accordingly expands with our wealth and technological resources. And the questions to be asked about any fraternal act are: will it work? And will it not only benefit the recipient but also leave him free of obligation and domination? By such standards Mrs Jellyby's project might well have been a model (assuming of course that it was economically viable and not some Victorian groundnuts scheme). The natives were to be taught to grow coffee and to fend for themselves; they were not to be subjected to the continued tyrannical and unhygienic proximity of an old white father, an awful brooding presence in the bush. The Good Samaritan is a parable of brotherhood. But it is also a parable of otherhood.

There is implicit in the idea of Brotherhood both a moving towards and a moving away, like that of soldiers dressing their ranks. The distance between each person and the next must be kept exactly equal. To allow undue proximity is to risk the re-forming of old domination and ancient selfishness. Those elements of intensity, constancy, and concentration which characterise passionate love are the elements most harmful to solidarity. Conversely, tepidity, mutability and diffusion are the inescapable qualities of fraternal relations.

We need no longer wonder why even those who believe most strongly in fraternity are so reluctant to analyse it, preferring the outline of the idea to remain vague and misty. The ideas of Freedom and Equality are far more rewarding topics. For freedom and equality are rhetorically intensifiable. The orator can promise *more* of them, just as he can promise more guns or more butter, without losing any intensity in the quality of what is promised.

But to promise more fraternity in general is to promise a weaker link between each particular pair of brothers. It is a promise to dilute the wine rather than to turn the water into wine. And in the last analysis, that is not much of a marriage feast to offer.

Those who have lived by the ideal of fraternity have tasted the watered wine. Beyond all the practical drawbacks of the commune – the hostility of the outside world, the difficulty of finding suitable land, problems of health and diet, squabbles, free-loaders – there often lies, barely acknowledged, a still more bitter disappointment with the tepidity of communal life. Frank Musgrove says that one of the sharp lessons the Counter-Culture has had to learn in recent years is that, 'Instead of promoting meaningful relationships, communes can often survive only by keeping relationships shallow.'[29] To live an open, fluid, free-floating life without limit imposes its own limits. The commune offers liberation from conventional ties; but 'shallowness' is the price to be paid for that liberation. To form deeper relationships is to re-impose the old ties; indeed it is just this idea of being tied or stuck to (or 'stuck on') another person which we call 'love'. The language of love is the language of bondage: attachment, affection, embrace. 'Those whom God hath joined together let not man put asunder.' But the commune is sunder-land or it is nothing. It is a desolate place.

Old-fashioned moralists like to imagine communes as perpetually fragmented by conflict. Fragmented they may be, but more by drift than by explosion. People just move on. After all, there is nothing to keep them in one place rather than another, no compelling reason to continue loving one person rather than another. Shallowness hardens into indifference. In the last analysis nothing matters because everything is the same. It is the tragedy of the fraternal ideal that the longing for a fuller life should so often finish in emptiness, and that what began in enthusiasm should end in apathy.

12

THE RECOVERY OF DIVORCE

This watered-down quality can, however, be made more of a virtue if it is contrasted with an institution which is the complete opposite. And it is an essential part of the fraternalist case to present marriage and the nuclear family as a horrifically cramped prison from which there is no escape. Unless you summon up the courage to make a complete break with your family, you will never breathe freely.

Look at the traditional family: bound together in one smoky hovel with grown-up and married brothers and sisters and even your grandparents hemming you in from dawn to dusk. Now, as we have seen, this is a caricature of Western family life. There was always rather more freedom and independence than used to be supposed. Adult sons and daughters did leave home, in fact were often *forced* to leave and seek work at a tender age; grandparents did not often live in the same house as their grandchildren. To have more than one married couple in a household – except in direst necessity – was in most societies a rarity.

All these qualifications will no doubt be met by the single rejoinder: *but there was no divorce.* Except for the very rich, you were tied to the same spouse for life. Even if we admit that marriages very often did break up, that wives were often deserted and often starved if they had no kin to return to, there still remains the huge fact of the legal indissolubility of marriage and the impossibility of remarriage.

And if we do away with that indissolubility and permit remarriage, are we not then destroying the very essence of traditional marriage? Even if men and women still choose to live together and exchange vows and bring up children, is their relationship not so different in kind from traditional marriage that we might as well call it something else? Can 'marriage' be merely a private contract which can be ended at the will of either party?

The answer is that, throughout a great deal if not most of recorded history, that is precisely what it was.

The most regular and universal feature of non-Christian or pre-Christian marriage is the relative ease of divorce. Certainly in Western Europe, what marks out the Christian era from earlier and later times is the insistence that marriage should *invariably* be 'till death us do part'. It is this which makes the dramatic contrast with the marriage customs of virtually all the peoples who were to be Christianised over the centuries, the Romans no less than the Anglo-Saxons, the Celts in the Dark Ages no less than most of the inhabitants of Africa and Asia who were to be converted by missionaries a thousand years later. Only the Hindus seem to have maintained anything like the strictness of the Catholic Church towards divorce.

These marriage customs were so different that it was often centuries before the Christians managed to exert effective control. Take the example of Ireland: in our time, Ireland has been the most uniformly obedient daughter of the Church and even today has not followed the rest of Northern Europe in relaxing the law of divorce.

Yet in ancient Ireland, centuries after the conversion to Christianity, divorce was freely allowed. A marriage might always be ended by mutual consent.[1] Similarly, in mediaeval Wales, the couple might, in practice, separate at the will of either or by mutual consent; the division of the household goods depended on the time and circumstances of the separation – the length of the marriage, the cause of the split and so on. Custody of the children was divided between the parents.

The rules were much the same among the Anglo-Saxons. The 'dooms of Ethelbert', albeit Christian, admit divorce by mutual consent or even at the will of one party. Even the *Penitential* of the great Archbishop Theodore in the seventh century offers a string of grounds for divorce, including adultery; he imposed only a year's delay on a woman not previously married, whose husband had been condemned to penal servitude. F. M. Stenton in *Anglo-Saxon England* says of Theodore: 'The whole tenor of his canons shows his anxiety that a moral life should not be made impossible for those whose marriages were broken by disaster.'[2]

Or take the Visigoths who created in Spain, Portugal and Southern France the most sophisticated of all the half-Roman, half-barbarian states to arise out of the ruins of the Western Empire. They were Christians, but followers of the Arian heresy. For the Visigoths, marriage or *coniugium* 'described, as it had done in Roman times, a state of union existing as a matter of social fact and created solely by the will, manifested in action, of particular individuals'.[3] It was not a church sacrament and not a state institution – although naturally it had legal consequences for both the married couple and other people.

There was undoubtedly a sexual double standard of the most extreme kind. A husband who caught his wife with her lover might kill them both. On the other hand, an erring husband was not punished at all for committing adultery with a slave girl, although he could be punished if he committed bigamy with a free woman. But in matters of divorce, the wife did have comparable rights. She could remarry if her husband committed homosexuality or bigamy. And neither husband nor wife could repudiate an unoffending spouse without his or her consent; a husband who attempted to trick his wife into giving such consent was liable to forfeit all his property to her or the children. Both wife and children had statutory rights to maintenance during the husband's lifetime and to inheritance at his death. The prime method of divorce – as in most pre-Christian and non-Christian societies – was by mutual consent, either given in writing or before witnesses.

These customs, far from being peculiar to the Teutonic and Celtic tribes of Northern Europe in times past, follow the pattern of the great majority of the human race at all times. Almost everywhere in Africa, there is divorce by mutual consent. A husband can usually divorce his wife unilaterally and without legal formality; a wife tends to need her guardian's permission.

Roman emperors from Augustus onward laid down grounds for divorce in a sequence of edicts. In the most common form of marriage, either party could end the marriage at will.

We may go back as far as the Hittites in c. 1200 B.C. and even to the Hammurabi Code in Babylon of c. 2000 B.C., and we shall still find roughly the same arrangements. In Babylon, a man might always divorce his wife at will, but he had to restore her dowry and provide for the maintenance of children. To receive this ancient alimony, however, the wife had to prove that she had fulfilled her duty. The wife could also obtain judicial separation for cruelty or neglect, but she sued at her peril, for if the fault was found to be hers, she could incur the penalty of death by drowning.

Almost everywhere we find provisions for divorce by mutual consent, divorce at the husband's wish and rather more restricted grounds on which the wife could sue – reflecting her inferior public position. Almost everywhere too, we find elaborate arrangements for the maintenance of divorced women and of the children.

Pre-Christian societies in general recognise two rights: the underlying right of individuals to divorce and remarry, and the right to compensation and maintenance of those adversely affected by the divorce.

The right of divorce was gradually eroded by the Church in its long struggle to gain control of matrimony. As we have seen, the purpose of that struggle was certainly not to elevate marriage and make it a holy thing. It was only in the twelfth century that the formula of the seven sacraments was drawn up and not until the Council of Trent in the sixteenth century that it was imposed. The purpose of controlling marriage was to minimise the uncleanness of sexual intercourse, to regularise sex for those who could not aspire to the superior state of celibacy. Council after council attempted to forbid, or to persuade the reigning Emperor to forbid divorce by mutual consent and remarriage. Yet the old customs persisted throughout the so-called Dark Ages. Marriage was so far from being a sacrament that there was no obligation to be married in church. Until about the tenth century, in most places divorce continued to be a private and secular, almost domestic matter. It was not until the so-called Hildebrandine reforms of the eleventh century that the Papacy (in the person of Hildebrand, who became Pope Gregory VII) both assumed control of the institution of marriage and managed to insist on its indissolubility. By about 1300 this control was complete.

The two centuries of Europe-without-divorce which followed were not notable for purity of morals. The licentiousness of clergy and laity alike and the even greater scandal of the Pope's agents tramping his spiritual domains hawking dispensations for annulments (the Papal Palace at Avignon was said to have been largely built on the proceeds) – all these were an important part of the reformers' case. And one of the reformers' earliest demands was for the restoration of divorce. Three years after nailing his theses to the door of Wittenberg Church, Luther pronounced marriage 'a holy thing' but not a sacrament and asserted that divorce on the grounds of adultery was plainly permitted in the Gospels. Later he went further and declared marriage 'a worldly, external thing like one's wife, child, house, garden, and so on, and therefore it belongs to the secular authorities'. Most of the reformers drew the logical conclusion that both husband and wife should be able to sue for divorce. In much of Northern Europe – Holland, Switzerland, Denmark, Norway, Sweden – marriage was soon after re-civil-ised, and laws of divorce began to develop.

In England, Cranmer's scheme of 'Reform of the Ecclesiastical Laws' envisaged dissolution for adultery, desertion, cruelty and 'where there is a fatal enmity between the spouses'. Alas, Edward VI died too soon for this to become law; and England kept a system of divorce law almost unchanged from canon law until the twentieth century.

Until the nineteenth century the Church with its control of the written word very largely managed to blanket the resentments of the unhappily married.

We can gather only by implication how ordinary people felt about the Church's restriction on divorce; complaints about the hypocrisy and licentiousness of the monastic orders, the resistance to the enforcement of clerical celibacy, criticism of the way in which papal dispensations were granted or denied for political reasons – all suggest only a grudging obedience.

The Church's rules concerning the annulment of marriage were always hotly questioned, both inside and outside the Church. Throughout the Middle Ages, it was a highly complicated and expensive business to define exactly what did constitute a valid marriage. It might be necessary to conduct a series of law-suits to clear away possible barriers. Those who married in haste then still had the convenient possibility of having the marriage subsequently declared invalid, usually on the grounds that the couple were too closely related. As Professor Colin Morris points out:

> It is a remarkable fact that almost every English king between 1066 and 1216 found himself in a matrimonial-legal tangle of this sort,

and England was in no way exceptional . . . William I and Henry I both had great difficulty in obtaining clearance from the Church for their proposed marriages. Henry II married a divorcee, Richard had major difficulties over his marriage contract with the French royal house, and John, having been once divorced, contracted a second marriage of dubious legality.[4]

The most celebrated example of the lengths to which these prohibited degrees of affinity could stretch was that a man could not marry his god-daughter and that, if such a relationship came to light, the marriage had to be dissolved.

The canon law had spawned a huge divorce industry. The efforts made on behalf of Henry VIII's struggle for a divorce from Catherine of Aragon ranged over the whole of Europe. As J. J. Scarisbrick writes:

A galaxy of Greek and Hebrew scholars, Christian and Jew, of theologians and canonists, of religious houses and universities, first in England and then on the Continent, were to be called upon to provide evidence for the king. Soon English agents were abroad, in France and Italy especially, quizzing and cajoling, ransacking libraries, interrogating university faculties, drawing up lists of signatories in this or that friary, urging canonists and Scripture scholars to take up the pen. By the end they had assembled a weighty corpus of *libelli*, tracts, opinions and *obiter dicta* from scores of scholars and institutions. Meanwhile, of course, the other side had been no less energetic. Men great and small rallied to defend Queen Catherine, meeting tract with tract, opinion with opinion. By 1529–30 the king's divorce had occasioned an international debate as violent and swift-moving, though on a much smaller scale, as the contemporary conflict between Catholic and Protestant polemicists.[5]

Was Henry's marriage to Catherine invalid because she had earlier been betrothed to Henry's brother, Arthur, since deceased? Had that marriage been consummated? If it had, did the Pope have the right to issue a dispensation? The answer depended on the interpretation of two sentences in Leviticus and one in Deuteronomy. Was the prohibition in Leviticus on marrying your deceased brother's wife the word of God and the positive instruction in Deuteronomy to marry her (to carry on the family) merely a Jewish custom, as Henry's supporters claimed? Or was Deuteronomy the word of God too and, what's more, the word which applied precisely to Henry's circumstances, as argued by Catherine's supporters, a far more numerous and distinguished assembly? Bishop Fisher of Rochester fearlessly wrote no less than seven books on Catherine's behalf; as Professor Scarisbrick remarks, 'One can only marvel that ultimate retribution was delayed until 1535.'[6]

Is it really an accident that the reformation of religion should have been based on, or at least been triggered by, a divorce – and a divorce not impelled by dynastic and political considerations alone, but by a fat man's lust? A divorce, in short, that ought to have been and was the scandal of Europe. Henry's case in canon law was a bad one; it is possible that if Catherine had not been the Emperor's aunt and Italy had not been under the Emperor's thumb, the divorce might have been granted – though even today historians disagree about that.[7] But what can we deduce from the relative ease with which Henry was able to shake off the rule of Rome? For though historians disagree too about the precise motives behind the revolt which we call the Pilgrimage of Grace – was it regional discontent mingled with attachment to the old religion? – in retrospect, it is the *lack* of opposition which strikes us most. The monasteries dissolved, the king installed as head of the Church, the Bishop of Rome shrugged off – and the English appeared to remain signally phlegmatic.

Was this a matter of general religious indifference? Or was it the result of a long tradition of resentment of rule from Rome (yet England had been regarded as among the more Papalist realms of Europe)? Or can we discern, within the unmistakable growth of anti-clericalism, a resentment at the particular claims of the Church to decide all matters relating to marriage? Did that specific intrusion into the private sphere contribute to the feeling that the Pope was an alien power meddling in matters which were, in some ill-defined sense, none of his business?

The documentary evidence is scant and oblique. All that can be said is that, as soon as we encounter men who are looking at marriage from a humanist point of view, we hear a completely modern tone of voice.

At the time of Henry's struggle for a divorce, Erasmus had already in effect consigned canon law to the dustbin and was writing:

Forcing a couple to stay together when they detest one another is dangerous. It may end in poison. Those whose marriage is already on the rocks should be granted a divorce and permitted to remarry. Paul's dictum that it is better to marry than to be tormented by passion is not inapplicable to persons once unhappily married and now separated.[8]

This was the consequence, not a contradiction, of Erasmus's high view of marriage, although he never married himself:

What more sweet than to live with her with whom you are united in body and soul, who talks with you in secret affection, to whom you have committed all your faith and your fortune? What in all nature is lovelier? You are bound to friends in affection. How much more to a wife in the highest love, with union of the body, the bond of the sacrament and the sharing of your goods! In other friendships how much there is of simulation and perfidy! Friends flit like swallows. Few continue to the end. But a wife is faithful and only death dissolves marriage, if indeed it does . . . You say, 'Your children may die.' But do you think you will have no sorrows if you are celibate? Nothing is more safe, felicitous, tranquil, pleasant and lovable than marriage.[9]

Erasmus was personally embarrassed by the dispute between Henry and Catherine; he had admired both; to Catherine he had dedicated his *Treatise on Matrimony*. He tried to avoid giving an opinion on the divorce when it was sought, as it inevitably was, although in private he robustly remarked, 'I would rather that Jupiter take two Junos than that he put away one' – in other words, he opted for bigamy.

But he distinguished between the position of a king who had to carry on a dynasty and secure the safety of a realm and the position of ordinary people contemplating marriage. In his *Colloquies* – didactic and humorous playlets – the arguments in favour of marriage always win. They are full of stories of how forgiveness and mutual tolerance can repair marital rifts, of the need to be tolerant of your in-laws and to put yourself in their shoes, of the delights of both sexual and spiritual love. Sometimes, the dialogue sounds like the advice column in *Woman's Own*.

To Xanthippe who wants to know how to make her husband kind and faithful, Eulalia replies:

> . . . See that everything at home is neat and clean and there's no trouble that will drive him out of doors. Show yourself affable to him, always mindful of the respect owed by wife to husband. Avoid gloominess and irritability. Don't be disgusting or wanton. Keep the house spick and span. You know your husband's taste; cook what he likes best. Be cordial and courteous to his favorite friends, too. Invite them to dinner frequently, and see that everything is cheerful and gay there. Finally, if he strums his guitar when he's a bit tipsy, accompany him with your singing. Thus you'll get your husband used to staying at home and you'll reduce expenses. At long last he'll think, 'I'm a damned fool to waste my money and reputation away from home on a drab when I have at home a wife much nicer and much fonder of me.'[10]

Over and over again – perhaps on the basis of his own unhappy experience of monastic life – Erasmus insists that for those without a true vocation, the monastery will be a prison and that in any case virginity is not a superior state. God does not insist or expect that man should be celibate.

Now the conventional reaction of historians and theologians to all this has been to regard Erasmus as an extreme intellectual radical; his views are described as provocative and offensive to the faithful, without the faithful being exactly defined. Ordinary people, we are led to infer, still believed what their priests told them; yet the *tone* of the *Colloquies* conveys a rather different impression, for the images and allusions are *popular*. Erasmus constantly appeals to the experience of ordinary people. His arguments invoke shared problems and relationships – babies born after three months of marriage, hostile mothers-in-law, selfish husbands; wives are told not to start a quarrel in the bedroom and not to make tactless complaints during sexual intercourse. His style of argument is rather to suggest that people ought to have the confidence of their own experience, to take hold of their own lives, and not to be afraid of deducing moral values from human instincts – among which desire is to be included as well as charity, altruism and self-denial. Erasmus, if only by implication, claims to be telling people things about life that they already know in their hearts. He crystallises into literary form the everyday assumptions of ordinary speech.

And if Erasmus is to be pigeonholed as an erratic extremist, what are we to think about Sir Thomas More? More's honesty, steadfastness and good humour are miraculously preserved for us in the anecdotes told about him and the record of his trial; it is precisely his reluctance to flatter and bow to fashion that makes him immortal. Yet in his *Utopia*, marriage follows much the same pattern as Erasmus set:

> Most married couples are parted only by death, except in the case of adultery or intolerably bad behaviour, when the innocent party may get permission from the Council to marry someone else – the guilty party is disgraced, and condemned to celibacy for life. But in no circumstances can a man divorce his wife simply because, through no fault of her own, she has deteriorated physically. Quite apart from the cruelty of deserting a person at the very time when she most needs sympathy, they think that, if this sort of thing were allowed, there'd be no security whatever for old age, which not only brings many diseases with it, but is really a disease in itself.
>
> Occasionally, though, divorce by mutual consent is allowed on grounds of incompatibility, when both husband and wife have found alternative partners that seem likely to make them happier. But this requires special permission, which can only be got after a thorough investigation by the Bencheaters and their wives. Even then they're 'rather reluctant to give it, for they think there's nothing less calculated to strengthen the marriage tie than the prospect of easy divorce.[11]

In many ways, Utopia is a cruel and puritanical place. Adultery, for example, is punished by imprisonment; a second conviction means capital punishment. There are echoes not merely of New England but of *1984* in parts of More's ideal state. But his treatment of marriage and divorce – and in particular of the plight of the abandoned wife – is gentle and sympathetic. We should not always take literary utopias literally, but in this section I think we can be sure that More was setting out his views quite straightforwardly. There is nothing in modern conceptions of marriage that could be said to be more 'humane' than the ideas of the Renaissance humanists. For the humanists were not simply criticising the rigidity of canon law and the corruption of the Church. They were, step by step, developing a critique of the Church's control of marriage – and of the way this control had *devalued* the natural qualities of marriage. Ultimately, their objection was that the Church had degraded the marriage bond by turning it into a mechanical performance of sexual duty.

These criticisms widened and deepened over the next century, with more scholars such as Fagius, Grotius and Selden joining the fray, until the grumble became a trumpet call in the hands of John Milton.

No person before or since has so thoroughly, eloquently and wholeheartedly defended the rights of men and women to divorce at will. *The Doctrine and Discipline of Divorce* makes many twentieth-century pleas for relaxation or abolition of the constraints on divorce seem modest and faint-hearted. Was his passion influenced by the calamitous start to his own first marriage – his wife left him after a few months? Perhaps, perhaps not. At any rate, his arguments are generally agreed to be grounded in the tradition of Grotius and Selden; and his elevation of the rights of conscience was his own abiding passion and that of his time.

What Milton sets out to prove is:

> That indisposition, unfitness, or contrariety of mind, arising from a cause in nature unchangeable, hindering, and ever likely to hinder the main benefits of conjugal society, which are solace and peace, is a greater reason of divorce than natural frigidity, especially if there be no children, and that there be mutual consent.[12]

Again and again, Milton asserts that certain people are simply not suited to be married either to each other or to anyone. They have 'unconjugal minds'. It often happens 'that those who have thoroughly discerned each others disposition, which ofttimes cannot be till after matrimony, shall then find a powerful reluctance and recoil of nature on either side, blasting all the content of their mutual society'.[13] The trouble is that 'Every one who happens to marry hath not the calling.'[14]

Especially interesting to modern readers is the way in which Milton goes on to enumerate the consequences of an unhappy marriage. 'All corporal delight will soon become unsavoury and contemptible.' The unhappily married man is lonelier than the single man:

> For in single life the absence and remoteness of a helper might inure him to expect his own comforts out of himself, or to seek with hope; but here the continual sight of his deluded thoughts, without cure, must needs be to him, if especially his complexion incline him to

melancholy, a daily trouble and pain of loss, in some degree like that which reprobates feel.[15]

He may seek 'to piece up his lost contentment by visiting the stews, or stepping to his neighbour's bed which is the common shift in this misfortune; or else by suffering his useful life to waste away.'[16]

Here Milton paraphrases modern ideas which would not seem out of place in the works of R. D. Laing: 'This doubtless is the reason of those lapses, and that melancholy despair, which we see in many wedded persons, tho they understand it not, or pretend other causes, because they know no remedy, and is of extreme danger.'[17]

Just as in his reference to 'those who have not the calling to marry unless nothing be requisite thereto but a mere instrumental body', Milton might be regarded as referring to natural celibates and even to homosexuals, so here he implies, as a modern doctor would, that a close connection exists between physical health and marital happiness: 'It is no less than cruelty to force to remain in that state as the solace of his life, which he and his friends know will be either the undoing or the disheartening of his life.'[18]

Here we have travelled a long way from the avoidance of fornication and the procreation of children, the first two of the Church's three main purposes of marriage. For Milton, 'the mutual society, help and comfort' is not merely the dominant, overriding purpose of marriage; it is nearly the most central and crucial thing in a man's life. It penetrates and irradiates his entire being, emotional, physical and spiritual. Indeed, we might almost say that marriage *is* a man's life. To confine him within an unhappy marriage is in effect to kill him.

This Puritan doctrine of marriage has the most radical implications. 'Love in marriage cannot love nor subsist unless it be mutual; and where love cannot be, there can be left of wedlock nothing but the empty husk of an outside matrimony, as undelightful and unpleasing to God as any other kind of hypocrisy.'[19]

But only we ourselves can judge whether we are in love; and since Milton says that you cannot be forced to love – or force yourself to love – someone who turns out to be incompatible or has an unconjugal mind, then every individual must logically have the right to say whether he or she shall stay married. Marriage cannot properly be incorporated into some social or ecclesiastical edifice; it is an entirely private and individual matter to be resolved between man and wife:

Another act of papal encroachment it was to pluck the power and arbitrement of divorce from the master of the family, into whose hands God and the law of all nations had put it, and Christ so left it, preaching only to the conscience, and not authorising a judicial court to toss about and divulge the unaccountable and secret reason of disaffection between man and wife, as a thing most improperly answerable to any such kind of trial. But the popes of Rome, perceiving the great revenue and high authority it would give them even over princes, to have the judging and deciding of such a main consequence in the life of man as was divorce; wrought so upon the superstition of those ages, as to divest them of that right, which God from the beginning had entrusted to the husband: by which means they subjected that ancient and naturally domestic prerogative to an external and unbefitting judicature.[20]

The role of the courts is properly confined to the external social consequences of marriage and divorce:

For although differences in divorce about dowries, jointures, and the like, besides the punishing of adultery, ought not to pass without referring, if need be, to the magistrate; yet that the absolute and final hindering of divorce cannot belong to any civil or earthly power, against the will and consent of both parties, or of the husband alone.[21]

Only in his assumption of male supremacy does Milton differ from what we think of as a modern attitude to divorce. The courts are for the awarding of alimony and the protection of children; 'the law can to no rational purpose forbid divorce, it can only take care that the conditions of divorce be not injurious.'[22] It may be added that even Milton's male supremacism is qualified and uneven; the emphasis on mutual consent and on the individual conscience naturally implies that women have an equal right to choose whether to marry or unmarry.

All these ideas which sound to us so modern and surprising are three hundred years old. But Milton himself regarded them as much older. For he shared the common view of the seventeenth-century radicals that the laws of divorce, like almost every other deplorable kind of bossiness, interference and domination, were part of the 'Norman yoke'. He pours scorn on 'canonical ignorance', and 'the narrow intellectuals of quotationists and common places', and calls on the Parliament of England ('worthy senators') to rescue Moses 'from the shallow commenting of scholastics and canonists', to 'reach out your steady hands to the misinformed and wearied life of man; to restore this his lost heritage into the household state'.[23]

In a splendid patriotic rhapsody, Milton reaches back beyond the Normans to the English fathers of true Christianity:

> Who was it but our English Constantine that baptised the Roman empire? Who but the Northumbrian Willibrode, and Winifride of Devon, with their followers, were the first apostles of Germany? Who but Alcuin and Wickliff, our countrymen, opened the eyes of Europe, the one in arts, the other in religion? Let not England forget her precedence of teaching nations how to live.[24]

How many people who have quoted that glorious boast remember that it occurs in the introduction to a passionate plea for divorce by consent? For England's 'precedence' was apparently that we had been first with liberal divorce laws. Our 'lost heritage' was the heritage of easy divorce.

While it may be historically unsound to claim any such precedence, Milton was at least right in saying that divorce had been easier before the Norman Conquest. Can we also claim that the Saxons felt as passionately about marriage as Milton did? That might be going too far. But we can say that the theory of the Norman yoke stretched back long before Puritan days. According to Christopher Hill,[25] some theory of the sort may well have had a continuous underground history since 1066. Less than fifty years after the Conquest, Henry I had tried to win popular support by confirming what were inaccurately called 'the laws of St. Edward the Confessor', and so helped to build the mythology of a golden Saxon past, which played its part in the struggles for Magna Carta. Now and then over the next couple of centuries, we come across odd documents which refer wistfully to the democratic justice of Saxon laws and Saxon parliaments. Evidence of this egalitarian, libertarian tradition may be scant; but how many pleas for the restoration of private property would you find in the back numbers of *Pravda*? It is certainly a reasonable surmise that the more relaxed or realistic view of divorce was regarded as one of our lost liberties.

We could perhaps also say that the rise of the Church as a secular power, followed by the rise of the absolutist State, and the intertwining and colluding of the two, have imposed a double yoke upon the independence and *privacy* of the married couple. There is a general difference between the pre-Conquest, pre-Christian marriage laws and the canon law tradition which governed marriage in England until the Divorce Reform Act of 1969. Saxon – or Celtic, or Roman – rules do seem to have been more *external*, more confined to the material consequences of a marriage for the transmission of property, and less trying to reach *inside* a marriage, to control the emotional life of the married couple. The modern, de-Churched State has withdrawn to the ancient limits of interference – not willingly and not without a struggle, but it has withdrawn. The interior emotional life of a married couple is now universally regarded as their own affair. The State's only role is, as Milton said it should be, to 'take care that the conditions of divorce be not injurious'.

Yet the seventeenth-century Establishment was right to see this retreat by Church and State as a strategic disaster. For in conceding that marriage is *too important* to allow politicians, churchmen and judges to meddle in it, the Establishment has accepted and legitimised a rival power centre. And it is this rival power centre which is the real abiding threat in the modern world to all ideologies, religions and patriotisms – namely, the family. And the right of divorce at will – which is the right to decide what does and what does not constitute a valid, living marriage – is the symptom of that power.

Only in 1981 has the Church of England Synod finally and reluctantly conceded that there are circumstances in which it would be right for a priest to remarry a divorced person in church. The Anglican recovery of divorce has taken nine centuries. The Roman Catholics have not yet recovered it.

We are told that this development is either a symptom of or a cause of the *decline* of marriage. There are two distinct groups making this criticism. On the one hand, there are traditional churchmen and conservatives who assert that easy divorce heralds the 'breakdown of family life' and poses a 'threat to social stability'. They agree with the second group – as does almost everyone else – in pointing to the 'appalling social costs' of the break-up of a marriage, and in particular to its psychological effects upon the children.

The second group, consisting of Marxists, radicals and various other communitarians, regards marriage as a fleeting historical phase in human history, caused by capitalism or repression or some other outside force. For this group, marriage is on the way out – and a good thing too for the psychic health of all of us. The right to divorce is a necessary step but only a step towards the destruction of the idea of a lifetime commitment to one partner and towards the fading-away of the selfish nuclear family.

In this book, we have been looking so far only at divorce from the inside, at the historical struggle of married couples to recover for themselves the right to decide when a marriage may be broken. Ought we not also to look at the question from the outside, from 'the wider view of society as a whole'?

Very well. But first we must observe that these outsiders who are drawing our attention to the social consequences are a curious coalition; they appear to be a mixture of those who believe marriage to be too sacred to be dissolved, except in exceptional circumstances, and of those who regard marriage as an oppressive institution, a 'prison' which is liable to cramp the spirit, poison the soul, and twist the mind. In reality, however, they are all enemies of marriage as an independent power base. In one way or another, they wish to bring our private sexual and parental arrangements under closer moral, social and legal supervision.

Their criticisms are therefore suspect from the start. The criticisms of the Church are suspect because churchmen very rarely make the necessary preliminary – of accepting the mountainous burden of guilt piled up over the centuries for the Church's barbarous cruelty to illegitimate children, pregnant unmarried women, unhappily married couples and indeed any other category which fell foul of its rules; the 'psychic casualties' of the Church's teaching on marriage can certainly rival the casualties which may result from the relaxation of the divorce laws. The comparison between a mythical past of happily married couples and a modern world of fleeting unions and abandoned children can be sustained only by historical stone-blindness or bad faith.

The historical bad faith of the second group – the overtly anti-family group – is rather different. Here it is a case of historical materialists who seem curiously reluctant to apply simple historical and economic analysis to the history of divorce.

What has happened is that, for the first time in this millennium, the working class has gained control of marriage and divorce. The huge rise in the number of divorces is not because bourgeois life is inherently unsatisfying, or because marriage is hell, or because man is lost without external controls on his behaviour. It is simply because divorce is now cheap and simple.

In the Middle Ages, divorces could be obtained only by princes who hired a good canon lawyer. In the seventeenth and eighteenth centuries, a few noblemen obtained divorces by means of private Acts of Parliament which were extremely expensive. In the nineteenth and early twentieth centuries, the upper-middle classes could obtain divorces, and solicitors and barristers grew fat on the takings. In the Middle Ages and in the Vatican to this day, the divorce (or, as we now say, annulment) had to be wangled by finding obscure reasons why the marriage had never been valid; in the nineteenth and early twentieth centuries, the divorce had to be wangled by fictitious adulteries in Brighton hotels.

This slow expansion of the divorcing classes has rapidly and irreversibly speeded up since the Second World War. In England and Wales, the number of divorces has increased from fewer than 10,000 a year before 1939 to 58,000 in 1970 and about 140,000 a year at the end of the 1970s. At least four practical causes spring to mind.

First, the introduction of legal aid for divorce in 1950. The income limits were changed in 1960 and have been changed again since. The legal costs to couples who wish to divorce have been reduced to negligible proportions.

Second, the Divorce Reform Act of 1969 made divorce easier, simpler and less painful. Not only were the grounds for obtaining divorce widened, but the adversarial, hostile nature of divorce proceedings was softened. The introduction of the concept of 'irretrievable breakdown' removed much of the viciousness and the hypocrisy. Divorce by mutual consent after two years' separation and by the wish of one partner alone after five years apart reduced lawyers' fees as well.

Third, the Welfare State from 1948 onwards provided a safety net for divorced wives which was at any rate an improvement on the old Poor Law and the pre-war Public Assistance. If ex-husbands could not or would not maintain their wives, the wives would not starve. The working-class couple was no longer forced to cling together to stay alive.

Fourth, general affluence meant that couples could afford to marry at an earlier age. They did not have to wait so long to save up the money necessary to start married life. This not only contributed to the immense overall increase in the number of marriages, but it must also have much inflated the number of hasty, ill-advised matches which are more liable to break up.

These are huge changes. Similar changes have taken place in many Western countries; almost all the Northern or predominately Protestant countries of Europe have divorce laws which are as relaxed as Britain's, if not more so; Mediterranean, Catholic countries follow at a slower pace.

To account for how these changes came to be made, we do not need to assume a change in 'attitudes'. This is unmistakably a change in the balance of social *power*. Universal suffrage has broken through to provide the mass of voters with the access to divorce which was previously reserved for the rich; affluence has enabled the necessary arrangements to be made out of public funds.

What we have experienced is a simple, once-for-all jump from divorce controlled by the State and the Church to divorce controlled by the married couple. We cannot even fairly compare the behaviour of ordinary people today with, say, the behaviour of princes or noblemen in time past, because even the most powerful aristocrats were marrying and divorcing within the assumptions and with the permission of the controlling authorities; their freedom was conditional upon a general observance of the pieties and formalities.

Free and universal access to divorce is something quite new in the Christian era – as remarkable a social change as free and universal access to reliable contraception. This is the first time in modern history that the married couple has enjoyed the power to make its own judicial decisions.

Once it is understood that we are dealing with a change in power relationships between the married couple and society, certain other things become apparent.

Public, visible power brings with it inescapable responsibility. Once it is seen that power to do something, to refrain from doing it or to do it in a different way rests with a specific person, the scope to commit one's own mistakes is thereby widened, one's ability to dodge the blame for them thereby reduced.

In one way, freely available divorce does reduce the stigma of marriage failure. Divorce becomes more common; 'everyone gets divorced these days'. The law itself tries to soften the humiliation by talking of 'incompatibility' or 'breakdown' rather than 'blame'. Splitting couples are regarded as comparable to colours that clash or cars that break down. The Americans even borrow a term from car insurance; Senator Edward Kennedy and his wife were reported as planning a 'no-fault divorce'.

Yet in another way, the humiliation is far deeper than it was. For married couples have taken control of marriage; their weddings are not arranged for them by their families, their parents' permission is not often sought, sometimes the parents are not informed. If the wedding is held in church, it is normally held on the couple's own terms, as a family celebration; often no religious commitment is sought or given. These outward and visible signs mirror an inner conviction that marriage is too important to allow any outside force to meddle with it; this Milton-like view raises both the commitment to and the expectation of marriage. When a marriage breaks down, it is as great a fall as Lucifer's.

How great a personal calamity the break-up of a marriage usually is often comes as a shock both to the divorced couple and their friends and relations. Profound depression or terrifying mania, or both, often strike apparently equable temperaments in the aftermath. We are surprised, I suppose, because the practical ease of divorce has led us, perhaps unconsciously, to believe that the whole business is now rather casual; 'attitudes have changed'; 'marriage is just a piece of paper' – and divorce another piece of paper. For most people, the reality is not like that.

They often feel they have failed in the most precious business of life. Indeed, this change in marriage-power is not unlike the change from being an employee to running one's own business. If the satisfactions increase, so do the worries and the risks. Marriage becomes a career, something to be worked at, rather than something you are.

Many people, particularly in the United States, argue that marriage cannot bear the weight placed upon it. They claim that the failure rate is too high and that many people would be happier living in a less intense, looser relationship with more than one person.

Before committing ourselves too deeply to the consideration of alternatives to marriage, we must be aware of our own historical context. We ought to recognise how new and startling is this liberation of marriage from its control by Church and State and from its constriction by economic scarcity. In Britain, this liberation is barely ten years old. Many of the first effects have been the result of pent-up demand. Thousands of people were divorced who would have been divorced years ago, had divorce been easier. Over the past forty years, there has been a huge increase in the numbers of people marrying in their teens and early twenties – a departure from previous known history in Western Europe. This increase must be connected with the greater economic and social freedom of the young, and this too may have contributed to the increase in the divorce rate. Most important of all, a far higher proportion of the population gets married at some stage in their lives than ever before. There are simply far more marriages. In short, the huge increase in the divorce statistics may be attributed to plenty of practical reasons which have nothing to do with the emotional intensity of modern marriage. As Ronald Fletcher argues persuasively in *The Family and Marriage in Britain*, there is simply no evidence which would permit us to speak of the breakdown of the family or the growing instability of family life.

Freedom is alarming; all individual power carries with it a certain loneliness. The freedom to marry at will carries with it the risk of failure. So do most commitments. Indeed, that is implicit in our speaking of someone's being committed to something – a cause, a group, a belief, another person. We mean that he or she is *risking* a part of his or her life. The risk may be expressed in terms of emotion, time or money. But the element of risk is essential.

The rate of divorce is not in itself an argument against marriage, any more than the number of bad poems is an argument against poetry. The risk of failure is not to be avoided. What modern divorce laws ensure is that at least the risks are known. If, in spite of these risks being so publicly advertised, young people persist in rushing into this perilous enterprise, there is, in a democracy, little more to be said. All efforts to bring marriage back under some kind of public control are, quite simply, illegitimate. For if freedom is perilous, it is also irreplaceable and unanswerable.

13

WOMEN, POWER AND MARRIAGE

The history of the family is more like a tug-of-war than a long march. All the evidence that we have put together here suggests that the struggle between the family and the 'alternative family' of brotherhood – Church, State or commune – goes back as far as we have any recorded knowledge. During some periods, often lasting centuries, as with the Church's control of marriage in the Middle Ages, the alternative family is on top. According to the monastic ideal, brothers and sisters are nearer to God than husbands and wives. In England, between the Norman conquest and the dissolution of the monasteries, it must have seemed unlikely that the popular view of marriage would ever manage to reshape law and custom to suit its purposes. Indeed, it has taken nine centuries for the law of divorce to be relaxed so as to serve human and not divine ends. But just as the popular view of marriage has come to dominate law and politics in the twentieth century, so the old impatience with the constraints and obligations of family life has cropped up again among the young. The alternative families mushroom again in workshops, squats and communes, all radiating the innocent assumption that this is all happening for the first time. The tug-of-war continues.

The material we have been considering may seem not only unfamiliar but oddly selected. I have scarcely mentioned any of the subjects which you might expect to see discussed in a study of marriage; endogamy versus exogamy, the incest taboo, the property arrangements surrounding marriage – bride price, dowries, jointures and so on – and, above all, the legal and social position of women. Simone de Beauvoir and Germaine Greer have scarcely had a look-in.

This is not because I regard either 'feminist history' or the economic approach to history as trivial or irrelevant to the history of the family. But both present a danger which is that, if you start from that end, you are liable to suffocate the evidence of the inner life of the family. You are liable also to take it for granted that this inner life is directly and exclusively shaped and controlled by economic and political circumstance.

If, for example, you start from the evidence of property arrangements, you may conclude that women in traditional society were usually considered primarily as pieces of property. From the legal point of view, this may well be true of certain societies – although we shall need to modify the conventional view on this too – but the economic preparations for marriage need not and cannot wholly determine what happens after marriage. The fact of living together in the same household inescapably creates emotional connections. We know this to be true even in cases where the relationship is one of officially sanctioned, legal oppression. How much greater is the possibility in relations within a family consisting of two and only two adults of the same class living together for twenty or thirty years, until one of them dies.

The intensity of emotion must be related to the size of the family. Attempts to dismiss household size as a statistical triviality fly in the face of all human experience. And we know that the two-adult family has been the norm throughout Western history. Moreover, although death cut many marriages shorter than it does today, Peter Laslett estimates that, in England between 1500 and 1849, people lived on average with their first spouses for a period of twenty years.[1] Contrary to the claim by Philippe Ariès that marriages seldom lasted more than twenty years at most, a fifth of all marriages in traditional England lasted thirty-five years or more – a good run even in our own time. It simply is not true that, as an earlier generation of historians argued, marriage could not last long enough to provide the basis for family life or to 'socialise' the child.

Moreover, from the start of recorded history, people have understood perfectly well the way in which living together creates emotional connection. In one of his dialogues on the family, Leon Battista

Alberti – who, although a great architect, is generally regarded as a rather pedestrian 'bourgeois' writer from whom great psychological insights are not often to be expected – has one of his speakers describe the state of marriage in 1432:

> We may consider the love of husband and wife greatest of all. If pleasure generates benevolence, marriage gives an abundance of all sorts of pleasure and delight: if intimacy increases good will, no one has so close and continued a familiarity with anyone as with his wife; if close bonds and a united will arise through the revelation and communication of your feelings and desires, there is no one to whom you have more opportunity to communicate fully and reveal your mind than to your own wife, your constant companion . . .
>
> Children are born, and it would take a long time to expound the mutual and mighty bond which these provide. They surely ally their parents' mind in a union of will and thought.[2]

We have seen how much people minded about unhappy marriages at all times in our past; we have seen too how highly prized married happiness was, even by the Church. To suggest that the degree of happiness or unhappiness was only a minor element in life compared with, say, the salvation of the immortal soul is to assume a great deal more than we know.

Feminist historians – particularly the earlier ones – have often relied on suspect evidence. They have tended to follow, although with some reservations, the well-trodden trail: the patriarchal family, the troubadours, the rise of capitalism, Engels. This is scarcely surprising. There was, after all, until recently little other history for them to work on. It is noticeable that the more recent writings of, say, Sheila Rowbotham and Betty Friedan are rather more cautious and qualified in tone.

But the dubious nature of some of their historical sources would not necessarily disprove their general thesis: that the legal and economic subjection of women has historically evolved a certain type of 'feminine' personality. Women, we are told, are expected and often compelled by the economic system to be secondary, negative, modest, unassertive, directed towards marriage and the pleasure and service of men; they have been successfully moulded by the system to play this role, even in a sense to *be* like that. Even if feminist historians may have given an imperfect account of how women came to be oppressed, that oppression may be none the less real and the result of a developing historical process.

On the other hand, the effect of oppression upon behaviour may not be as simple and direct as historians presume. Feminists themselves have often noticed disquieting examples of assertive women within the most blatantly oppressive structures – the harem, for example. Again and again, we come across fragments and wisps of evidence which suggest that the external oppression by laws and command-ments fails to keep women totally downtrodden. Indeed, at times in the Middle Ages we are almost deafened by complaints of hen-pecked men, of women bored by their dreary and repulsive husbands, of women asserting their right to choose husbands or lovers. Men are constantly made to look fools, much as they are in Hollywood comedies. None of this means that the treatment of women was not oppressive, unfair and sometimes horrifyingly cruel; but to describe women as downtrodden and nothing else, or at least to suggest that all women stayed downtrodden, seems less than the truth.

What I think is wrong is not so much the unreliability of the history as the crudity of the connection between the way women were treated and the effect upon their spirits and their attitudes. This crude materialist account of feminine psychology produces what I will call the 'mute thesis' about women before the twentieth century.

The mute thesis argues that women were in fact silent and unasser-tive as men wanted them to be. Women stayed mum and did what they were told. They did not choose their husbands; they did not even ask to choose their husbands. They did not expect to love their husbands or to be loved by them; they did not, until comparatively recent times, expect to find a satisfying human relationship as between equals. They exerted no power within the household; they were simply the crea-tures of their husbands, one step up from the servants.

And because of these entrenched expectations of little or no emo-tional satisfaction in marriage, their other responses, we are told, tended to shrivel too; they became impoverished human beings. They expressed little emotion even at the death of their children. As for the deaths of their husbands, their mourning was purely formal and merely conformed to the norms of grief prescribed by the dominant menfolk.

There is even a myth, which has been a long time dying, that women in times past were mostly unacquainted with sexual pleasure;

equality of orgasm was said to be a discovery of the twentieth century. Now this myth of course could not stand up to the slightest historical examination; only by restricting enquiry to the official propaganda of polite society in the high Victorian age did it even *look* plausible. However far you go back, it is difficult to see much evidence of inequality of ardour. If anything, the literature of the past assumes that women are by nature more amorous. Chaucer and Boccaccio, Montaigne and Brantôme are filled with stories of men who are too old or too puny to satisfy their women. When Montaigne discusses the advisability of arousing women's sexual desire, it is not because their desire is feeble or unnatural but, on the contrary, because it is so terrifyingly powerful that all sorts of calamitous consequences may follow.

Simone de Beauvoir herself quotes Montaigne's estimate of women: 'They are incomparably more capable and ardent than we in the act of love.'[3] Madame de Beauvoir does not go in for vulgar comparisons; however, her own characterisation is equally damning to insecure men:

> Because no definite term is set, woman's sex feeling extends towards infinity; it is often nervous or cardiac fatigue or psychic satiety that limits woman's erotic possibilities, rather than a specific gratification; even when overwhelmed, exhausted, she may never find full deliverance: *lassata nondum satiata*, as Juvenal put it.[4]

Finally to dispose of the myth that until recent times, Western men were unacquainted with female sexuality or that female sexuality was in some way a secret, let us refer to Brantôme, a successful soldier, courtier and traveller in the sixteenth century. In *Les Dames galantes*, this coarse Renaissance clubman appears to have collected every scabrous anecdote and popular *canard* about sex that had been floating around French society for the past half century. Here he invents a dialogue between a man and a woman as to who ought to be on top during intercourse and quotes the case of a pretty lady:

> Who was once waked by her husband from a profound sleep to do it. After he had done, she said to him: 'you've done it and I haven't.' And because she was on top of him, she bound him with her arms, hands, feet and intertwined legs and said: 'I'll teach you to wake me up again' and battering, shaking and shoving beyond endurance her

poor husband who was underneath her and who could not even uncouple and who sweated, panted, grew weary and cried mercy, she made him do it again against his will.[5]

Aubrey's tale of Sir Walter Raleigh gives some idea of the vulgar view in the sixteenth and seventeenth centuries:

He loved a wench well; and one time getting one of the Maids of Honour up against a tree in a wood ('twas his first lady) who seemed at first boarding to be something fearful of her honour, and modest, she cried, 'Sweet Sir Walter, what do you me ask? Will you undo me? Nay, sweet Sir Walter! Sweet Sir Walter! Sir Walter!' At last, as the danger and the pleasure at the same time grew higher, she cried in the ecstasy, 'Swisser Swatter, Swisser Swatter!'[6]

Perhaps most remarkable of all is the description given by the Abbess Hildegard in her medical handbook written in the middle of the twelfth century:

For when the storm of passion rises in a man, it churns around him as though in a mill. His sexual organs are then like the smithy in which the marrow delivers its fire. Then that forge passes the fire onto the male member and makes it flame up mightily. By contrast when the breath of lust rises up from the woman's marrow, it comes into the womb, which hangs below the navel and stimulates the woman's blood into a state of excitement. But since the womb occupies a large and relatively open space in the abdomen, that force is able to spread throughout the woman's abdominal region and so fires her with passion less violently, although more frequently because of the moistness.[7]

Hildegard (1098–1179) was an abbess in the Rhineland, later sanctified, a pious and respected figure who corresponded with popes and emperors. Her handbook contains the best medical advice then available. Far from regarding her as a crank, abbots and bishops sought out her company and advice. Her description of the physiological effects of sexual intercourse apparently raised no eyebrows.

But Hildegard's interest in sex was not merely physiological. She was an eloquent proponent of *mutuality* in love between man and woman, based upon physical union. 'It is the power of eternity itself that has created physical union and decreed that two human beings should become physically one.' Each partner can attain divinity through the other's love. 'The man and the woman are therefore so joined together that each is the other's work of art and could not exist without the other.'[8]

She carries through this belief in marriage as a reciprocal act of creation by investigating how the different types of men affect the women they fall in love with. The kind of men most apt for love, for example,

> can have an honourable and fruitful association with women, but they can also restrain themselves, and regard them with looks of affection and moderation. For the eyes of such men come admirably into accord [*symphonizant*] with those women, whereas the eyes of other men are fixed on them like arrows. And whereas the voices of the others seem to women like a raging storm, theirs are like the sound of a lute; where the thoughts of those others break out like hurricanes, these are known as sensitive lovers and highly honoured. Often they too suffer deeply when they practise this restraint as far as they can, but there is in them a temperate kind of prudence which is a womanly art and which they draw from the feminine element in their nature. For they possess a sensitive understanding.[9]

Could any modern treatise on marriage, whether written by priest, doctor or counsellor, convey more exactly the implications, for women, of the ideal of mutual love? The range of views held on marriage, in both its physical and its emotional aspects, at the beginning of the twelfth century seems to have been rather wider than we were taught. And the 'discovery' and encouragement of the feminine element in male persons seem to have taken place rather earlier. So too does the idea of marriage as a symphonic process.

Today, historians have quietly dropped the myth that women in times past either were ignorant of sexual matters, or pretended ignorance or experienced little or no sexual pleasure. Only the shell of that myth lingers on in the implication that somehow men always used to remain *in control* of women's enjoyment. But how was this achieved if so many men were terrified and exhausted by women's sexual demands – as folklore indicates?

Yet surely the non-sexuality myth is vital for the full feminist case. For if women *were* experiencing sexual pleasure – demanding it in

225

fact and complaining when they did not get it – then they cannot have been quite as unequal in the most intimate and central aspects of marriage as we were told they were. And if they were expressing their sexual demands so uninhibitedly, it seems reasonable to assume that they were expressing themselves in other ways too, by letting their husbands know whether they loved or hated them, by shouting at their families, by loving and caressing their children and by grieving for them when they died. If mediaeval women were so sexually assertive, what becomes of the mute thesis?

I hasten to repeat that none of this is intended to suggest that the oppression of women – or of any category of people – is lessened or made tolerable simply because its victims are not totally crushed by it. My argument is directed solely to the crude materialism which is almost always Marx-ish even when it is not explicitly Marxist. What is objectionable is the assumption that material circumstances always crush and deform people in a uniform and historically predictable way. Most people are resilient some of the time; some people are resilient all of the time. Women are supposed to be more resilient than men. By saying that, I do not mean that everyone is equally resilient; some people do have the spirit or the life crushed out of them; huge emotional costs are paid. But to assume that women have no life in them beyond what society allows or trains them to express is to *dehumanise* women by reducing them to men's computer print-outs.

I want only to rely on the evidence. And the evidence shows two things, as clearly as can be expected of any evidence concerned with times which are remote and with thoughts and feelings which are unlikely to be documented in the Public Record Office: first, as far back as we have any evidence at all, in Western Europe the ideals of love *and* equality were both present in the popular view of marriage; second, among ordinary people, to be happily married was always regarded as one of the most important pieces of good fortune in life. The Church, the State, systems of inheritance and other aspects of law and custom might present obstacles, but no ordinary person ever imagined that marriage was unimportant.

Throughout the Middle Ages – as before and since – there was an *argument* about marriage going on. To take the anti-marriage, anti-woman stuff as showing *the* attitude of the times is to miss out half the evidence; it is also to miss the whole atmosphere of the debate –

combative, ironic, indignant, passionate, playful.

At the beginning of the fourteenth century Jean de Meung, who wrote the second part of the *Roman de la Rose*, pointed out a stream of mocking abuse of women and marriage and of contrasting praise of carefree lechery. This grisly French tradition was carried on throughout the fourteenth century by writers such as Eustache Deschamps in such works as *The Darkness of Marriage*, *The Complaint of the Newly Wed Man* and *The Mirror of Marriage*. Women were denounced at interminable length as being unpredictable, garrulous, fickle, shrewish – and, of course, whores. Reading this stuff is like being forced to listen to an endless series of stand-up comics making jokes about The Wife and The Mother-in-law.

At the same time, though, there was a vigorous counter-attack in progress. The most famous feminist of the time was Christine de Pisan (c. 1364–c. 1430), the daughter of an Italian physician in the service of Charles V. She was brought up in Paris, became a keen French patriot, married and was left widowed at the age of twenty-five. Widowhood, she said, had made her fall 'from freedom into slavery'; she was 'a turtle dove without a mate', 'a sheep without a shepherd', 'a ship without a skipper, languishing in orphanhood'. She took on what she called a manly role with energy, writing poems and treatises on popular subjects from the education of women to the laws of chivalry, although she continued to claim that she would rather have been a wife again.

Christine tried to expose the dreary shallowness of Jean de Meung's praise of Don-Juanism by asking: 'Would it really grieve you less to pretend to love me in order to have your pleasure with my body than to lose time and money, soul and sense by falling in love?'[10]

For her own part, Christine said she would prefer that her son should fall completely in love with a good woman rather than that he should deceive several. After all, who were these women who were to be deceived? Were they wild beasts to be caught in traps? 'By God, these are your mothers, your sisters, your daughters, your wives, your friends; they are yourselves and you are themselves. Go on then, deceive them if you like.'[11]

Christine was not and did not claim to be a lone voice. The arguments she put were put by plenty of others, most notably by Jean Charlier de Gerson, chancellor of the University of Paris, one of the greatest humanist scholars of his day. Gerson asked whether any man would be stupid enough to go and tell a prince that his wife was a whore or to tell the prince's daughters, 'I advise you to abandon yourselves entirely to the pleasures of the flesh and to any man who will pay you a decent price.' Women were not to be regarded merely as instruments for male pleasure; and the simplest way of pointing out the lecher's hypocrisy was to ask him: 'How would you like it if it was your daughter who . . . ?'[12]

To take Jean de Meung and Deschamps as the only or the dominant voices of their time is like taking Hugh Hefner and his '*Playboy* philosophy' as the dominant twentieth-century attitude towards women. At a more elevated literary level, this is just what Kate Millett does in *Sexual Politics* when she uses D. H. Lawrence, Henry Miller and Norman Mailer as prime examples of male attitudes to women. Now I do not see how any rational reader could fail to notice how the imaginative powers of Lawrence and, to a lesser extent, of Mailer, are continually being damaged if not destroyed by a terrible egotistic insensitivity to other people and so by a near-total inability to portray characters or relationships in the round; what they write about women is at best patronising, at worst bestial and usually loopy. The adolescent narcissism which produces such unpleasant fantasies is neither new nor confined to good writers.

Such writers cannot honestly be taken, now any more than in the thirteenth and fourteenth centuries, as accurate or comprehensive guides to the emotional realities of marriage in their societies – any more than the marriages of Lawrence, Mailer and Miller themselves could be taken as typical.

But if we once concede that traditional marriage, however flawed, could have some emotional life of its own – could indeed scarcely help having some emotional life and generating some kind of two-way relationship between husband and wife – then we ought surely to look at the connection between marriage and society *from the inside out*. Instead of marriage being a puppet show created by one huge, eternal, all-powerful masculine enemy, entirely for his own pleasure and convenience, we may begin to see marriage as an autonomous, natural and moral institution threatened and often oppressed from outside by a series of enemies thrown up by history. On this interpretation, it is not the family which represents a passing historical phase or sequence of phases – but rather its enemies.

Take, for example, the way in which Church and State combined in the sixteenth century to insist on the supreme authority of the Husband and Father. The head of the household was supposed to mirror in the family the authority of the King in his kingdom and, above the King, of God in His universe. Any hint of equality within the family would have undermined the crucial symmetry of this hierarchical pyramid. As remnants of democratic institutions were gradually being stamped out all over Europe during the rise of the absolutist monarchies in the sixteenth and seventeenth centuries, so kings and bishops too laid increasing stress upon paternal authority in the household.

Paternal authority was, of course, not an innovation. It was established in both the Old and New Testament in the image of God and Father and in the institution of the papacy. And yet throughout the Middle Ages, there had been an alternative pattern of marriage – a pattern of equality between husband and wife. How else could there have been these endless and often wearisome debates as to who should rule the household? Now this equality may seem to modern feminists inadequate and partial; in material terms, it was more a question of recognising and delimiting a domestic sphere in which the wife might reign supreme. In the outside world, male supremacy was not to be threatened. Nevertheless, the equality was presented, as we have seen in Chaucer, as an emotional and spiritual thing; and this the Church too could not entirely refute, as it was implicit in the Christian doctrine of the equal worth of every human soul and of the remembered equality of women in the early Church.

And in the real world it was impossible that men should continually reign supreme in *every* household. Many households were ruled by widows; in others, men were away at the wars. There were feeble men, like most of the Wife of Bath's five husbands. The wife's dominance might be not only domestic but managerial too; under certain conditions, she might run the farm. A huge variety of situations evaded the official orthodoxy.

Most of the time, what we are listening to is the voice of officialdom. Our reading-matter consists almost exclusively of the equivalents of *Pravda* and *Izvestia*; only the occasional refugee or smuggled-out *samizdat* suggests the complexity of reality or the extent of resistance to the regime.

There is always a danger in relying too naïvely on official propaganda; in trusting too much in the claims of Church and State to have subjugated half the human race within a totally controlled institution of marriage.

We accept that, in Soviet Russia, only careerists believe in Communism; ordinary Russian citizens, we know, are cynical, drunk or otherwise preoccupied with children, sport or religion. Yet it is widely assumed that Men have succeeded completely in subjugating Women throughout most of recorded history, not merely to the extent of making them stay at home, clean, cook and look after children, but managing totally to dominate their minds.

If, on the other hand, we once accept that women retained a considerable amount of emotional autonomy, we may wish to re-examine the conventional assumptions about their lack of practical and material independence.

In fact, if you actually consult mediaeval historians – instead of relying on sentimental myths about the Middle Ages – you may find surprises. The great F. W. Maitland in his *History of English Law* points out that, although a woman could hold no public office, 'After the Norman Conquest the woman of full age who has no husband is in England a fully competent person for all the purposes of private law; she sues and is sued, makes feoffments, seals bonds, and all without any guardian . . . '[13]

Later on, in the thirteenth century,

Women are now 'in' all private law, and are the equals of men. The law of inheritance, it is true, shows a preference for males over females; but not a very strong preference, for a daughter will exclude a brother of the dead man, and the law of wardship and marriage, though it makes some difference between the male and the female ward, is almost equally severe for both. But the woman can hold land, even by military tenure, can own chattels, make a will, make a contract, can sue and be sued. She sues and is sued in person without the interposition of a guardian; she can plead with her own voice if she pleases; indeed – and this is a strong case – a married woman will sometimes appear as her husband's attorney. A widow will often be the guardian of her own children; a lady will often be the guardian of the children of her tenants.[14]

Dr Alan Macfarlane in *The Origin of English Individualism* offers further evidence that women were not without some measure of independence. Eileen Power, writing about 'The Position of Women',[15] points out that there were women villeins and cotters in most manors; some of these were widows, but others were obviously unmarried. In the fifteenth century, women harvest workers were often paid the same daily rate as the men. In the manorial courts not only did women conduct their own lawsuits, but also women were occasionally revealed as village money-lenders. In the manor of Battle, Sussex, in the thirteenth century, women could and did 'remain unmarried land-holders, buying and selling lands and rent charges as freely and often with no less rigour than men'.[16]

And this measure of power and influence was not a novelty some-how connected with the Norman Conquest. In Anglo-Saxon England, as among the Franks, it was upon the King's wife that the Pope often relied for the King's conversion. The Pope, for example, wrote to Ethelburga, the Christian wife of Edwin, the pagan king of North-umbria, enclosing a silver mirror and an ivory and gold mirror, asking her to use her influence to bring her husband into the Church. Edwin was indeed converted, though whether by his wife or by the mission-ary Paulinus we cannot be sure. Ethelburga was the daughter of Ethelbert, king of Kent, whose conversion by St Augustine had itself been influenced by his Christian wife, Bertha. Now Bertha was the great-granddaughter of Clovis, King of the Franks, whose wife Clotilde had much to do with his own conversion. If we look back to the first great royal conversion, that of the Emperor Constantine under the influence of his mother Helena, we cannot help noticing not only the crucial importance of this royal 'chain effect' for the spread of Christianity but also the unmistakable importance of women in the spiritual and domestic spheres. In countries such as Denmark and Norway, without such feminine influence, Christianity failed to make headway until two or three centuries later.

And when death precipitated women into those positions of su-preme public power from which otherwise the system tried to debar them, they did not hesitate to exercise their authority. Alfred the Great's eldest daughter ruled Mercia with an iron hand after her father's death and put up fierce resistance to the Vikings. Between the middle of the ninth century and the middle of the tenth century, the Holy Roman Empire was effectively governed for most of the time by a succession of queen mothers, who were honoured by such titles as *imperatrix augusta*. Even before being widowed, these powerful consorts of Otto I, Otto II, Otto III and Henry II were often described as co-rulers.

In the ecclesiastical sphere, abbesses no less than abbots were liable to become overmighty magnates. The Pope had to instruct Charlemagne to issue an edict forbidding both abbots and abbesses to keep either a pack of hounds or a private jester. And it was not unknown for abbesses to rebel against exclusion from the priesthood. Again, Charlemagne had to issue an edict forbidding abbesses to give the blessing, lay on hands or place the veil on novices.

Anglo-Saxon women were often large land-owners in their own right, as place names such as Wolverhampton (Wulfrun's chief estate) and Adderbury, Oxfordshire (Eadburg's manor) still attest. It is also clear that women had considerable freedom to dispose of their estates as they pleased, as the following court case shows:

> At a shire meeting at Aylton, Herefordshire, in the early eleventh century one Edwin, Enniaun's son, brought a claim against his mother for possession of a piece of land. The meeting sent three thanes to examine the woman's case, 'and she became very angry with her son, and summoned her kinswoman Leofflaed, Thorkil's wife, and said to her in their presence, "Here sits my kinswoman Leofflaed to whom I grant after my death my land, my gold, my clothing and apparel, and everything I own." And then she said to the thanes, "Act like thanes, and announce truthfully my message in the presence of all the worthy men at the meeting. Tell them to whom I have granted my land and all my possessions, leaving nothing at all to my own son. Ask them to be witnesses of this." ' The thanes made their report, and Thorkil claimed the land, asking the meeting to reject Edwin's counter claim, which they did.[17]

These property rights naturally corresponded to and were interwoven with occupational rights and interests, as the great trading cities of the Middle Ages began to flourish. In the laws of many mediaeval German cities, equality between men and women in business matters is explicitly stated; in Munich, for example, 'A woman who stands in the market and buys and sells is to enjoy all the rights which her husband enjoys in relation to inheritance and property.' How could it be otherwise, since husband and wife were so often effectively business partners? The wife would run the firm while the husband was away buying stock in Venice or Genoa; she might trade on her own behalf in fine textiles; she often kept the accounts. Her rights grew out of the fact of her indispensability, just as the concrete power of the abbess posed a recurring threat to the male supremacist theory of the Church. Even where Man unremittingly strove to prevent Woman from rearing her head in public, individual men failed or did not try to make their supposed supremacy stick.

In classical times, although Man in both Greece and Rome was constantly passing laws to restrict women's rights to inherit, own or manage property, somehow Woman continued to accumulate land. What happened was that individual men found ways of getting round the laws in order to look after their own wives and daughters. In Rome, for example, the father of an only daughter might make over his whole property, as a trust, to a male friend on the understanding that he would later transfer the whole estate as a gift to the daughter. This was a risky device, for the trust was not enforceable at law, and a treacherous trustee could simply hang on to the property.

With the coming of the Empire, the law was replaced, and thereafter a daughter could inherit straightforwardly. There were complicated rules surrounding the wills of married women, but unmarried people and women without children were free to dispose of their property as they wished.

In Greece, at least in Hellenic times, the situation was roughly comparable. The private imperatives – of a man's desire to look after his female dependants and to recognise their closeness and affection, the reality of a woman's power over her property, and the reality too of the power of an heiress over a man who had married her for money – these all kept breaking through and nullifying the power of Official Man to keep women in a condition of public rightlessness and servility.

This conflict between the public and the private condition of women did not pass unnoticed. It is clearly evident in the advice on marriage given in Plutarch's *Moralia*:

> . . . it is an excellent thing for the wife to feel sympathy with her husband in his affairs and for the husband to feel in the same way for his wife. So, as ropes twined together gain strength from one another, the two of them will each contribute his or her share of goodwill and by their joint action the partnership will be preserved.[18]

Already this may surprise those who remember being taught at school that Roman wives were expected to be servile husband-pleasers. But Plutarch's conception of marriage goes beyond mutual companionability:

> Man and woman are joined together physically so that the woman may take and blend together elements derived from each and so give birth to a child which is common to them both, so that neither of the two can tell or distinguish what in particular is his or hers. It is very right too that married people should have the same kind of partnership in property. They should put everything they have into a common fund; neither of the two should think of one part as belonging to him and the other as not belonging; instead each should think of it all as his own, and none of it as not belonging to him.[19]

Plutarch (A.D. 45–125) has been described by generations of academics as 'second-rate' and 'superficial'. Yet it is Plutarch who foreshadows here modern conceptions of the joint bank account. Our reading of the classics is so heavily weighted towards political, military and philosophical works, towards Plato, Cicero, Thucydides and Caesar, that we are liable to form a somewhat unrealistic picture of popular attitudes towards marriage and the family, rather as if 500 years hence people had to rely on the works of Winston Churchill and Wittgenstein to find out about twentieth-century attitudes to marriage and the family.

Yet Plutarch had also to take account of the public condition of women. And so he adds hastily: 'As a mixture of wine and water is called "wine" even though the larger part of it is water, so the property and the house should be said to be the husband's, even though the wife has contributed the larger share.'[20]

The feminist may reasonably comment that this sounds like typical masculine trickery, and that domestic equality is a poor exchange for public serfdom. And yet there is no doubt that what Plutarch meant was that the core of marriage was internal and private and that the public arrangements were secondary matters of convenience. For he goes on:

> A couple who are in love with each other form an organic unity; those who marry for the sake of a dowry or in order to have children

form a union of component parts; and those who merely sleep in the same bed form merely a connexion of separate individuals who would be described more correctly as sleeping together than as living together. Scientists tell us that when liquids are mixed together the mixture is total and entire. It should be the same with married people – a mutual blending of bodies, property, friends and relations.[21]

Because Plutarch is so prosaic, we can take him as a reliable guide to how ordinary people looked on marriage in the first century after Christ. There is nothing here of the casual attitudes of the imperial debauchees; and if confirmation is wanted of the general contempt in which the manners of the court were held, we have only to look at the more highbrow writers such as Juvenal and Tacitus who mourned the purer manners of the Republic and idealised the treatment of women among savage nations like the Germans.

The position of women certainly had its terrible downs as well as its partial ups. Maitland warns us against the assumption that 'from the age of savagery until the present age every change in marital law has been favourable to the wife.' The straight-line theory of historical development is just as misleading when applied to the position of women as to most other topics. It may well be that, on balance, the property rights of women gradually *diminished* until the late Victorian period. But at all times, there seems to have been what E. P. Thompson calls 'a considerable feminine presence'. In this fine Marxist historian, we note a certain honest uneasiness at this evidence which fits so ill with the conventional theories of the *total* subjection of women. Thompson argues strongly against the assumption that feminine tenures were only fictionally so:

This was certainly not true at the top of society, which saw the formidable presence of such women as Sarah, duchess of Marlborough, or of Ruperta Howe, the ranger of Alice Holt Forest. And we must all have encountered evidence which suggests that women of the yeoman class acquitted themselves, at the head of farming households, with equal vigour. In the early eighteenth century a steward of St. John's was engaged in a protracted and inconclusive negotiation with one infuriating tenant, whose evasions always left her in possession of all the points at issue: 'I had rather' (he wrote) 'have business with three men than one woman.'[22]

In Berkshire wills of the 1720s, Thompson could find no evidence of bias against female kin. And if female freeholds did decline during that period, that was because of the severe decline in the yeoman class generally. Throughout the Middle Ages and later, according to Cicely Howell, in the English Midlands the tendency was to leave the residue of the estate to the widow, sometimes jointly with her son; only in a minority of cases was the land left to the son alone.[23]

Not merely is the wife particularly well provided for in early English wills; sometimes the husband would appoint her as his sole executor. Of the *Fifty Earliest English Wills*, in more than half the cases where there might have been a wife to inherit, she was the residuary legatee; in the others, she almost always shared the inheritance with the children in general or the eldest son as principal heir with portions set aside for the other children.[24]

All this reflects not simply the husband's debt of affection to his wife and his concern for her future but also an acknowledgment of her role in the *management* of the family fortune, far exceeding the property she might have brought with her on marriage.

In the letters she wrote and received, Honor Lisle has left us the most complete portrait we have of the life and duties of an English gentlewoman in the first half of the sixteenth century. Not only was she responsible for bringing up and placing her numerous family and running her households, both in England and *en poste* in Calais; she also managed her English estates with a beady eye. She acted for and with her husband, an experienced soldier and courtier, in all diplomatic and political affairs – often a matter of life and death in the perilous later years of Henry VIII.

As Muriel St Clare Byrne remarks in her introduction to the *Lisle Letters*, Honor 'reflects in quite a remarkable manner the difference between the theory of woman's place in the scheme of things as set forth in the mass of sixteenth-century treatises on the subject, and the reality as we encounter it both in the lives of noblewomen and gentlewomen and in their letters'.[25] In theory, woman was subordinate, submissive. She occupied a lower rung on that hierarchy of absolutism which subjected man to God and commoner to king. In practice, she had the freedom to act independently and the capacity to assert her legal rights in her own name. Honor Lisle spoke to and negotiated with men of her own class as an equal, and in business matters she acted as her husband's partner, not his servant.

We must above all rid ourselves of the picture of our own times as the culmination of a process of steady development in a straight line. The twentieth century is not, for example, unique in the high proportion of property held by women – more than half in the United States. It is estimated that almost half the agricultural land in Sparta was held by women in the fourth century B.C.

Nor is it possible to say that women have been becoming steadily more independent and assertive over the centuries, still less that this assertiveness spread gradually from the Anglo-Saxon world to the more tradition-bound male supremacies of the Mediterranean. Emmanuel Le Roy Ladurie identifies a considerable number of matriarchs in the French Pyrenean village of Montaillou at the beginning of the fourteenth century. These matriarchs might either have inherited a house from their own family, or created one for themselves or simply run it after the death of their husbands. They are to be recognised by the fact that their names, given a feminine ending of -a, are preceded by Na, short for *domina* or mistress. Their occupations were various: Na Roqua was one of the mothers of the Cathar Church and adviser to heads of families; I imagine she was rather the equivalent of an elder of the Kirk. Na Ferriola owned a house and a flock of goats. Many of the inns were run by hostesses. Other matriarchs might be the village purveyors of wine or cheese.

Perhaps the most interesting case preserved for us in the Inquisitor's record is that of Guillemette Maury. She married Bernard Marty of Montaillou, who had a *domus* there. After the persecution of 1308, the Martys fled from Montaillou and wandered from town to town in Catalonia, from one temporary dwelling to another. Bernard died. With her two now grown-up sons, she settled in San Mateo, a more 'lucrative' town. They earned a good living and bought a smallholding which consisted of a farm with a courtyard, a garden, a cornfield, vineyards, pastures, an ass and a mule and sheep. Guillemette used to entertain twelve or fifteen guests at a time. The family earned extra money by working the wool from their sheep and by hiring themselves out to other farmers at harvest-time. This farm had nothing to do with the deceased Bernard, who was so far forgotten that Guillemette reverted to her maiden name of Maury, by which surname her sons were also known. Guillemette became 'Her Grace, Madame Guillemette', unmistakably the mistress of this new household. Her brother Pierre played an essential part in the household, but she was the mistress and she it was who accepted or refused proposals of marriage for her grown-up sons.

From these snapshots of mediaeval life, what emerges is the distinction between the public and private spheres. From the public life of Church and State women were largely, sometimes wholly debarred. But in private matters of property and marriage, women had clearly established legal and customary rights and exercised those rights vigorously. Certainly they did rank behind men in most questions of inheritance and precedence, but they were not debarred, still less regarded as livestock or articles of property. Indeed, in the management of property, the sharpest distinction often appears to be one of age and marital status rather than one of sex. The wife might be said to rank after the husband but before the unmarried son as well as the unmarried daughter. The hierarchy of subjection was as much parental as sexual. Age brought authority and respect to both sexes. But in England anyway, even the unmarried daughter was, it seems, not regarded as a piece of sexual property in quite the way we used to think; she could often own and manage property with as much freedom as anyone else.

I do not wish to over-correct. It would be just as misleading to substitute a counter-myth of an underlying civil equality between men and women. But it does seem as though our false impressions of women in times past as totally powerless sex-objects derive, in part at least, from a wish to impose a straight-line pattern on history; our images of patriarchy and female subjugation are encrusted with sentimental embellishment.

Modern sociologists too are sometimes just as surprised as historians by how little their images of the position of women correspond to reality. Perhaps the greatest classic of post-war British sociology is *Family and Kinship in East London*, a description of working-class life in Bethnal Green and on a new housing estate in Essex, by Michael Young and Peter Willmott. The note throughout this investigation is one of surprise. 'We were surprised to discover that the wider family, far from having disappeared, was still very much alive in the middle of England.' The supposed shrinking of the family had simply not taken place; the Industrial Revolution had failed to separate families from each other.

Then there was the surprise of the shared responsibility of husband and wife; 'we cannot reconcile our other impressions with the stereotype of the working-class husband' – violent, usually drunk, callous and neglectful, 'a sort of absentee husband, showing his wife neither responsibility nor affection, partner only of the bed.'

But not merely did life in Bethnal Green seem to correspond more to the supposedly discarded pattern of the 'extended family', there was no doubt who was the head of this family:

> The mother is the head and centre of the extended family, her home its meeting place. 'Mum's is the family rendez-vous', as one wife said. Her daughters congregate at the mother's, visiting her more often than she visits any one of them: 68 per cent of married women last saw their mother at her home, and only 27 per cent at their own . . .
>
> In addition to the weekly meetings there are special family gatherings at the mother's house for birthdays and wedding anniversaries, Mum's own birthday being one of the occasions of the year . . .
>
> It almost goes without saying that where Mum plays so large a part in the lives of her descendants, she should be honoured for what she does. The very word, and the warmth with which it is uttered, somehow conveys the respect in which she is held.[26]

No doubt the new picture is in turn sentimentalised. All the same, it repeats in recognisable form our snapshots of mediaeval life. The wife and mother is still denied *formal* public power. Her husband still receives the pay packet, often doling out the housekeeping money without telling her how much he earns; and he is the legal householder and taxpayer. Yet informally, privately, she is the matriarch, unmistakably the heart and controlling intelligence of the family.

Now working-class Bethnal Green may be a dying place; even by the 1950s, great numbers of families had moved to housing estates in Essex where they found green fields, bathrooms, telephones but less warmth and fewer 'kinship contacts', according to Young and Willmott. But the point is that it is places like Bethnal Green which have always been regarded as providing the classic examples of women's powerlessness.

It would make no sense to use this counter-evidence to argue that history shows that private power was a substitute for or 'as good as' public power. None of the foregoing alters or diminishes by one jot the case for permitting women equal rights in any sphere: politics, property, taxation, religion, the bringing-up of children or the running of a household. If democracy is desirable, then we must will the means to it; and democracy is patently a charade unless it attempts to maximise both civic liberty and civic equality.

In some fields, such as education or income tax, the problems of ascertaining the best possible mixture of liberty and equality are very difficult. When is individual liberty severely infringed? How far is equality of income part of being a full citizen? In the case of women's rights, however, no such difficulties arise. Both civic liberty and civic equality demand, directly and unconditionally, that women have the right to participate fully and equally in all civic institutions. Questions as to whether or not women are always capable of so participating are entirely irrelevant; even if it were proved that women make poor stockbrokers, racehorse trainers, weight-lifters or bishops, that would be no reason to debar them from such posts and occupations, or to deny them the opportunity to train and qualify for them.

But that is not the same as saying that civic rights and public power are an indispensable precondition for the genuine exercise of private power. It is part of the feminist case that women are eunuchs because they are denied full civic rights; marriage is a prison and the family a fraudulent hell because women are second-class citizens.

This completely misses the *opposition* between the family and society. Some feminists assume an unbroken continuity extending from the intimate core of the family to the widest network of civic obligations; but this is precisely to mimic the arguments of the Enemy – that is, of male supremacy, whether expressed in the State or the Church. For it is the State and Church which constantly assert the right to regulate so-called private relationships and to reach into the most intimate nooks of a marriage and of individual hearts. It often seems almost as if feminists are yearning for a new Christendom, a reborn Respublica Christiana, only with an Almighty She.

The defenders of the family argue the precise opposite. They assert always the privacy and independence of the family, its biological individuality and its right to live according to its natural instincts. It is for this reason that, even in societies where male supremacy is officially total, the family asserts its own maternal values. This assertion is fudged and confused by anthropologists who describe whole societies as 'matriarchal' or 'matrilineal' as if these epithets were enough to describe both the public and private aspects of life, as if indeed there were little need to distinguish between the two. Again, there is a sentimental myth of Wholeness at work here; in primitive society, there is said to be no distinction between public and private, hence no ideas of shame or jealousy or possession. This myth too now seems to be coming under more critical examination. But for our own purposes it is of dubious relevance; for after examining the history and reality of the Western family, we can at least be sure that, with us, there *has* always been a distinction between public and private.

The distinction between public and private law in mediaeval times shows unmistakably two worlds for women: the public world of modesty, silence, subjection and rightlessness; and the private world of responsibility for children and household, of rights to property and to a hearing at law, of authority over children and of assertiveness in commercial dealings, no less than in marital discussion and decision.

Women's rights to equality are unassailable because women are human beings. We may hope and expect that as a result the spirit of civic equality may seep through into the private world of marriage and blot out the patches of inequality and consequent resentment that disfigure it. But we should also recognise that these inequalities themselves originally seeped through into marriage from the outside, from the public world. For it is *within* marriage that the notions of equality and open-heartedness have existed long before they became part of a political programme. This does not mean of course that those notions generally or even frequently came within measurable distance of being realised. But they remained ideals of what might be achieved and enjoyed.

It was never suggested that they could be achieved without forbearance and self-sacrifice. In the mediaeval and Renaissance texts we have quoted, mutual forbearance and respect are regarded as inescapably connected with and consequent upon the equality of true marriage. The old ideals of marriage were not and are not opposed to women's rights; indeed, it is in them that we first find those rights asserted. What the old ideals were and are opposed to is *egotism*, whether male or female. They assume a biological ethic – a series of duties of nest-gathering, nursing, feeding, protecting and teaching, all involving the sacrifice of self.

By distinguishing between the public and private roles of women in past time, we can see more clearly that extreme feminists are fighting on two entirely distinct fronts: more obviously, they are fighting on the public front against patriarchy and Man, and for equal rights. In this struggle, the values of the family offer auxiliary support as a pattern and reminder of the natural, complementary equality of the sexes.

But some feminists are also fighting on a private front: against the biological ethic, against self-sacrifice for husband and children, and for the unrestrained free play of the ego. The difference between the public and the private battle is, if you like, the difference between Mrs Pankhurst and Shulamith Firestone, between reformist feminism and utopian feminism.

In *The Dialectic of Sex*, Shulamith Firestone calls for 'the freeing of women from the tyranny of reproduction by every means possible'. Child-bearing could be taken over by technology. And child-rearing could be diffused to society as a whole, to men and other children as well as other women. The 'repressive socialisation process' of family life as we know it 'would now be unnecessary in a society in which the interests of the individual coincided with those of the larger society'. The blood tie of the mother would eventually be severed,

> so that pregnancy, now freely acknowledged as clumsy, inefficient and painful, would be indulged in, if at all, only as a tongue-in-cheek archaism, just as already women today wear virginal white to their weddings. A cybernetic communism would abolish economic classes, and all forms of labour exploitation, by granting all people a livelihood based only on material needs. Eventually work (drudge jobs) would be eliminated in favour of (complex) play, activity done for its own sake, by adults as well as children. With the disappearance of motherhood, and the obstructing incest taboo, sexuality would be re-integrated, allowing love to flow unimpeded.[27]

A more endearing, less mechanistic version of this utopia is to be found in *The Female Eunuch*: musing on the problems of persuading 'brilliant women' to 'reproduce', Germaine Greer writes:

> No child ought to grow up alone with a single resentful girl who is struggling to work hard enough to provide for herself and him. I thought again of the children I knew in Calabria and hit upon the plan to buy, with the help of some friends with similar problems, a farmhouse in Italy where we could stay when circumstances permit-

ted, and where our children would be born. Their fathers and other people would also visit the house as often as they could, to rest and enjoy the children and even work a bit. Perhaps some of us might live there for quite long periods, as long as we wanted to. The house and garden would be worked by a local family who lived in the house. The children would have a region to explore and dominate, and different skills to learn from all of us. It would not be paradise, but it would be a little community with a chance of survival, with parents of both sexes and a multitude of roles to choose from.[28]

Within this relaxed community the possessive aspects of motherhood would melt away: 'If necessary the child need not even know that I was his womb-mother and I could have relationships with the other children as well. If my child expressed a wish to try London and New York or go to formal school somewhere, that could also be tried without committal.'[29]

This exactly mirrors the goals and methods of the male utopias of all preceding centuries: responsibility is abolished by being spread throughout the community; 'mine' and 'thine' are abolished; no person is tied more to one person than to another; relationships are thinned and diffused; the children have no ties, to people or place; when they are bored, they simply move on. At the same time, work is turned into play; scarcity is no longer an insistent pressure; jobs are softened into 'roles' which can be chosen and discarded at will; by implication, it is clear that any unpleasant work will be mopped up by the 'local family' – a remnant of the slave class which is to be found in many utopias but which is often supposed to wither away as technology increasingly performs the boring or unpleasant tasks for us. These communities are naturally to be located in idyllic surroundings. This is only logical, for if struggle, conflict and effort have disappeared and no longer preoccupy us, this liberation which grants us the time and the serenity to enjoy, perceive and absorb must also demand that we have pleasant and beautiful objects around us: cypress trees, sunburnt children, limitless flasks of Chianti.

This is true utopian anarchism, unfamiliar to past generations only because it includes pregnancy, childbirth and child-rearing among the painful drudgeries which are to be swept away. Bliss is to be eternal, unconstrained, *sexless*. Women, and men too, are to become winged, irresponsible, undifferentiated beings . . . like, well, like angels.

' . . . There is neither male nor female: for ye are all one in Christ Jesus.'[30] In the end, all enemies of the family turn out to be the same enemy. And every liberation turns out to be the same liberation, the same attempt to jump out of your skin and soar. And all heavens are the same heaven, in which the interests of the individual miraculously and naturally coincide with those of the larger society.

And every return to earth is the same return, to skin and blood and bone – and the same recall to singularity and the same recognition of specific duty and particular love.

Utopian feminism *needs* Marxism. Without the underlying theory that economic conditions ultimately and basically determine social existence, feminism runs up against biology. The family has to be entirely created and thoroughly penetrated by the economic process; otherwise, we shall have to concede that it has a life of its own, that in some sense the family is *natural*. Hence the tremendous emphasis on 'the nuclear family' as something fleeting, artificial and accidental; hence, too, the insistence on the necessary and sufficient connection between the supposed rise of the nuclear family and the rise of 'capitalism'. There has to be some impersonal, inhuman force which is responsible for the imprisonment and oppression of women. This connection has to be desperately maintained against all new pieces of historical ammunition.

But if the public world and the private world do develop in their separate ways and at differing paces, then there must be something to be gained by looking at them separately. Many reformist feminists accept the duties of care prescribed by the biological ethic; but they do not see why these duties should bar them from civic equality, nor why civic inequality should be allowed to corrode marital equality.

It is this separation which utopian feminism sternly resists. Woman's Misery is one and indivisible. Her condition is an integral thing. Either consciously or unconsciously, the utopian feminist grasps the tactical necessity not to split up her complaints. For example, Germaine Greer catalogues the medical risks and the physical discomforts of contraception which women have to put up with:

> As long as women have to think about contraception every day, and worry about pills, sheaths, and devices of all kinds, and then worry

every time a period is due, more irrationality will appear in their behaviour. The almost universal problem of menstrual tension is certainly aggravated for today's woman, and added neurasthenia makes it more acute. Misery, misery, misery.[31]

Now it is true that these miseries are loaded on to women; but at least part of them, those surrounding menstruation, have some biological element in them which cannot be said to be Man's 'fault'. However, Dr Greer does not stop there but sweeps into attack on a broader front:

> There are more women who attempt suicide than men, more women in mental hospitals than men; there are hundreds of children injured by desperate parents every year, and even cases of infants bloodily put to death by deranged mothers. Post-natal weeps are a recognized syndrome; some women have suffered them for as long as a year after the birth of the child. The tiny scandalous minority of baby-bashers and husband-murderers get into the press. The majority of women drag along from day to day in an apathetic twilight, hoping that they are doing the right thing, vaguely expecting a reward some day. The working wife waits for the children to grow up and do well to vindicate her drudgery, and sees them do as they please, move away, get into strange habits, and reject their parents.[32]

The indictment muddles three separable types of misery: the misery resulting from the unequal treatment of women, the misery resulting from biology and the misery which is experienced by men too. Drugs may cure or relieve 'post-natal weeps'. Opportunities to get out of the house for work, pleasure or education may relieve women's drudgery and put them more on a level with men. But there remains a large quantum of misery which is experienced with equal severity by men.

What about the *men* who attempt suicide or spend time in mental hospitals or batter babies or murder their wives or live lives of drudgery or quiet desperation or are disappointed or rejected by their children? Can any of these miseries really be described as distinctly or exclusively female? Surely not all this misery can be attributed to the corruption of the relationship between the sexes. And the more women liberate themselves from being eunuchs and unpeople, surely the more they will share in male misery. Is it not conceivable that there may exist varieties of misery – perhaps even of happiness too – which have little or nothing to do with sex or even with belonging to a family?

No doubt civic oppression, at least in the upper-middle classes of a hundred years ago, has always made it more likely that the unhappiness in an unhappy family would be concentrated upon a wife or daughter who had less practical chance of escaping. But even R. D. Laing's theory of the 'family scapegoat', upon whom the accumulated misery and tension of the family is piled until he or she goes mad (or, in Laing's version, goes sane), does not deny that the victim may be of either sex.

The removal of civic oppression may well even up the sex ratio of misery. If it is no longer always the wife who stays at home, or looks after the sick grandparent, then the chances of being the vulnerable link in the family chain may be spread more evenly – although the liberated female members are liable to be taking on fresh strains outside the family.

But as the evening-up develops, as women's civic rights slowly begin to become undisputed facts, utopian feminism is itself put under pressure. For it has always relied on the plain, shocking facts of civic oppression to support its apocalyptic arguments. It was the arranged marriage, the denial of the vote, the inequality of legal rights, the brutish masculinity of Church and State that fed the yearning for a marriageless, de-sexed utopia.

The feminine variety of utopia has survived longer than other utopias because it started so much later and because it had such unanswerable evidence of male brutality and oppression to produce. In its exhilarating destructiveness, it encompasses the sweeping away not merely of class and poverty and cruelty and forced labour but of all distinctions of sex or age, for children too must be liberated from childish dependence – otherwise women could not be liberated from motherhood. It is the ultimate utopia, unnerving and bewildering to most men, as it is meant to be.

Yet all utopias have only a limited life, like shooting stars. They become boring, in the same way that orbiting in space becomes boring. Their exhilarating quality derives from struggle, from encounters with hostile forces: the organisers of beauty contests, reactionary politicians, brutish husbands.

I do not mean that feminist communes, co-operatives and workshops are likely to disappear overnight as soon as civic equality of the sexes is achieved. But what is likely to happen, what may indeed be already happening is that attention begins to stray from the extreme version of the feminist utopia. For the great majority of people – including many feminists – what is more interesting is the future of marriage.

14

AND AFTERWARDS?

Guessing the future is fun. Describing the present is harder work. Precision is difficult, certainty more difficult still, and there is an ever-present danger of being either misled by false pictures of the past or distracted by interesting visions of the future. The kindest thing we can do to the future, therefore, is to be as careful and accurate as we can about the present.

'The Continuing Decline of Marriage' was the title of a leading article in *The Times* (11th May 1981). 'Marriage', *The Times* said, 'in so far as it can be measured, is in decline.' The number of people getting married in England and Wales had been steadily falling throughout the 1970s. 'Fewer single people are getting married and when they do it is later in life.' Living together outside marriage was becoming more acceptable. 'The social stigma of bearing a child out of wedlock has diminished considerably, and more than one in ten births is now illegitimate.' Divorce was quick and easy. The psychological effects of the breakdown of marriage on the children involved were traumatic. On the other hand, 'making divorce harder again would no doubt improve the statistics of marriage, but it would not necessarily be for the good either of society or of those unfortunates, and their children, trapped in a loveless union.'

That, I imagine, would be how the majority of people see the times we live in: marriage declining, divorce increasing, more and more children distraught because their parents are splitting up. Yet there can be no going back to legal indissolubility. This picture is certainly not wholly false, but it is not wholly, true either. We need to look a little more closely at the figures.

Marriage rates in England and Wales have gone up and down frequently throughout the twentieth century (see the appendix).

The two peaks were reached in the years immediately before, during and after the two world wars. The all-time high was reached in the period 1936–40. After the war there was a further peak during the late 1960s and early 1970s. After that the marriage rate went down sharply, then up again a little at the end of the 1970s. These figures are probably roughly comparable with the experience of other Western countries, although exact comparisons are tricky because of different legal and social conditions.

Marriage rates, however, only measure the number of *weddings* per year. If we take *marital condition* – the number of people who are married – we find a rather different picture. The percentage of the population which is married rises steadily from 1901 to 1971 and then begins to fall, slowly but steadily. This is clearly the consequence of the rapid rise in the number of divorced people from 1970 onwards, following the 1969 Divorce Reform Act. The proportion of single persons – those who have never been married – falls steadily and steeply between 1907 and 1971 and then stays constant.

At the peak for weddings, in 1971, the percentage of married, widowed and divorced people in the population as against the percentage of single people was much the same as it is now. What has happened is not so much that marriage has gone out of fashion as that divorce has become readily available to all unhappily married couples.

Within these totals, the pattern of when people get married and how often has certainly changed quite markedly. The mean average age of marriage steadily went down between 1907 and 1971. Since then, it has climbed again. This is partly because both single men and women are getting married later and because of the increasing number of remarriages. Even so, bachelors and spinsters today still tend to marry *younger* than they did at the turn of the century: 25 for men as against 27 in 1901, 22 for women as against 25 in 1901.

I think there can be little doubt, either about the reason why the age went down or about the reason why it has gone up again. In the first case, it was economic; people could afford to marry younger. In the second, sexual freedom permitted respectable persons to experiment in living together without being married.

Far more people are or have been married today than ever before. The fact that easier divorce laws have increased the percentage of 'have beens' as against the 'ares' scarcely makes it possible to talk of a decline in marriage. At present only 1.9 per cent of the population is divorced, while 2.8 is widowed, 51.8 is married and 43.6 is single (three-quarters of these being children). It is hardly surprising that a vast increase in the proportion of people attempting marriage should also mean an increase in the number of failed marriages.

There is also something in Lawrence Stone's point that 'modern divorce is little more than a functional substitute for death.' Modern marriages do last longer than marriages in times past, even in Britain or the United States, because people live so much longer.

In England, for example, the proportion of divorced-or-widowed men has only in the last few years overtaken the comparable percentage at the turn of the century – then, of course, almost exclusively composed of widowers. For women, the figures are more startling still. The proportions of both married people and widows have increased by half as much again since 1900.

What the 'marital condition' figures conceal, however, is the huge increase in the number of remarriages in the twentieth century. In about a quarter of all marriages, either the bride or groom or both has been married before. At the turn of the century, in only one-eighth of marriages, one or other partner or both had been married before. This figure, though, was considerably higher in the days before the rapid improvement in life expectancy during the nineteenth century.

Mediaeval society was a network of remarriages. In the sixteenth and seventeenth centuries, about a quarter of all marriages were a remarriage for the bride or groom – exactly the same proportion as in the 1980s. In Manchester in the 1650s, in no less than one-third of all marriages one of the partners had been married before.[1]

Neither then nor now can remarriage be regarded as a sign of marriage being in decline. If people remarry as soon as possible, whether after burying or after divorcing their first spouse, it does not suggest positive revulsion from the married state – even if commercial considerations were not absent in the courting of a widow who had been left nicely provided for. Indeed, early remarriage after being widowed is widely regarded as a compliment to the dead spouse.

There is one other measure which may have something to tell us about the popularity of marriage. And this is the illegitimacy rate. This has been rising more or less steadily since about 1940, after having fallen equally steadily from a peak round about 1850. There had been a previous lower peak somewhere in the region of 1600.[2]

Was the peak in 1850 the result of a revolution in sexual behaviour and the subsequent decline in illegitimacy the result of the spread of contraception, only to be overwhelmed by a second post-1940 sexual revolution, which finally removed the restraint on premarital sexual relations, as Shorter argues? Quite possibly, but for our purposes what matters more is why women today do not insist, wherever possible, on getting married before bearing a child and why, in the last ten years at any rate, they have often preferred to take the risk of bearing a child despite the availability of free contraception and abortion.

There are three possible factors: first, the decline in the social pressure to get married; the lessening of the moral and religious stigma of illegitimacy is reinforced by popular opinion as well as by changes in the law. Second, more is expected of marriage; the 'shotgun marriage' is despised, just as the arranged marriage was in earlier times; it is thought, often by the mother's parents as well as by the mother herself, that the child will be better off being brought up by the mother alone rather than in a loveless or shaky marriage. Finally, some mothers regard all marriage as hypocritical and constricting and prefer to bring up a child in a milieu where relationships are impermanent, and so unforced and sincere. It is a matter of opinion, but my impression is that this last is the view of a minority and, in the majority of cases where the mother could choose either to marry or not to marry, she chooses to bring up her child on her own because she believes that marriage to that particular man would be a mistake, not because marriage in general is a mistake.

This is to take a higher view of marriage, not a lower one. At a moment when, even today, the advantages of marriage are considerable in material terms, particularly for the support of the child, the mother prefers to avoid a marriage undertaken for the wrong, that is, the purely material reason.

The statistics thus can equally well be used to prove a rather different case. More people are or have been married today than ever before; more people remarry than ever before, undeterred by unsuccessful first or even subsequent marriages. At the same time, there is less and less material advantage in the married state. Sex can be regularly enjoyed without benefit of clergy or registrar. More and more women go out to work and, albeit very slowly, their earnings begin to approach those of men. And even in cases where there are still considerable advantages in being married – namely when there is a baby to look after – women, it seems, are reluctant to marry someone whom they would not have wanted to marry if there had been no baby on the way. None of that suggests a decline in the aspiration to achieve a happy marriage.

Yet if we can at least prevent statistics from misleading us, we cannot expect them to answer the ultimate question, which revolves around what we expect out of marriage.

We cannot really say whether marriage is or is not in decline, until we say precisely what we mean by marriage.

Do we mean 'Christian marriage' – that is, a lifelong, divinely ordered, indissoluble relationship within which *all* sexual activity and all child-bearing must take place? That unrealised, unrealisable ideal is certainly fading. But we must beware of assuming that it ever dominated people's minds quite as comprehensively as it was supposed to. Of course, people hoped and expected that their marriage would be lifelong and regarded that as the best outcome for themselves and for their children; people still do. But at the same time they knew how often marriages came to grief, whatever Church and State might say; they knew how easy it was for a girl to get in the family way and how many pregnancies were terminated more or less illegally.

At almost all times, for example, the illegitimacy rates were far higher than the Church was willing to admit; and often popular attitudes towards unmarried mothers were rather more charitable than those of the official promoters of charity. It may also be that the present rate of unmarried couples living together is historically quite so remarkable only by comparison with official Victorian standards in Western Europe. At other times and in other places, marriage has been far more 'blurred at the edges'; the number of couples living together without benefit of clergy or registrar (though never as great as today) has always been a sizeable social hinterland scarcely explored.

For example, in Montaillou, around 1300–1320, the records show us that at least five or six of the fifty-odd couples in the village were illicit. Despite the supposedly complete grip of the Church, a minimum of ten per cent of couples were living in sin. At other more prudish times, the proportion may have been equally high, but the sinners may have been more careful to hide their status, and respectable people may have averted their eyes.

In many places, older, less formal attitudes towards marriage persisted until recent times. Of New York in the 1890s, for example, it was said that 'if two parties, living together, speak of each other as husband and wife, this public acknowledgment is all that is requisite to constitute their relation in the eyes of the law a perfectly valid marriage.'[3] The notion of the 'common-law marriage', in which the law recognises a couple as in effect married although no ceremony has taken place, persists because the reality of it persists. This concept of marriage as the recognition of a social fact rather than as the concluding of a contract dates back to classical Greece and Rome, and no doubt earlier.

Scandinavian historians go so far as to say that 'in old peasant society, the arrival of a child seems to have been the occasion for official marriage.'[4] Peter Laslett describes this attitude as 'literally celebratory'. The marriage exists; all that the festivities or the wedding service or the baptism, or the whole lot together, achieve is to celebrate the fact.

Throughout its centuries of theoretical control of marriage, the Church has had widely varying success in enforcing its code of conduct. Illegitimacy rates have ranged from near zero in nineteenth-century Ireland to over 50 per cent in the Austrian province of Styria, also Catholic, in the same period. In England, Laslett estimates that the proportion of first children conceived extra-maritally (bastards plus 'shotgun wedding' children) may have reached three-fifths in the supposedly tight-laced nineteenth century. Historians even argue whether there was or was not a 'bastardy-prone sub-society' composed of women who bore several illegitimate children who in turn produced more illegitimate children of their own.

At the very least, we have to reckon at all times in our history with a large 'unrespectable' population, composed of separated spouses, unmarried mothers and illegitimate persons, young and old, who made their own rules, cheerfully indifferent to the rulings of Church and State. And we have to recognise too that their attitudes towards marriage and the family were often shared by many of those who were 'properly' married with benefit of clergy. Amongst this multifarious overlapping assortment of habits and attitudes, there may be discerned something which can justly be called 'popular marriage' – more realistic and tolerant of failure, more concerned with rubbing along with and physically looking after your family, less interested in spiritual purity, earthier, less ambitious.

A society in which less than two-fifths of mothers were virgins on their wedding day cannot claim to be wholly dedicated to the Church's views on pre-marital chastity. Mothers whose unmarried daughters so regularly found themselves pregnant surely cannot have imagined that their own flesh and blood were all damned to eternity for their lapses. And indeed we have evidence that they did not so imagine.

I choose out of the abundant literary and sociological evidence of working-class tolerance in such matters the evidence in Christopher Smout's startling essay on 'Sexual Behaviour in Nineteenth-century Scotland', simply because it shows how little effect even the most extreme religious prohibitions on fornication had on working-class women at the supposed peak of Victorian puritanism. Dr J. M. Strachan of Dollar, in an exhaustively researched series of articles for the *Scotsman* in 1870, wrote that there was no discouragement to illegitimacy in rural Scotland because 'Previous unchasteness even with another individual does not form a very serious bar to marriage.' In 1886, William Cramond's pamphlet *Illegitimacy in Banffshire* recorded the following replies to a circular asking for views on the causes of local immorality:

'Notwithstanding all our preaching and teaching, this sin is not at all seen in its true light, in fact it is thought very little of – scarcely thought a sin at all, just a mistake, rather annoying and hard when the father does not take with the child and pay for it . . .': parish minister.

'A woman once said to me with reference to her erring daughter, "It was not so bad as if she had taken twopence that was not her own." That woman was a fair type of the average church member in this district, neither better nor worse': parish minister.

'I have heard many a mother of this kind say, "It's nae sae bad as steeling, or deein' awa' wi' the puir craters"': bank official.

The Committee on Religion and Morals of the Free Church was even forced to admit of the supposed stain of bastardy that 'the people hardly regard it as a sin. They seem to think that marriage covers all.'[5]

In the light of such comprehensive admissions from people who would be professionally disinclined to admit total failure to influence the minds of their parishioners, the control of the minister or the priest begins to look more formal than real. Legal and economic penalties might make bearing a child out of wedlock a terrible mistake, but it was hard to persuade the working class at least that it was as bad as stealing twopence. The tolerant attitudes of popular marriage refused to be stamped out.

So do we mean by marriage not official Christian marriage but 'popular marriage' – a relationship which is also sealed by a vow of lifelong fidelity between adults who know their own minds, but which, like all earthly relationships, is prone to disasters which must be allowed for? Popular marriage is designed for two of the same objects as Christian marriage, namely, the procreation and protection of children and the mutual help and affection of the couple, but it does not realistically expect to monopolise procreation or affection. Popular marriage sees itself as the most natural and preferable of social arrangements rather than as a spiritual ideal. Above all, it is a *voluntary* arrangement which derives its virtue from the exercise of free choice.

There is logically no reason to expect that the married state should exhaust the varieties of actual behaviour, once you assume that marriage is an independent institution controlled by a voluntary partnership of two persons. If people can choose whether to marry, who to marry and whether to unmarry, then we ought to expect that noticeable quantity of people will choose not to marry or remarry. Freedom provokes such variety. And while this book has been concerned to stress the natural independence of the biological imperative, I do not want to over-correct so much that we substitute the premise of an irresistible biological urge for that of an irresistible economic process. Marriage, like most other things in life, is a mixture of choice, accident and circumstance. And most people know it.

Yet it remains true that the dominant force in the Western world is the desire of the urban working class to fulfil its own aspirations. And among the first of those aspirations, most intimate and ancient, is the desire for equality, privacy and independence *in marriage*. Why is it that this desire for the independence of marriage should continue to look stronger than the desire for personal independence – which is so often said to be the dominant trend of our times? Why do people still wish to submerge, at least partially, their personalities in marriage and devote a great part of their lives, perhaps the major part, to 'working at' this battered old form of human relationship?

It can only be said, in the most hesitant fashion possible, that it may be because marriage still seems to be the most *interesting* enterprise which most of us come across. With all its tediums and horrors, it has both more variety and more continuity than any other commitment we can make. Its time-scale is far grander; there are still marriages alive which are older than the Bolshevik Revolution. Its passions, both of love and hatred, are more intense. Its outcomes – children, grandchildren, heirlooms of flesh and blood – stretch away over the horizon; they are the only identifiable achievements which most of us are likely to leave behind us, even if, like many achievements, they are liable to be flawed and only partially within our control. Marriage and the family make other experiences, both pleasant and unpleasant, seem a little tame and bloodless. And it is difficult to resist the conclusion that a way of living which is both so intense and so enduring must somehow come naturally to us, that it is part of being human.

APPENDIX

The data contained in these tables is reproduced, with the permission of the Controller of Her Majesty's Stationery Office, from *Marriage and Divorce Statistics: Review of the Registrar General on Marriages and Divorces in England and Wales, 1979* (HMSO, 1981), tables 2.1 and 1.1b.

Appendix

Table 1 Marriages and Divorces: summary, 1901–79

Period	Marriages			Divorces
	Total	First marriage of both parties	Remarriage of both parties	Total
1901–05	1,300,851	1,139,258	43,215	2,816
1906–10	1,339,664	1,181,184	41,324	3,118
1911–15	1,500,646	1,326,633	45,006	3,280
1916–20	1,575,257	1,314,651	65,320	7,548
1921–25	1,504,889	1,300,067	51,894	13,668
1926–30	1,519,883	1,341,273	47,839	16,789
1931–35	1,629,065	1,454,421	44,644	20,056
1936–40	1,985,815	1,783,679	51,302	30,903
1941–45	1,755,437	1,518,961	62,832	51,944
1946–50	1,917,238	1,517,749	107,561	199,507
1951–55	1,754,579	1,432,217	104,779	147,858
1956–60	1,723,500	1,452,971	95,870	128,858
1961–65	1,776,173	1,495,700	104,454	159,034
1966–70	1,990,604	1,647,342	133,363	237,503
1971–75	1,996,422	1,457,924	231,229	533,487
1969	396,746	326,950	27,622	51,310
1970	415,487	339,873	29,853	58,239
1971	404,737	320,347	34,126	74,437
1972	426,241	312,957	47,856	119,025
1973	400,435	288,003	48,752	106,003
1974	384,389	271,672	49,164	113,500
1975	380,620	264,945	51,331	120,522
1976	358,567	243,770	51,362	126,694
1977	356,954	237,961	53,654	129,053
1978	368,258	240,512	58,666	143,667
1979	368,853	240,744	58,445	138,706

Table 2 Male Marital Condition:
population estimates, proportions out of 1,000, 1901–79

Year	Single	Married	Widowed	Divorced
1901	608	357	35	
1911	593	372	35	
1921	550	414	36	0
1931	517	444	38	1
1951	441	520	35	4
1961	438	527	30	5
1971	439	525	28	8
1975	436	522	28	14
1976	436	520	28	16
1977	436	520	28	17
1978	436	518	28	19
1979	436	515	28	20

Table 3 Female Marital Condition:
population estimates, proportions out of 1,000, 1901–79

Year	Single	Married	Widowed	Divorced
1901	586	340	74	
1911	571	356	73	
1921	535	383	82	0
1931	500	413	86	1
1951	405	487	102	6
1961	389	497	106	8
1971	380	497	111	12
1975	372	496	113	19
1976	370	495	113	21
1977	369	495	114	22
1978	368	493	115	24
1979	367	491	115	26

NOTES

Introduction
1 D. H. Lawrence, *Apropos of Lady Chatterley's Lover*, London, Phoenix edn 1961, p. 27.
2 Shulamith Firestone, *The Dialectic of Sex*, Women's Press edn 1979, p. 75.
3 Germaine Greer, *The Female Eunuch*, Granada edn 1971, p. 221.
4 E. R. Leach, in Nicholas Pole (ed.), *Environmental Solutions*, Cambridge, 1972, p. 105.
5 Rachel Moss (ed.), *God's Yes to Sexuality*, London, 1981, pp. 130, 132.

1 Marriage and the Church
1 Luke 14: 26.
2 Matthew 10: 34–7.
3 John 2: 1–11.
4 Mark 10: 1–12.
5 Colossians 3: 19.
6 Ephesians 5: 22–3.
7 Titus 2: 4–5.
8 I Corinthians 7: 1, 7–9, 31–4.
9 Hans Lietzmann, *History of the Early Church*, London, 1961, Vol. I, p. 136
10 J. Daniélou and H. Marrou, *The Christian Centuries*, London, 1964, Vol. I, p. 121.
11 Ibid., p. 142.
12 Ibid., p. 176.

13 T. H. L. Parker, *John Calvin*, Berkhamsted, Herts, 1975, p. 121.
14 Ernst Troeltsch, *Social Teaching of the Christian Churches*, London, 1931, p. 131.
15 Ibid., p. 313.
16 Matthew 19: 9.
17 I Corinthians 7: 27.
18 Quoted, Laurence Lerner, *Love and Marriage: Literature and Its Social Context*, London, 1979, p. 162.
19 John Milton, *Prose Writings, The Doctrine and Discipline of Divorce*, Everyman edn 1927, pp. 255–6.
20 *The Times*, 9th October 1980.
21 A. Werth and C. S. Mihanovich (eds), *Papal Pronouncements on Marriage and the Family*, Milwaukee, 1955, pp. 64–7.
22 J. L. Flandrin, *Families in Former Times*, Cambridge, 1979, p. 160.
23 Quoted, ibid., p. 164.
24 Ibid., p. 206.
25 Rachel Moss (ed.), *God's Yes to Sexuality*, London, 1981, p. 59.
26 Ibid., pp. 45–6.
27 Ibid., p. 73.
28 Ibid., p. 72.
29 Ibid., p. 135.
30 Ibid., p. 158.
31 Ibid., pp. 137–8.
32 Matthew 6: 19, 26, 28–9, 34.

2 The State and the Family

1 Karl Marx and Friedrich Engels, *Communist Manifesto*, Pelican edn 1967, pp. 100–1.
2 Adolf Hitler, *Mein Kampf*, Munich, 1929, p. 276.
3 Ibid., p. 445.
4 Ibid.
5 Nora Waln, *Reaching for the Stars*, London, 1939, p. 178.
6 Quoted, Ronald Fletcher, *The Family and Marriage in Britain*, Pelican edn 1973, p. 38.
7 Quoted, H. Kent Geiger, *The Family in Soviet Russia*, Cambridge, Mass., 1968, pp. 44–5.
8 Ibid., pp. 47–8.
9 Ibid., p. 68.
10 Ibid.
11 V. I. Lenin, *On the Emancipation of Women*, Moscow, 1965, p. 106.
12 Ibid., p. 107.
13 Ibid., p. 104.
14 Geiger, *Family in Soviet Russia*, p. 77.
15 Beatrice and Sidney Webb, *Soviet Communism: A New Civilisation?*, London, 1935, p. 849.

16 Geiger, *Family in Soviet Russia*, p. 94.
17 Quoted, ibid., p. 104.
18 E. R. Leach, in Nicholas Pole (ed.), *Environmental Solutions*, Cambridge, 1972, p. 105.
19 Lawrence Stone, *The Family, Sex and Marriage in England 1500–1800*, Pelican edn 1979, p. 428.
20 Edward Shorter, *The Making of the Modern Family*, Fontana edn 1977, p. 273.
21 Society of Conservative Lawyers, *The Future of Marriage*, 1981.
22 See chapter 12, 'The Recovery of Divorce'.
23 Acts 2: 44 and 4: 32.
24 Plato, *The Republic*, V, 464.

3 Is the Family an Historical Freak?

1 Friedrich Engels, *The Origin of the Family, Private Property and the State*, London, 1972, p. 97.
2 Ibid., p. 100.
3 J. Beecher and R. Bienvenu (eds), *The Utopian Vision of Charles Fourier*, Boston, 1971, p. 333.
4 A. Werth and C. S. Mihanovich (eds), *Papal Pronouncements on Marriage and the Family*, Milwaukee, 1955, pp. 2–4.
5 Engels, *Origin of the Family*, p. 111.
6 Ibid., pp. 112–13.
7 Ibid., pp. 120–1.
8 Ibid., p. 112.
9 Ibid., p. 128.
10 E. Westermarck, *History of Marriage*, London, 1891, 3 vols, Vol. I, p. 503.
11 Meyer Fortes, *Kinship and the Social Order*, London, 1969, p. 5.
12 Robert H. Lowie, *Primitive Society*, London, 1929, pp. 52–3.
13 Ibid., pp. 148, 59, 63.
14 David McLellan, *Engels*, London, 1977, p. 37.
15 Sheila Rowbotham, *Women, Resistance and Revolution*, Pelican edn 1974, p. 69.

4 The Myth of the Extended Family

1 Peter Laslett, introduction to Peter Laslett and Richard Wall (eds), *Household and Family in Past Time*, Cambridge, 1972, p. 40.
2 Quoted, ibid., p. 105.
3 See Anderson, ibid., pp. 216–40.
4 Peter Laslett, Karla Oosterveen and Richard M. Smith (eds), *Bastardy and Its Comparative History*, London, 1980, p. 27.
5 Ibid., pp. 63–4.
6 See, in particular, the early chapters of E. P. Thompson, *The Making of the English Working Class*, Pelican edn 1968.

7 Laslett and Wall (eds), *Household and Family*, p. 110.
8 Summarised, ibid., pp. 335–427.
9 Ibid., p. 124.
10 Rodney Hilton, *Bondmen Made Free*, London, 1973, University Paperback edn 1977, p. 27.
11 Ibid., p. 27.
12 Laslett and Wall (eds), *Household and Family*, p. 73.
13 Lawrence Stone, *The Family, Sex and Marriage in England 1500–1800*, Pelican edn 1979, publisher's blurb.
14 Ibid., p. 26.
15 Ibid., p. 382.
16 Ibid., pp. 77, 80.
17 Christopher Falkus (ed.), *The Private Lives of the Tudor Monarchs*, London, 1974, p. 31.
18 Barbara Beuys, *Familienleben in Deutschland*, Hamburg, 1980, pp. 173–4.
19 Edward Shorter, *The Making of the Modern Family*, Fontana edn 1977, preface.
20 Ibid., p. 12.
21 Ibid., p. 68.
22 Ibid., p. 170.

5 Matchmaking and Lovemaking

1 Shakespeare, *The Merry Wives of Windsor*, III, iv.
2 Ibid., V, v.
3 Quoted, Alan Macfarlane, *The Origin of English Individualism*, Oxford, 1978, p. 156.
4 Lawrence Stone, *The Family, Sex and Marriage in England 1500–1800*, Pelican edn 1979, p. 42.
5 Peter Laslett, *The World We Have Lost*, London, 1965, p. 84.
6 Ibid.
7 Stone, *Family, Sex and Marriage*, p. 134.
8 Quoted, C. L. Powell, *English Domestic Relations 1487–1653*, New York, 1917, p. 15.
9 Quoted, ibid., p. 105.
10 Sebastian Brant, *The Ship of Fools*, trans. W. Gillis, London, Folio Society edn 1971, p. 129.
11 Stanley Bennett, *The Pastons and Their England*, Cambridge, 1922, p. 28.
12 *The Paston Letters*, ed. John Warrington, London, Everyman edn 1975, II, p. 160.
13 Ibid., II, p. 199.
14 Ibid., II, p. 189.
15 Ibid., II, p. 207.
16 Quoted, Bennett, *Pastons and Their England*, p. 60.
17 *Lisle Letters*, ed. Muriel St Clare Byrne, Chicago, 1981, 6 vols.
18 Ibid., V, p. 655.
19 Ibid., V, p. 652.

20 Ibid., II, p. 352.
21 *Stonor Letters and Papers*, ed. C. L. Kingsford, 1919, nos 169 and 173.
22 *Lisle Letters*, III, p. 294.
23 Ibid., IV, p. 361.
24 Ibid., IV, p. 387.
25 Quoted, Bennett, *Pastons and Their England*, p. 29
26 *Paston Letters*, I, p. 28.
27 Ibid., II, p. 76.
28 Ibid., II, p. 67.
29 Quoted, Bennett, *Pastons and Their England*, p. 44.
30 Quoted, R. H. Helmholz, *Marriage Litigation in Medieval England*, Cambridge, 1974, p. 89.
31 Quoted, ibid.
32 Quoted, ibid., pp. 28–9.
33 Ibid., pp. 32–3.
34 Quoted, ibid., p. 33.
35 Quoted, ibid., p. 7.
36 Ibid., pp. 199–201.
37 *Stonor Letters*, ed. Kingsford, no. 166.
38 Chaucer, *Troilus and Criseyde*, Penguin edn, trans. Nevill Coghill, 1971, pp. 45–6.
39 Chaucer, *Canterbury Tales*, Penguin edn, trans. Nevill Coghill, 1951, p. 118.
40 Ibid., p. 290.
41 Ibid., p. 298.
42 Ibid., p. 428.
43 Ibid., pp. 428–9.
44 Richard Gough, *The History of Myddle*, ed. Peter Razzell, Firle, Sussex, 1979, p. 96.
45 Ibid., p. 35.
46 Ibid., p. 122.
47 Ivy Pinchbeck and Margaret Hewitt, *Childhood in English Society, Vol. I, From Tudor Times to the Nineteenth Century*, London, 1969, p. 126.
48 Oliver Heywood, *The Autobiography of Oliver Heywood*, ed. J. H. Turner, Brighouse, Yorks, 1882, Vol. I, p. 62.
49 Roger Lowe, *Diary of Roger Lowe*, ed. W. L. Sachse, London, 1938, pp. 14, 20, 21, 23–4, 28.
50 Ibid., pp. 68–9, 105, 106.

6 The Troubadour Myth

1 C. S. Lewis, *The Allegory of Love*, Oxford, 1936, pp. 2, 4, 11.
2 Friedrich Engels, *The Origin of the Family, Private Property and the State*, London, 1972, pp. 133, 139–41.
3 E. T. Donaldson, *Speaking of Chaucer*, London, 1970, chapter 11.
4 D. N. Robertson, 'The Concept of Courtly Love as an Impediment to the

Understanding of Mediaeval Texts', in D. N. Robertson (ed.), *The Meaning of Courtly Love*, New York, 1968, p. 1.

5 John F. Benton, 'Clio and Venus: An Historical View of Medieval Love', in Robertson (ed.), *Meaning of Courtly Love*, pp. 36–7.

6 H. A. Kelly, *Love and Marriage in the Age of Chaucer*, Cornell, 1975, p. 52.

7 D. Scheludko, 'Über den Frauenkult der Troubadours', *Neuphil. Mitt.* XXXV, 1934, quoted in Peter Dronke, *Medieval Latin and the Rise of European Love-lyric*, Oxford, 1965, p. 55n.

8 Laurence Lerner, *Love and Marriage: Literature and Its Social Context*, London, 1979, pp. xiii, xiv.

9 Ibid., p. 13.

10 Ibid., pp. 13–14.

11 Dronke, *Medieval Latin*, p. xvii.

12 Ibid., p. 10.

13 Ibid.

14 Ibid., p. 8.

15 Ibid., p. 136.

16 Ibid., p. 171.

17 'The Wife's Lament', in *A Choice of Anglo-Saxon Verse*, sel. and trans. Richard Hamer, London, 1970, pp. 73–5.

18 Dronke, *Medieval Latin*, p. 45.

7 The Myth of the Indifferent Mother

1 Edward Shorter, *The Making of the Modern Family*, Fontana edn 1977, p. 170.

2 Ibid.

3 Ibid., p. 171.

4 Philippe Ariès, *Centuries of Childhood: A Social History of Family Life*, Peregrine edn 1979, p. 362.

5 Ibid., p. 37.

6 Montaigne, *Essays*, Penguin edn 1958, pp. 139–40.

7 Ibid., p. 142.

8 Ibid., pp. 149–50.

9 Shorter, *Making of the Modern Family*, pp. 173–4.

10 Lawrence Stone, *The Family, Sex and Marriage in England 1500–1800*, Pelican edn 1979, pp. 287, 288.

11 Ibid., pp. 289–92.

12 Emmanuel Le Roy Ladurie, *Montaillou: Cathars and Catholics in a French Village*, London, 1978, p. 212.

13 Ibid., p. 210.

14 Ibid.

15 Ibid., p. 211.

16 Ibid., p. 212.

17 Ibid., p. 186.

18 Ibid., p. 187.

19 Ibid., pp. 187–8.

20 Chaucer, *Canterbury Tales*, trans. Nevill Coghill, Penguin edn 1951, pp. 369–70.
21 Quoted, Barbara Beuys, *Familienleben in Deutschland*, Hamburg, 1980, p. 225.
22 Quoted, Christopher Falkus (ed.), *Private Lives of the Tudor Monarchs*, London, 1974, pp. 12–13.
23 Quoted, Arthur Ponsonby (ed.), *English Diaries*, London, 1923, p. 79.
24 Quoted, ibid., pp. 104–5.
25 Plutarch, *Moral Essays*, trans. Rex Warner, Penguin edn 1971, p. 177.
26 Ibid., p. 178.
27 Ariès, *Centuries of Childhood*, p. 332.
28 Ibid.
29 E. V. Lucas, *A Wanderer in Venice*, London, 1914, p. 70.
30 Lloyd de Mause (ed.), *The History of Childhood*, London, 1976, p. 54.
31 Quoted, ibid., p. 127.
32 Quoted, ibid., p. 131.
33 Quoted, ibid., p. 168.
34 Quoted, ibid., p. 128.
35 Quoted, ibid., p. 124.
36 Quoted, Beuys, *Familienleben in Deutschland*, p. 166.
37 Quoted, de Mause (ed.), *History of Childhood*, p. 89.
38 Quoted, ibid., p. 81.
39 James Bruce Ross, 'The Middle-class Child in Urban Italy, 14th to early 16th century', ibid., pp. 183–228.
40 Quoted, ibid., p. 183.
41 Ariès, *Centuries of Childhood*, p. 393.
42 Ibid., p. 379.
43 Ibid., p. 395.

8 Where Did the Historians Go Wrong?

1 Chaucer, *Canterbury Tales*, trans. Nevill Coghill, Penguin edn 1951, p. 507.
2 R. T. Davies, *Medieval English Lyrics*, London, 1963, introduction.
3 Ibid., p. 31.
4 *The Oxford Book of English Verse 1250–1918*, chosen and ed. Sir Arthur Quiller-Couch, p. 2, no. 3.
5 Victor E. Neuburg, *Popular Literature*, London, 1977, p. 48.
6 Quoted, ibid., p. 39.
7 Quoted, Philippe Ariès, *Centuries of Childhood: A Social History of Family Life*, Peregrine edn 1979, p. 84.
8 Quoted, ibid., p. 152.
9 Peter Laslett, *The World We Have Lost*, London, 1965, p. 91.
10 Edward Shorter, *The Making of the Modern Family*, Fontana edn 1977, p. 175.
11 Ivy Pinchbeck and Margaret Hewitt, *Childhood in English Society, Vol. I, From Tudor Times to the Nineteenth Century*, London, 1969, p. 201.

12 Ibid., p. 203.
13 Ibid.
14 Alan Macfarlane, 'Illegitimacy and Illegitimates in English History', in Peter Laslett, Karla Oosterveen and Richard M. Smith (eds), *Bastardy and Its Comparative History*, London, 1980, pp. 75–6.
15 Jean Meyer, 'Illegitimates and Foundlings in Pre-industrial France', ibid., p. 249.
16 *Daily Telegraph*, 7th February 1981.
17 *Daily Express*, 24th January 1981.
18 Shorter, *Making of the Modern Family*, p. 66.
19 See chapter 13, 'Women, Power and Marriage'.
20 See chapter 12, 'The Recovery of Divorce'.
21 Renate Bridenthal and Claudia Koonz (eds), *Becoming Visible: Women in European History*, Boston, 1977, introduction.
22 I Chronicles 2: 10–11.
23 Ariès, *Centuries of Childhood*, p. 341.
24 Ibid., p. 125.
25 Ibid., p. 32.
26 Ibid., p. 33.
27 Ibid., pp. 37–8.
28 Ibid., p. 53.
29 Ibid., p. 55.
30 Johan Huizinga, *The Waning of the Middle Ages*, Penguin edn 1955, p. 10.
31 Ariès, *Centuries of Childhood*, p. 301.
32 Ibid., p. 96.
33 Quoted, Joseph Strutt, *The Sports and Pastimes of the People of England*, London, 1830, p. 92.
34 Quoted, *Football*, Badminton Library, London, 1904, pp. 4–5.
35 Quoted, ibid., p. 6.
36 Quoted, ibid., p. 9.
37 Ariès, *Centuries of Childhood*, p. 351.

9 The Family-haters

1 Plato, *The Republic*, trans. Jowett, Oxford, 1908, III, pp. 414–15.
2 Ibid., V, p. 464.
3 Quoted, Norman Cohn, *The Pursuit of the Millennium*, Paladin edn 1970, p. 189.
4 Quoted, ibid., p. 194.
5 Quoted, ibid., p. 270.
6 Quoted, ibid., p. 328.
7 Quoted, ibid., p. 329.
8 E. R. Leach, *A Runaway World*, London, 1968, p. 44. These lectures are a classic statement of the old myths about the family: 'History and ethnography provide very few examples of societies constructed around a loose assemblage of isolated groups of parents and children . . . Children need to grow up in larger, more relaxed domestic groups centred on the

community rather than on mother's kitchen; something like an Israeli kibbutz perhaps, or a Chinese commune' (p. 45). Leach's attempts to qualify these statements (pp. 44, 45 fns and postscript) do not alter his views much.

9 Friedrich Engels, *The Origin of the Family, Private Property and the State*, London, 1972, pp. 134–5.
10 F. T. Marinetti, *Selected Writings*, ed. R. W. Flint, New York, 1972, pp. 76–7.
11 William Gerhardie, *God's Fifth Column*, ed. M. Holroyd and R. Skidelsky, London, 1981, pp. 131–2.
12 Cyril Connolly, *Enemies of Promise*, London, 1938, revised edn 1949, chapter 14, pp. 115, 116.
13 *Spectator*, 4th April 1981.

10 Privacy and the Working Class

1 Karl Marx, *Das Kapital*, London, 1889, p. 495.
2 Ibid., p. 496.
3 John 17: 20–3.
4 Jeremy Seabrook, *What Went Wrong: Working People and the Ideals of the Labour Movement*, London, 1978, p. 14.
5 Ibid., p. 246.
6 Ibid., p. 285.
7 Ibid., pp. 23, 25.
8 Ibid., p. 95.
9 Ibid., p. 279.
10 Quoted, M. Beer, *A History of British Socialism*, London, 1920, Vol. II, pp. 221–2.
11 C. A. R. Crosland, *The Future of Socialism*, revised paperback edn 1964, p. 255.
12 Ibid., p. 255.
13 Edmund Burke, *Works*, London, 1808–13, Vol. V, *Reflections on the French Revolution*, pp. 100, 252–3.

11 The Dilution of Fraternity

1 E. J. Hobsbawm, 'Fraternity', *New Society*, 27th November 1975.
2 P. B. Shelley, *Prometheus Unbound*, III, ix, 194–8.
3 Edward Bond, 'Scenes of Death and Money', *Bingo*, London, 1974.
4 Galatians 3: 28.
5 Enoch Powell, *The Times*, 20th July 1973.
6 John Locke, *Two Treatises of Government*, ed. Peter Laslett, Cambridge, 1960, II, p. 58.
7 Ibid., p. 59.
8 Ibid., p. 65.
9 Aristotle, *Politics*, trans. Jowett, Oxford, 1921, II, p. 4.
10 Shelley, *Prometheus Unbound*, III, iv.

11 D. H. Lawrence, *Lady Chatterley's Lover*, London, Phoenix edn 1963, p. 204.
12 Sir Henry Maine, *Village Communities*, London, fourth edn 1881, pp. 226, 228.
13 B. N. Nelson, *The Idea of Usury*, Princeton, 1949, p. 136.
14 Ibid., p. 137.
15 Carl R. Rogers, *Encounter Groups*, Harmondsworth, Penguin edn 1973.
16 Friedrich Engels, *The Origin of the Family, Private Property and the State*, London, 1972, p. 145.
17 Christopher Caudwell, *Studies in a Dying Culture*, London, 1938, pp. 152–3.
18 Ibid., p. 155.
19 Ibid.
20 Engels, *Origin of the Family*, p. 145.
21 Quoted, James Joll, *The Anarchists*, London, 1979, p. 253.
22 Quoted, *Guardian*, 26th August 1974.
23 Colossians 3: 5.
24 Clem Gorman, *Making Communes*, Bottisham, Cambridge, 1972, p. 90.
25 Bruno Bettelheim, *The Children of the Dream*, Paladin edn 1971, p. 31.
26 Ibid., p. 222.
27 Luke 10: 34.
28 Luke 10: 35.
29 Frank Musgrove, *Ecstasy and Holiness – Counter Culture and the Open Society*, London, 1974.

12 The Recovery of Divorce

1 See Myles Dillon and Nora Chadwick, *The Celtic Realms*, London, 1967.
2 F. M. Stenton, *Anglo-Saxon England*, Oxford, 1943, p. 140.
3 P. D. King, *Law and Society in the Visigothic Kingdom*, Cambridge, 1972, p. 224.
4 Colin Morris, *The Discovery of the Individual 1050–1200*, New York, 1972, p. 107 and footnote.
5 J. J. Scarisbrick, *Henry VIII*, London, 1968, p. 219.
6 Ibid., p. 167.
7 See Scarisbrick, op. cit.; G. R. Elton, *Reform and Reformation*, London, 1977; and C. S. L. Davies, *Peace, Print and Protestantism*, London, 1977, for different emphases.
8 Roland H. Bainton, *Erasmus of Christendom*, London, 1970, p. 278.
9 *De Conscribendis Epistolis*, abridged, ibid., pp. 71–2.
10 Erasmus, *Colloquies*, ed. Craig Thompson, Chicago, 1965, pp. 126–7.
11 Thomas More, *Utopia*, trans. Paul Turner, Folio Society edn 1965, pp. 104–5.
12 John Milton, *Prose Writings*, Everyman edn 1927, p. 259.
13 Ibid., p. 277.
14 Ibid., p. 280.

15 Ibid., p. 261.
16 Ibid.
17 Ibid., p. 267.
18 Ibid., p. 280.
19 Ibid., p. 268.
20 Ibid., p. 309.
21 Ibid.
22 Ibid., p. 313.
23 Ibid., p. 252.
24 Ibid., p. 253.
25 Christopher Hill, *Puritanism and Revolution*, Panther edn 1968, p. 65.

13 Women, Power and Marriage

1 *Encounter*, March 1976.
2 Leon Battista Alberti, *I Libri della famiglia*, trans. R. N. Watkins, *The Family in Renaissance Florence*, Columbia, South Carolina, 1969, p. 98.
3 Simone de Beauvoir, *The Second Sex*, Penguin edn 1972, p. 415.
4 Ibid., p. 416.
5 Brantôme, *Les Dames galantes*, Paris, 1962, p. 43.
6 John Aubrey, *Brief Lives*, Michigan, 1962, pp. 255–6.
7 Quoted, Barbara Beuys, *Familienleben in Deutschland*, Hamburg, 1980, p. 189.
8 Quoted, Peter Dronke, *Medieval Latin and the Rise of European Love-lyric*, Oxford, 1965, p. 68.
9 Abbess Hildegard, *Causae et Curae*, ed. Kaiser, Leipzig, 1903, p. 136.
10 R. Rigaud, *Les Idées féministes de Christine de Pisan*, Neuchâtel, 1911, p. 66.
11 Ibid., p. 67.
12 Ibid., p. 101.
13 F. W. Maitland, *History of English Law*, Vol. I, p. 482.
14 Ibid.
15 Eileen Power, 'The Position of Women', in G. C. Crump and F. F. Jacobs (eds), *The Legacy of the Middle Ages*, Oxford, 1926.
16 Alan Macfarlane, *The Origin of English Individualism*, Oxford, 1978, p. 134.
17 R. I. Page, *Life in Anglo-Saxon England*, London, 1970, p. 71.
18 Plutarch, *Moral Essays*, trans. Rex Warner, Penguin edn 1971, p. 18.
19 Ibid.
20 Ibid.
21 Ibid., p. 23.
22 E. P. Thompson, in Jack Goody, Joan Thirsk and E. P. Thompson (eds), *Family and Inheritance*, Cambridge, 1976, p. 349.
23 Ibid., pp. 112–55.
24 *Fifty Earliest English Wills*, ed. F. J. Furnivall, 1882.
25 *Lisle Letters*, ed. Muriel St Clare Byrne, Chicago, 1981, 6 vols, I, p. 28.

26 Michael Young and Peter Willmott, *Family and Kinship in East London*, Pelican edn 1962, p. 49.
27 Shulamith Firestone, *The Dialectic of Sex*, Women's Press edn 1979, p. 224.
28 Germaine Greer, *The Female Eunuch*, Granada edn 1971, p. 235.
29 Ibid.
30 Galatians 3: 28.
31 Greer, *Female Eunuch*, p. 281.
32 Ibid.

14 And Afterwards?
1 Lawrence Stone, *The Family, Sex and Marriage in England 1500–1800*, Pelican edn 1979, pp. 47–8.
2 Peter Laslett, Karla Oosterveen and Richard M. Smith (eds), *Bastardy and its Comparative History*, London, 1980, pp. 1–65, and Edward Shorter, *The Making of the Modern Family*, Fontana edn 1977, chapter 3.
3 Quoted, Laslett, Oosterveen and Smith (eds), *Bastardy and Its Comparative History*, p. 11.
4 Quoted, ibid., p. 56.
5 All examples quoted, ibid., pp. 192–216.

SELECT
BIBLIOGRAPHY

This list contains the books which I have found most helpful and relevant to the past and present of marriage and the family. I have not included general literary sources such as Chaucer or Jane Austen. Books marked with an asterisk contain useful bibliographies in their field.

Alberti, Leon Battista: *The Family in Renaissance Florence*, trans. and ed. R. N. Watkins, Columbia, South Carolina, 1969.

Anderson, Michael: *Family Structure in Nineteenth Century Lancashire*, Cambridge, 1971

*Ariès, Philippe: *Centuries of Childhood*, London, 1962, Peregrine edn 1979; originally *L'Enfant et la vie familiale sous l'Ancien Régime*, Paris, 1960

Aubrey, John: *Brief Lives* (ed. 1898), Michigan, 1962; ed. Oliver Lawson Dick, London, 1969, Penguin edn 1972

Bainton, Roland H.: *Erasmus of Christendom*, New York, 1969, London, 1970

Balsdon, J. P. V. D.: *Life and Leisure in Ancient Rome*, London, 1969

Beauvoir, Simone de: *The Second Sex*, London, 1953, Penguin edn 1972; Paris, 1949.

Beecher, J., and Bienvenu, R.: *The Utopian Vision of Charles Fourier*, Boston, 1971, London, 1975

Bennett, H. S.: *The Pastons and Their England*, Cambridge, 1922

Bettelheim, Bruno: *The Children of the Dream*, London, 1969, Paladin edn 1971

*Beuys, Barbara: *Familienleben in Deutschland*, Hamburg, 1980

Bloch, Marc: *Feudal Society*, London, 1962

Brantôme: *Les Dames galantes*, Paris, 1962

Brewer, D. S.: *Love and Marriage in the Age of Chaucer*, Cornell, 1975

Bridenthal, Renate, and Koonz, Claudia (eds): *Becoming Visible: Women in European History*, Boston, 1977
Byrne, Muriel St Clare (ed.): *The Lisle Letters*, Chicago, 1981, 6 vols

Caudwell, Christopher: *Studies in a Dying Culture*, London, 1938
Cohn, Norman: *The Pursuit of the Millennium*, London, 1959, Paladin edn 1970
Crosland, C. A. R.: *The Future of Socialism*, London, 1956, revised paperback edn 1964, reissued 1981
Crump, G. C., and Jacobs, F. F.: *The Legacy of the Middle Ages*, Oxford, 1926

Daniélou, J., and Marrou, H.: *The Christian Centuries*, Vol. I, London, 1964
Davies, R. T.: *Medieval English Lyrics*, London, 1963
de Mause, Lloyd (ed.): *The History of Childhood*, U.S., 1974, London, 1976
Dillon, Myles, and Chadwick, Nora: *The Celtic Realms*, London, 1967
Donaldson, E. T.: *Speaking of Chaucer*, London, 1970
Dreitzel, H. P. (ed); *Family, Marriage and the Struggle of the Sexes*, New York, 1972.
Dronke, Peter: *Medieval Latin and the Rise of European Love-lyric*, Oxford, 1965

Engels, Friedrich: *The Origin of the Family, Private Property and the State*, trans. A. West, London, 1972
Erasmus: *Colloquies* (1516–36), ed. Craig Thompson, Chicago, 1965

Falkus, Christopher (ed.): *Private Lives of the Tudor Monarchs*, London, 1974
Firestone, Shulamith: *The Dialectic of Sex*, U.S. 1970, London, 1971, Women's Press edn 1979
Flandrin, J. L.: *Families in Former Times: Kinship, Household and Sexuality*, Cambridge, 1979; originally *Familles: parenté, maison, sexualité dans l'ancienne société*, Paris, 1976
Fletcher, Ronald: *The Family and Marriage in Britain*, London, 1962
Fortes, Meyer: *Kinship and the Social Order*, London, 1969
Friedan, Betty: *The Feminine Mystique*, New York and London, 1963

Geiger, H. Kent: *The Family in Soviet Russia*, Cambridge, Mass., 1968
Goody, Jack, Thirsk, Joan, and Thompson, E. P. (eds): *Family and Inheritance: Rural Society in Western Europe 1200–1800*, Cambridge, 1976
Gough, Richard: *The History of Myddle*, ed. Peter Razzell, Caliban Books, Firle, Sussex, 1979, Penguin edn 1981
Greer, Germaine: *The Female Eunuch*, London, 1970, Granada edn 1971

Hallam, H. G.: *Rural England 1066–1348*, London, 1981
Hamer, Richard (ed. and trans.): *A Choice of Anglo-Saxon Verse*, London, 1970
*Helmholz, R. H.: *Marriage Litigation in Medieval England*, Cambridge, 1974

Select Bibliography

Héroard, Jean: *Journal de Jean Héroard sur l'enfance et la jeunesse de Louis XIII*, ed. Soulié and E. de Barthélemy, Paris, 1868

Heywood, Oliver: *The Autobiography of Oliver Heywood*, ed. J. H. Turner, 1882

Hildegard, Abbess: *Causae et Curae*, ed. Kaiser, Leipzig, 1903

Hill, Christopher: *Puritanism and Revolution*, London, Panther edn 1968

Hilton, Rodney: *Bondmen Made Free*, London, 1973, University Paperback edn 1977

Hitler, Adolf: *Mein Kampf*, Munich, 1929

Homans, G. C.: *English Villagers of the Thirteenth Century*, Cambridge, Mass., 1942

Huizinga, Johan: *The Waning of the Middle Ages*, London, 1924, Penguin edn 1955

Josselin, Ralph: *Diary of Ralph Josselin*, ed. Alan Macfarlane, Cambridge, 1976

Joyce, G. H.: *Christian Marriage*, London, 1948

King, P. D.: *Law and Society in the Visigothic Kingdom*, Cambridge, 1972

Kingsford, C. L. (ed.): *Stonor Letters and Papers*, London, 1919, 2 vols

Kitchen, S. B.: *A History of Divorce*, London, 1912

Ladurie, Emmanuel Le Roy: *Montaillou: Cathars and Catholics in a French Village 1294–1324*, Paris, 1975, London, 1978

Landry, La Tour: *The Book of the Knight of La Tour Landry*, ed. T. Wright, London, 1868

*Laslett, Peter: *The World We Have Lost*, London, 1965

Laslett, Peter: *Family Life and Illicit Love in Earlier Generations*, Cambridge, 1977.

Laslett, Peter, Oosterveen, Karla, and Smith, Richard M. (eds): *Bastardy and its Comparative History*, London, 1980

*Laslett, Peter, and Wall, Richard (eds): *Household and Family in Past Time*, Cambridge, 1972

Lawrence, D. H.: *Lady Chatterley's Lover*, London, Phoenix edn 1961

Lenin, V. I.: *On the Emancipation of Women*, Moscow, 1965

Le Play, F.: *Les Ouvriers européens*, Paris, 1855, 1877–9

Lerner, Laurence: *Love and Marriage: Literature and Its Social Context*, London, 1979

Lewis, C. S.: *The Allegory of Love*, Oxford, 1936

Lietzmann, H.: *History of the Early Church*, London, 1961, 2 vols

Locke, John: *Two Treatises of Government*, ed. Peter Laslett, Cambridge, 1960

Lowe, Roger: *Diary of Roger Lowe*, ed. W. L. Sachse, London, 1938

Lowie, R. H.: *Primitive Society*, New York, 1920, London, 1929

Lyell, Laetitia (ed.): *A Mediaeval Postbag*, London, 1934

Macfarlane, Alan: *The Family Life of Ralph Josselin*, Cambridge, 1970

Macfarlane, Alan: *The Origin of English Individualism*, Oxford, 1978
McWilliams, W. C.: *The Idea of Fraternity in America*, Berkeley, 1973
Maine, Henry: *Ancient Law*, London, 1861
——: *Village Communities*, London, 4th edn 1881
*Mair, Lucy: *Marriage*, London, 1971
Marinetti, F. T.: *Selected Writings*, ed. R. W. Flint, New York, 1972
Marx, Karl: *Das Kapital*, London, 1889
Marx, Karl, and Engels, Friedrich: *Communist Manifesto* (1848), Harmondsworth, Pelican edn 1967
*Millett, Kate: *Sexual Politics*, U.S., 1969, London, 1971
Milton, John: *Prose Writings*, London, Everyman edn 1927 (includes *The Doctrine and Discipline of Divorce*)
More, Thomas: *Utopia* (1515), London, 1974
*Morgan, D. H. J.: *Social Theory and the Family*, London, 1975
Morgan, L. H.: *Ancient Society*, New York, 1877
Morris, Colin: *The Discovery of the Individual 1050–1200*, New York, 1972
Moss, Rachel (ed.): *God's Yes to Sexuality*, London, 1981

Nelson, B. N.: *The Idea of Usury*, Princeton, 1949
*Neuburg, V. E.: *Popular Literature*, London, 1977

Page, R. I.: *Life in Anglo-Saxon England*, London, 1970
The Paston Letters, ed. John Warrington, London, Everyman edn, 2 vols, 1924; reprinted 1975
Pepys, Samuel: *Diary*, ed. R. Latham and W. Matthews, London, 1974
*Pinchbeck, Ivy, and Hewitt, Margaret: *Childhood in English Society, Vol. I, From Tudor Times to the Nineteenth Century*, London, 1969
Plato: *The Republic*, trans. Jowett, Oxford, 1908
Plutarch: *Moral Essays*, trans. Rex Warner, Harmondsworth, Penguin edn 1971
Pole, Nicholas (ed.): *Environmental Solutions*, Cambridge, 1972
Pollock, F., and Maitland, F. W.: *History of English Law*, Cambridge, 1898, reissued 1968, 2 vols
Powell, C. L.: *English Domestic Relations 1487–1653*, New York, 1917

Rigaud, R.: *Les Idées féministes de Christine de Pisan*, Neuchâtel, 1911
Robertson, D. N. (ed.): *The Meaning of Courtly Love*, New York, 1968
Rogers, Carl R.: *Encounter Groups*, Harmondsworth, 1973
Rougemont, Denis de: *L'Amour et l'occident*, Paris, 1939; pub. in Britain, 1940, as *Passion and Society*, in U.S. as *Love in the Western World*
——: *Comme toi-même*, Paris, 1961; pub. in Britain as *The Myths of Love*, trans. R. Howard, London, 1964
*Rowbotham, Sheila: *Women, Resistance and Revolution*, London, 1972
——: *Women's Liberation and the New Politics*, Institute for Workers' Control, Nottingham, 1969

Select Bibliography

Scarisbrick, J. J.: *Henry VIII*, London, 1968

Seabrook, Jeremy: *What Went Wrong: Working People and the Ideals of the Labour Movement*, London, 1978

Shorter, Edward: *The Making of the Modern Family*, London, 1976, Fontana edn 1977

Stapleton, Thomas (ed.): *Plumpton Correspondence*, London, 1839

Stendhal: *De l'amour*, Paris, 1822; London, trans. T. S. and C. N. S. Woolf, 1915

Stenton, F. M.: *Anglo-Saxon England*, Oxford, 1943

Stephen, J. F.: *Liberty, Equality and Fraternity*, London, 1873

Stone, Lawrence: *The Family, Sex and Marriage in England 1500–1800*, London, 1977, Pelican edn 1979

Thompson, E. P.: *The Making of the English Working Class*, Harmondsworth, Pelican edn 1968

Troeltsch, Ernst: *Social Teaching of the Christian Churches*, London, 1931

Vinogradoff, P.: *Villeinage in Medieval England*, Oxford, 1923

Waddell, Helen: *Mediaeval Latin Lyrics*, London, 1952

Webb, Beatrice, and Webb, Sidney: *Soviet Communism: A New Civilisation?*, London, 1935, without question mark 1937, revised 1944

Werth, A., and Mihanovich, C. S.: *Papal Pronouncements on Marriage and the Family*, Milwaukee, 1955

Westermarck, E.: *History of Marriage*, London, 1891, 3 vols

*Young, Michael, and Willmott, Peter: *Family and Kinship in East London*, London, 1957, Pelican edn 1962

INDEX

277

Index

Index